Long-Term Solutions
for a Short-Term World

Long-Term Solutions for a Short-Term World

Canada and Research Development

Ronald N. Harpelle and
Bruce Muirhead, editors

WILFRID LAURIER
UNIVERSITY PRESS

Wilfrid Laurier University Press acknowledges the financial support of the International Development Research Centre for this publication. We acknowledge the financial support of the Government of Canada through its Canada Book Fund for its publishing activities.

Library and Archives Canada Cataloguing in Publication

Long-term solutions for a short-term world : Canada and research development / Ronald N. Harpelle and Bruce Muirhead, editors.

Includes bibliographical references and index.
Issued also in electronic format.
ISBN 978-1-55458-223-5

1. Economic development — Research—Developing countries — Case studies. 2. Economic assistance, Canadian—Developing countries. 3. Technical assistance, Canadian — Developing countries. I. Harpelle, Ronald N., 1957– II. Muirhead, Bruce

HD77.5.D4L66 2011   338.91'7101724   C2010-907876-4

Electronic formats
ISBN 978-1-55458-241-9 (PDF), ISBN 978-1-55458-353-9 (EPUB)

1. Economic development — Research — Developing countries — Case studies. 2. Economic assistance, Canadian — Developing countries. 3. Technical assistance, Canadian — Developing countries. I. Harpelle, Ronald N., 1957– II. Muirhead, Bruce

HD77.5.D4L66 2011a   338.91'7101724   C2010-907877-2

Cover design by Sandra Friesen. Cover photograph by Bruce Muirhead. Text design by Daiva Villa, Chris Rowat Design.

This book is printed on FSC recycled paper and is certified Ecologo. It is made from 100% post-consumer fibre, processed chlorine free, and manufactured using biogas energy.

Printed in Canada

RECYCLED
Paper made from
recycled material
FSC
www.fsc.org   FSC® C103567

Contents

Acknowledgements

This book is an offshoot of a project to write a history of the International Development Research Centre. Research on the IDRC History Project began in 2006 and over a three-year period we had the opportunity to meet scientists from around the world. We would like to thank all the contributors to this book for their efforts in making the conference they initially attended and this publication a success. The conference was entitled "Canada and Research for Development: Past, Present and Future," and it was organized with support from IDRC. With the support of Lauchlan Munro, IDRC vice-president, Corporate Strategy and Regional Management, and former president of IDRC, Maureen O'Neil, we were able to bring together this diverse group of researchers whose work has made a difference.

Along with encouragement from a number of other IDRC staff, we benefited from the support of the Centre for International Governance Innovation in Waterloo and staff at Wilfrid Laurier University Press. In particular, we would like to thank Rob Kohlmeier and Ryan Chynces through the publication process. Our anonymous reviewers provided a great deal of assistance in helping us corral ideas and better connect the submissions, which were written from a wide variety of social, ethnic, and political contexts. A great many thanks go to Laura Murray, who helped us edit and format generally pull the book together. We are indebted to our partners, Kelly Saxberg and Sandi Bair, who not only served as sounding boards for many ideas that did not see the light of day but who lived and relived the "drama" of many of the decisions that went into this book. We cannot hope to repay them for their patience and the sacrifices they made to see us through the entire IDRC History Project.

The International Development Research Centre and Research for Development

One of the most fascinating and inspiring aspects of international development is the dedication of individuals who are engaged finding solutions to the problems faced by the world's poor. In this age of globalization, we are never far from those that plague developing countries. From the extremes of poverty experienced by the majority of the world's population to the wealthiest of the wealthy, the problem of development affects us all because it is the single most important factor in the future of our world. Every other pressing global issue, from climate change to the civil unrest that engulfs much of the planet, can be said to centre on the problems of development. Although government agencies and celebrities are often seen as being at the forefront of the fight to assist the world's poor, there are thousands of people engaged in finding solutions.

An important group is the scientists who conduct research for development. They provide the foundation for the solutions proposed by the World Bank, Bob Geldof, Bill Gates, and others. *Long-Term Solutions for a Short-Term World* introduces some of the individuals whose dedication to research lights the elusive pathways to development. The book examines two important and understudied issues: the importance of research in international development and the work of the International Development Research Centre (IDRC).

In early 2006, Bruce Muirhead and Ron Harpelle were commissioned to write a history of IDRC, a small Canadian Crown corporation that is far better known among researchers in the developing world than it is at home. *IDRC: 40 Years of Ideas, Innovation, and Impact* (Wilfrid Laurier University Press, 2010) focuses on the political and administrative side of the story. Like all research projects, outcomes develop over time, and one of the supplements to our work is this collection of essays on the practitioners of research for development. The essays that follow tend to be descriptive, because our enquiries into the history of IDRC required an understanding of the evolutionary process of specific research projects with clear examples of how various kinds of research is conducted in the field.

As part of our research for the project we were tasked with travelling to IDRC's six regional offices, where we conducted interviews with, among others, dozens of past and present recipients of Canadian support for social science and scientific research for development. This kind of research is directed at immediate problems faced by societies in poor countries. Some is at the macro level, focused on regional, continental, and even global challenges, but most of the research we were exposed to had as its primary focus the amelioration of general living conditions or, in its more ambitious or farsighted characterization, the alleviation of poverty among the world's poor. Research for development is the search for long-term solutions to problems that persist despite the rapid changes taking place as the world accelerates into the twenty-first century.

Our interviews for the IDRC history focused on past support from this uniquely Canadian institution and its often overlooked, but highly successful, track record of building capacity among researchers in the developing world. However, we also took on the task of determining what kinds of research were being conducted at the present time; we visited laboratories and offices of individuals addressing long-term solutions to the ongoing challenges to development. Knowledge is the single most important means for a country to achieve development goals, and the monopoly on scientific knowledge enjoyed by advanced industrial countries such as Canada does not lend itself easily to solving the perplexing problems associated with poverty in the developing world.

Long-Term Solutions for a Short-Term World results from a conference held in September 2008 at the Centre for International Governance Innovation (CIGI) in Waterloo, Ontario. It was held over two days with an invited audience of researchers, students, and representatives from funding agencies and NGOs. The objective of the conference was to bring together a representative group of researchers to speak about their individual work as a means of conducting a cross-disciplinary and multinational dialogue on development. The presenters were invited because each had received critical acclaim for their work and because each represented one of six areas of research that provided the conference with a broad spectrum of issues and approaches to discuss. Our focus was on water, women, politics, health, information and communication technologies, and the BRIC's emerging economies. These themes coincided with a six-part documentary film series called *Citizens of the World* (directed by Kelly Saxberg) that grew out of meetings with some of the most dynamic development researchers of our time. In a sense, this book is a companion to the film series, but it's different, too, because we have allowed the researchers to present their own accounts of meeting development challenges head-on.

While international development is often dominated by policy-makers who create models that provide answers to the problem of poverty, the individuals highlighted in this book are the people who shape fields of research. As such, this book is not written as a challenge to current orthodoxies on development, nor does it claim to provide a clear path forward. We leave the debates about the literature on development and the grand solutions to those who wish to situate themselves within a broader and more critical context. *Long-Term Solutions for a Short-Term World* is about research from the perspective of the researchers themselves. None of the participants in the conference or the contributors to this book would ever claim a monopoly on knowledge about specific challenges to development, because their commitment is to research and making the small advances that build toward lasting change.

Our book is, therefore, inspired by the stories of people who have dedicated their lives to finding solutions to some of the challenges that confront the world's poor. Approaching various problems with what were often considered unorthodox approaches, each of the authors in this volume displays a dedication to research for development combined with self-sacrifice that merits our admiration. The authors of the following essays are not only accomplished leaders in their respective fields but people who have chosen paths that often bring them into conflict with authorities and systems that exist as obstacles to development. These are people who have taken risks (sometimes dangerous ones) to secure a better future for citizens of the Global South. They enjoy international stature for their work, but they toil in relative obscurity because theirs is research to benefit marginalized people. Some of these researchers focus on issues that are global or that have global implications, while others focus on issues that are local and immediate. Together their stories offer a cross-section of the kinds of research for development that is taking place across the Global South.

The researchers featured in the pages that follow have chosen to remain in their country of origin. These are individuals with qualifications from some of the best universities in the world who work for the benefit of their countries. They cannot be criticized for the sacrifices they have made or for not having read the latest literature that is generally published in English in journals that are increasingly controlled by large commercial publishing companies that are not in the business of providing universal access to information. These researchers also cannot afford to pay to have their work published with these same publishers, and this puts limits on their ability to stand out in the academic world or research. They are citizens of the world who are working in the field on problems that face humanity.

IDRC has made a reputation for itself by funding researchers with potential. Recipients of IDRC support are often younger scientists whose first big break comes from this little known Crown corporation. IDRC has led the way in supporting research in non-industrialized countries in order to increase the competitiveness of researchers in poor countries and help pave the way for a more sustainable scientific foundation among national institutions. Capacity-building is a slow process and, like science, the results often raise more questions than they answer. The researchers in this volume exemplify the success of IDRC; they have been given the tools to devote their attention to problems that plague the world.

This book serves to present a Canadian alternative to the global challenge of assisting developing countries in their search for solutions to the problems they face in the twenty-first century. The model for this approach is the International Development Research Centre. As Rohinton Medhora, one of its vice-presidents, has often pointed out, IDRC is in some ways like a university, an NGO, and a government department. Like a university it is intellectually curious and committed to scientific excellence; like an NGO it strongly believes in its mission and in the autonomy needed to carry it out; and like a government department it uses public funds and is publicly accountable for its actions and enjoys the confidence and protection of that official status. Without this hybridization the IDRC would not be what it is and would probably not have enjoyed the success it has.

Participants at the CIGI conference were invited to make personalized presentations that would provide the audience with insight into the experiences of researchers who have focused on some of the most important development questions of our time. The chapters in this book are written by people who have intimate knowledge of the challenges faced by individuals and communities in some of the poorest countries in the world. Their work does not always grab headlines or command the attention of governments, but it makes a vital contribution to our understanding of the many pathways to development and the improvement of the general conditions for people in the Global South. The authors are from several different regions of the world and they specialize in different fields of study, but they have one important thing in common — each of the research experiences described in this book was funded, in whole or in part, by Canada's International Development Research Centre.

The first chapter is written by Ron Harpelle, a specialist in Latin American history with a background in international development. His association with IDRC dates from 1998, when he was awarded a Canada and the World Grant to undertake a study of the West Indian community of Central America. Since then he has taught the history of international development and created course materials that help students understand the constraints placed on non-industrial societies around the world. Chapter One offers an overview of international development, looking at how it evolved in the aftermath of the collapse of European colonialism and within the context of the post-1945 world. Harpelle places a special emphasis on the history of Canada's role in development assistance and why the Canadian approach is in many ways different from that of other countries.

In Chapter Two, Bruce Muirhead offers a summary of the history of the International Development Research Centre from its inception in 1970 to the present. Bruce Muirhead is a professor of history and the Associate Dean of Graduate Studies and Research in the Faculty of Arts at the University of Waterloo. His current research is on the history of the International Development Research Centre, and he has undertaken the writing of a history of Canadian official development assistance policy from 1945 to 1984 with a grant from the Social Sciences and Humanities Research Council. He continues to work on the topic of the development of Canadian foreign economic policy in the 1960s and '70s. The story of IDRC is important because it is a uniquely Canadian approach to development problems, which reflects Muirhead's work.

Dipak Gyawali is an activist academic who is a member of the Royal Nepal Academy of Science and Technology as well as the research director of the Nepal Water Conservation Foundation and the editor of its interdisciplinary journal, *Water Nepal*. His research interests centre on the society–technology interface and deals primarily with water and energy issues. He was Nepal's Minister for Water Resources in 2002–3 and is currently vice-chair of the technical committee of UN's Third World Water Assessment. In Chapter Three, Gyawali offers an analysis of the difference between development research and development consultancy and raises critical questions about the difference between the two. He focuses on the problem of imported solutions that do not address the home-grown needs of the countries being "developed."

Chapter Four, by Zoubida Charrouf, who is a professor at the Mohammed V University in Rabat, and Dominique Guillaume, a professor of medicinal chemistry at the University of Reims Champagne–Ardenne, is about a fascinating research journey that saw the creation of a network of Argan oil-producing co-operatives run by women in Morocco. The efforts of these scientists to study the oil's properties has fed into the fight against desertification, resulting from the empowerment of poor women in the countryside through the valorization of a traditional commodity.

Chapter Five is by Rita Giacaman, a professor of public health at the Institute of Community and Public Health, Birzeit University, Viet Nguyen-Gillham, who has a background in social work and psychotherapy, and Yoke Rabaia, who conducts research with the mental health unit of the Institute of Community and Public Health, Birzeit University. Their chapter is about the study of trauma among Palestinian youth. Their work highlights an aspect of life under military occupation that is overlooked in other efforts to find a path toward state creation in Palestine.

Dr. Oumar Cissé is a civil engineer who holds an M.A. in environmental studies and a PhD in management from the University of Montreal. Since 1997, he has served as executive secretary of the African Institute for Urban Management (IAGU), where he has led a group of researchers in a study of the Mbeubeuss garbage dump and landfill in Dakar. In Chapter Six Cissé explains how his work has served to bring the daily challenges of some of the world's poorest people to national discussions of waste management in Senegal.

Chapter Seven, by Clotilde Fonseca, the Costa Rican Minister of Science and Technology and the former director and founder of the Programa de Informática Educativa de Costa Rica, tells an important story of bringing e-learning to remote regions of Central America. While Costa Rica was spared much of the turmoil of war and dislocation that characterized the region in the last decades of the twentieth century, the challenges of introducing digital technology and delivering education are daunting. Nevertheless, through Fonseca's efforts, individuals who would otherwise have been unable to obtain certain kinds of education and skills are now enjoying the prospect of a brighter future.

Palmira Ventosilla is an expert on tropical disease vectors from the Alexander von Humboldt Tropical Medicine Institute in Lima. In Chapter Eight she tells how a simple means of combating the spread of malaria was developed and how she was able to raise the awareness of an entire community, through its youth, about health issues. The means to this end was an educational program that has seen dozens of young people participate in making their community a healthier place in which to live. Their efforts to combat malaria have also led the community to a better understanding of other diseases and the negative effects of pesticide use.

Chapter Nine is by Heloise Emdon. She leads Acacia, an International Development Research Centre program that works with African partners to apply information and communication technologies to Africa's social and economic development. Emdon brings many years of experience in journalism and development in Southern Africa. Her chapter tells the story of connecting Africans to the world and how recent technological changes have served to bring millions of people into the global mainstream.

The last chapter is a story of how support for research for development has long-lasting political implications. Diego Piñeiro is a rural sociologist who is the former dean of the Faculty of Social Sciences, Universidad de la Republica, in Uruguay. In Chapter Ten he writes about his experiences and those of his colleagues under the military dictatorship in Uruguay from 1973 to 1985. Piñeiro discusses the role played by IDRC in maintaining research capacity in Uruguay and elsewhere in the Southern Cone region by supporting scientists who otherwise would have fled into exile or been prevented from continuing their investigations due to their pariah status as left-wing intellectuals living under right-wing dictatorships.

Long-Term Solutions for a Short-Term World was designed to engage international development specialists as well as students and the general public. Further information about the studies contained in this collection can be found online or in print. These chapters represent a small sample of the dynamic research currently being conducted in the developing world. The authors provide inspiration to those who are looking for examples of research that matters, and they provide insight into how scientists from different fields engage with problems that are common to poor people everywhere. Each of the following stories helps put a human face on research for development while at the same time explaining different facets of scientific investigation for the benefit of humanity.

— *Ron Harpelle and Bruce Muirhead*

CHAPTER ONE

The Underpinnings of Canadian Development Assistance

Ronald Harpelle

Defence, diplomacy, and development are the three pillars of Canadian foreign policy, and their use is in direct response to the needs or objectives of the Canadian government in a given country or region. Diplomacy and development work hand in hand to assist poor countries in strengthening their capacity to engage in democratization, human rights, rule of law, and public sector performance and accountability. Assistance in these key areas comes in many different forms, but support through Canada's Official Development Assistance (ODA) for research by scientists in poor countries to assist them in finding solutions to problems that confront their societies is an idea that was pioneered in Canada by the International Development Research Centre (IDRC). Capacity-building through research funding serves to strengthen and protect democratic institutions and civil society groups while at the same time providing tangible benefits to society as a whole. This investment in research has produced dividends throughout the non-industrialized world and has helped ensure that Canada is at the forefront of supporting research for development. A review of Canada's evolution as a donor country reveals ways in which the Canadian role in international development has been shaped by a history of accommodation.

Concern over the plight of the world's poor is enshrined in the Charter of United Nations, and it has been on the agenda of many bilateral and multilateral agencies for more than sixty years. In wealthy countries like Canada, many individuals and organizations have recognized that the struggle for development is one that we must participate in even though these challenges are mainly abroad. For example, Brock Chisholm, a Canadian who served as the first Director General of the World Health Organization, told an audience at the Empire Club in Toronto in 1952 that it was essential that "the peoples of the fortunate countries carry a greater load for the less fortunate who cannot carry loads for themselves." While this attitude resonates with the notion of the "white man's burden,"[1] development, along with defence and diplomacy, has evolved into one of the three pillars of Canadian foreign policy. Canada was not alone in following this trajectory toward a modern understanding of the global challenge of development and the place of international development in world affairs, but the Canadian experience was in many ways different. As part of the evolution of the thinking on the subject and with hindsight as a guide, international development practitioners in Canada and abroad have come to understand that the future is not only in the hands of those who carry a greater load, it is in the hands of us all. However, Canadians have stood out by creating the International Development Research Centre, a small Crown corporation whose mandate is to focus on research for development in poor countries.

IDRC's approach to international development is unique in that it funds research by researchers from and in developing countries and is guided by the straightforward idea that qualified researchers who live with the challenges of development are in the best position to explore solutions to the problems that confront the societies of which they are a part. A straightforward idea, but one that governments are reluctant to take up because it means spending money on research that will have no obvious or apparent benefit to the taxpayers of the donor country. Much of the development assistance offered to poor countries comes with strings attached; this is known as "tied aid." The ties may be minimal or they may benefit the donor country more than the recipient country, but international assistance almost always comes at a price. IDRC, however, is unique because it operates like a non-governmental foundation more than an extension of the Department of Foreign Affairs. Whereas the Canadian International Development Agency (CIDA) is known to Canadians because of its high profile and is seen to be working as an extension of the Canadian government abroad, IDRC has a much lower profile across Canada and in Ottawa. Chapter Two offers a detailed history of IDRC, but to better appreciate the milieu in which development research is conducted and the role Canada has played in assisting researchers in their quest for solutions, it is instructive to begin with a brief overview of the history of international development.

In Canada and other wealthy countries, development assistance has become a significant dimension of international relations, but this means of providing relief to the world's poor while at the same time projecting the ideology, technology, and values of industrial society on pre-industrial societies has been around for only about sixty years. Prior to the advent of the aid industry, the world was dominated by colonial powers whose aim was to maintain access to resources and markets through the more traditional means of building on existing power structures and who would use force when necessary. In almost every part of the world, European capital and colonial regimes dominated local economic and political systems. Latin America was an exception only in that Spanish power had all but ended by the 1820s and the United States came to dominate the region, playing a neo-colonial role. By 1900, virtually all of what came to be known in the 1960s as the "Third World" or "underdeveloped" was tied very directly to one or another of the European empires or to the nascent American empire. Then, in the first part of the twentieth century, global economic, political, and social changes began to take place at a rate that was unheard of in earlier centuries. The colonial world began to fall apart, the Russian Revolution created new challenges for societies everywhere, and new economic and political configurations confronted the dominance of the existing power brokers.

Through the first half of the twentieth century Europe was engulfed in the two bloodiest wars in history, the global economy endured a decade of depression, and approximately two-thirds of the world's population freed themselves from the yoke of European imperialism. Moreover, the Soviet Union was created and extended its power across Eastern Europe and elsewhere in the world, China underwent its own radical revolution and then excluded itself completely from Western influence, and a group of other countries, led in large part by India after its independence from Britain, formed the Non-Aligned Movement that came formally into existence in 1961. These events and thousands of other less spectacular changes took place around the world, causing significant disruption to the status quo of European and Euro-American capital and political domination. The international aid industry grew out of the turmoil caused by the changes brought on by the decline of Western Europe and shifting global power. International development assistance became the third pillar, along with diplomacy and defence, of Canada's and other industrial nations' foreign policy in the second half of the twentieth century.

This is not to say that the idea of assisting poor countries in developing their economic, political, and social foundations was a new idea. Throughout the nineteenth century, as Europeans expanded their colonial domination of Asia, Africa, and the Middle East, the plight of the world's poor was discussed among politicians and intellectuals, missionaries fanned out across the globe, and people with vision, like Simon Bolivar, dreamed of a more egalitarian world. However, the challenges of finding long-term solutions to poverty in a short-term world have been with us only since the end of the Second World War, when international development became a global concern. During this period, development specialists came slowly to appreciate the complexity of the problems faced by the world's poor. The early focus on infrastructure as a quick fix for development, which emphasized capital-intensive projects such as hydroelectric dams, roads, and the industrialization of agriculture, has given way to an appreciation of the social, ethnic, religious, and political complexities of poor countries. This, in turn, has given rise to the notion of helping others to help themselves. While education and training are obvious elements of such an approach, the facilitation of research on everyday problems is essential to capacity-building in less developed countries.[2]

IDRC was created in 1970 by the government of Canada as an arm's-length agency with a focus on research for development. Its mandate is to provide opportunities for researchers in poor countries to enable them to find solutions to the problems they see every day. By facilitating advances in research by researchers who are closest to the problem, IDRC aims to empower those who are best positioned to lead their communities and countries toward a better future. Since 1970 IDRC has supported research abroad through funding and various other forms of organizational support. The result is that legions of researchers from across the non-industrialized South, or what is more commonly known as the Global South, have benefited from its support over the past forty years. In addition to the advances that have been made through this kind of development assistance, there has been a significant increase in the capacity of individual researchers, their institutions, and societies as a whole to build on what has been accomplished. Importantly, funding provided by IDRC has enabled researchers to remain in their home countries, where their contributions extend far beyond the confines of the offices, laboratories, and classrooms in which they work. These are people who also participate in the affairs of societies in which they live and who often find themselves called upon to represent their country on the international stage.

IDRC is a little-known and often misunderstood arm of Canada's Official Development Assistance program with an impressive history. Most Canadians are familiar with CIDA, a scapegoat for many failed efforts at providing assistance to developing countries, but few have heard of IDRC, and, when they have, they have many misconceptions about its origins and its place in the world of development organizations. IDRC is rarely mentioned in the general histories of Canadian development assistance, and sometimes even highly regarded historians get the story wrong.[3] And, when they do get it right, IDRC is often shortchanged because it has a low profile in Ottawa. Unlike CIDA, IDRC does not have to worry about politicians showing up at its door demanding to know what it is going to do for his or her constituency, because IDRC spends little of its budget in Canada and its assistance is not tied aid.

To appreciate the evolution of international development thinking in Canada and the emergence of the idea of IDRC, it is instructive to begin with a look at the period between 1945 and the 1960, when Canada's External Aid Office was created. During the fifteen years between the end of hostilities in Europe and the launching of the Decade of Development by the United Nations, the world entered a new era. Canada and Canadian society underwent fundamental change, evolving slowly from a White-settler colony of the British Empire to a multicultural society made up by a large number of immigrants and first-generation Canadians from around the world. The changes made to Canada's immigration policy in 1962 were a reflection of the country's adaptation to a world that opened up in the aftermath of the Second World War. Canada emerged in the 1960s as a new country that was the product of virtually every history, culture, language, and religion in the world. Canada's recognition of the country's ethnic diversity through the adoption of multiculturalism as official policy in 1971 ensured that the country's present and future role in international development is tied to its diversity as a nation.

For the past sixty years, Canada's contributions to international development have, for the most part, followed a path similar to that of other leading donor countries. Initially, investment in development was exclusively scientific in nature, focusing Western knowledge and experience on what were seen by Western experts as the most obvious causes of poverty. The focus was on building infrastructure to facilitate production and trade. Massive hydroelectric, mining, and agricultural projects were financed and directed by Western governments using services and goods produced in the donor countries. No bones were made about it; development in the South was good for the North. Films like Donald Fraser's *Ten Years after the Colombo Plan*, produced by the National Film Board of Canada in 1961, make it clear that Canadian assistance helped Canadian industry. This approach to international development may have made sense to leading Western countries at the time, but it was born of the reconstruction efforts in Europe in the wake of the Second World War and was designed for countries with a pre-existing industrial base.

The problem of economic development in lower- and middle-income countries was then, as it is now, obviously extensive and persistent. According to the World Bank, 40 per cent of the world's population lives in low-income countries with an average GNP per capita of $410 per year; another 35 per cent live in lower-middle-income countries where the average per capita GNP is $1,200 per year. A total of 75 per cent of the people on earth live on less than four dollars a day, and more than half of these live on a little more than one dollar a day. Countries like Canada are included in the lucky 15 per cent of world population that is considered high-income. Another important aspect of the disparity between the rich and poor nations of the world is that the wealthiest countries in 1900 remain the wealthiest in the world today. One hundred years ago the richest countries were found in Western Europe and North America (minus Mexico), with Australia, New Zealand, and Japan rapidly catching up. Today we see the addition of some Eastern European countries, South Korea, and Taiwan, with Brazil, India, and China, and a few other, showing promise. Finally, the disparities between rich and poor countries and the disparities in individual wealth have also increased considerably in the last century, exacerbating the tensions between and within societies.

The origins of international development as we know it can be found in the Second World War, which undermined the capacity of Western European countries to govern the colonial world. Europe lay in ruins, two major Japanese cities were obliterated, and people throughout the southern hemisphere began to envision a new future. In Latin America, a wartime boom occasioned by import substitution policies created optimism for a prosperous future, while in Africa and Asia the yoke of European and Japanese imperialism spawned visions of political and economic independence. The vacuum created by the war paved the way for national liberation struggles throughout the colonial world. In the two decades that followed the end of the Second World War, membership in the United Nations more than doubled from 51 member countries to 117, most of which were carved out of former European empires.[4]

While the legacies of colonialism served as the foundation upon which the modern states of the Global South were built, it was the Second World War served as the catalyst for rapid change. The war destroyed the European foundations of the colonial world, and it provided opportunities for those who envisioned a future made up of nations functioning as equals and working together for a more equitable future. The war took its toll on Europe and on the rest of the world. Approximately 100 million people, soldiers and civilians alike, were killed, wounded, or disabled as a result of the war. Millions more were dislocated, left homeless and impoverished because of the conflict. Moreover, the German invasion of neighbouring countries, coupled with the imperial ambitions of Italy and Japan, shifted control over large parts of Africa and Asia to the Axis powers during the war. As a result, in the postwar period the British, French, Belgian, and Dutch governments were obliged to re-establish their imperial interests and attempt to reimpose control at a time when they could least afford it.

The Second World War also saw the United States and the Soviet Union emerge as the chief arbiters of international affairs. This new rivalry, born of Western fears of communism and hostility to the creation of the Soviet Union — nurtured through the Depression Era, when radical politics swept across Europe and North America, and concretized by the division of Europe into East and West at the end of the war — resulted in the emergence of the Cold War and a new global scramble for influence. The independence of India in 1947 — coupled with the success of the Chinese Revolution in 1949, the outbreak of the Korean War, and the difficulty of re-establishing European control over Indochina — initiated a move toward developing new means of sustaining Western dominance over the world. Development assistance emerged as a new tool that could help alleviate the pains of poverty while simultaneously protecting the economic and political interests of the capitalist world. While global politics in the period after 1945 was framed within the Cold War, domestic politics and economics were also important parts of the platform for development assistance.

The war provided the opportunity for Canada to distinguish itself in the eyes of the world. In joining the war effort in 1939, Canada was among the first nations to come to the defence of Britain and the other countries threatened by German aggression. During the course of the war, Canada, a country with a population of less than 12 million, had 1.1 million enlistments in its armed forces and saw more than 45,000 men and women perish in the conflict. By the end of the war, Canada possessed the third-largest military among the Allies, which ensured that the country played a significant role on the international stage both during and immediately after the war.[5] As a result of its sacrifices, Canada, a relatively insignificant country in 1939, became one of the leading arbiters of power in the post-war world. Respect for Canada as an ally, combined with other countries' perception that Canadians could be trusted, carried Canada forward, opening the door to founding membership in numerous international bodies. Along with other leading nations, Canada became a member of the United Nations in 1945, the Organisation for European Economic Co-operation and Development in 1948, and became an active contributor to other new institutions like the World Bank and the International Monetary Fund, created at the Bretton Woods Conference in 1944. Canadian representatives had a hand in creating the new global superstructure of organizations charged with leading the world toward a more prosperous and less dangerous future.

Although Canada's history of international development might be said to begin with the creation of the United Nations and its various agencies, far more significant to the evolution of a Canadian response to development problems was the launching of the Commonwealth of Nations and the establishment of the Colombo Plan for Co-operative Economic Development in South and Southeast Asia. According to V. Peyton Lyon, Canadian foreign assistance began as a desire to "assist the United Kingdom" in meeting its postwar obligations to past and present members of the British Empire.[6] The original British Commonwealth of Nations was an organization formed in the 1920s when the United Kingdom and its dominions — Canada, Newfoundland, Australia, and New Zealand — agreed they were equal in status and united by common allegiance to the Crown. With the end of the Second World War and the rapid growth in the number of colonies that gained their independence, the word British was dropped from the name and the Commonwealth of Nations was created. The Colombo Plan was agreed to in January 1950 following a meeting of Commonwealth foreign ministers. It was intended as a means of assisting countries in South Asia with their transition to independence and as a way of checking the spread of communism, which was thought of by Western powers to be an opportunistic ideology that took advantage of poverty. Consequently, the Colombo Plan focused on poverty reduction in the region, and Canada participated with an initial contribution of $25 million of assistance.

It is not surprising in the post-1945 world that among the primary reasons given for the establishment of the Colombo Plan was the need to shore up South Asia in order to prevent the spread of communism. This justification was framed by Nik Cavell, the administrator of Canadian participation in the plan, when he toured the country telling Canadians that although totalitarianism had been defeated in two world wars, a new, "more sinister, diabolical, world-wide totalitarian force" was confronting the world in the early 1950s. Cavell told his audiences that the free world had lost "Poland, Hungary, Rumania, Czechoslovakia, Bulgaria, Albania and East Germany in Europe; and that Communism has made a great inroad in Asia by taking over the 500 million people of China." He warned Canadians that communism was "busy day and night softening up, and preparing, other populations ready for the day when they too can be made satellites of an ever-growing world of terrible totalitarian slavery of the human mind and body."[7] Cavell and the Canadian government were playing on the sensitivity Canadians still had over the Second World War and on Cold War sentiments that were becoming a part of all international and many domestic decisions made by governments in the West.

While Canada's main motives for involvement in the Colombo Plan were to help Britain by helping other members of the Commonwealth and to staunch the tide of communism, another reason for Canada's international assistance was the need to bolster the Canadian economy. The Second World War had provided Canada, like the United States, with the economic stimulus to pull the country out of depression and significantly increase its industrial base. Canada's economic contribution to the war effort was third among the Allied nations, making up 5 per cent of total Allied war production.[8] Manufacturing centres like Toronto and Montreal saw their industrial output increase dramatically as Canada became an important supplier of military and non-military manufactures during the conflict. More remote regions of the country saw demand for foodstuffs and raw materials like timber and steel increase in tandem with the growth of the manufacturing sector. Cities across the country also saw their industrial output increase as the Allied forces demanded more *matériel* to replace that which was lost in war and to keep pace with the exponential growth in the size of their armed forces.

Canadian men and women participated in the boom as both workers and consumers, creating new demand in the domestic sector, and after 1945 wartime industries were retooled to meet continuing growth in the Canadian economy. In the decades that followed the Second World War, Canada experienced a significant expansion in its economy. Returning soldiers found jobs and settled down to start families. Throughout the 1950s and 1960s, unemployment levels remained low and Canada developed an economy that was able, in the 1960s, to support the creation of a number of state welfare programs. These changes in the role of government in people's lives also increased Canada's attractiveness as a destination for immigrants from around the world. In the immediate aftermath of the war the bulk of these immigrants came from war-torn Europe, but increasingly immigration to Canada came from non-European countries around the globe as opportunities arose in all fields of employment. But domestic markets alone could not absorb all that Canada could produce, and international markets became more and more important.

Canada became increasingly reliant on foreign markets for its commodities and manufactured products. Most of this external trade was with the United States, which became Canada's most important trading partner during the Second World War. In terms of foreign investment, the United States, with its booming manufacturing sector and rapidly increasing domestic markets, displaced Britain and became the Canada's principal foreign investor, contributing 75 per cent of all investments in the years after 1945. By 1951, 59 per cent of Canada's exports were to the United States, as compared with 16 per cent to Britain. Later, the 1957 Royal Commission on Canada's Economic Prospects, chaired by Walter Gordon, brought the country's reliance on U.S. markets to light and forced the Government of Canada to look at ways of limiting U.S. influence over the economy. But in the early 1950s, the government and business were increasingly aware that a significant portion of Canada's foreign trade was

with countries other than Britain and the United States, and this knowledge permitted the government to justify its investments in development
abroad.

With the broadening of markets abroad for Canadian manufacturing
and agricultural exports, the economy became more dependent on smaller
countries as outlets for goods. As a result, development assistance became
a means of increasing exports from Canada, and Southeast Asia was the
first area to be targeted for investment in development. Although trade
with the region was quite limited, the Canadian government was banking
on the future and saw an opportunity to support the domestic economy
through its largesse. In the early 1950s, Canada was purchasing $12 to 14
million worth of products from Ceylon, mostly tea, but Ceylon was unable
to reciprocate. Canadian assistance to Ceylon was the key to increasing
purchasing power and the importation of Canadian goods.[9] While Ceylon
was only a minor beneficiary of Canada's contributions to the Colombo
Plan, India and Pakistan received the bulk of Canadian assistance. In
1951–52, Canada gave India and Pakistan $25 million in assistance. Of the
$15 million in assistance given to India by Canada, $10 million was in the
form of wheat from the Canadian prairies and $5 million in the form of
Canadian-built buses and trucks for the Bombay Transportation Commission. Among the Canadian priorities for Pakistan was a $5 million
cement mill produced in Canada to meet demand for the construction of
irrigation canals and $3 million worth of Canadian-made railway ties.[10]
Thus, manufacturers and forest products companies in Canada benefited
as much from this assistance as the recipient countries. Canada also contributed $400,000 in technical assistance that allowed people to take
courses at universities and training schools in Canada, providing support
for the post-secondary education system in Canada and establishing long-
term relationships that would benefit everyone involved.

One of the most obvious features of Canada's early commitment to
development assistance was the result of the country being born into the
British Empire. As a result, almost all Canadian assistance went to Commonwealth countries during the immediate postwar period, and even in
1962–63, approximately 95 per cent of Canadian Bilateral ODA (Official
Development Assistance) flowed to India, Pakistan, and Ceylon.[11] More
specifically, 54 per cent of Canada's total contribution to the Colombo
Plan went to India and 37 per cent to Pakistan.[12] The emphasis on India
was in part because Canadian Prime Minister Louis St. Laurent was on

good terms with Indian Prime Minister Jawaharlal Nehru and because, in the context of the Cold War, India needed to be kept within the fold. Another factor that favoured South Asia was that Canadian assistance was limited to newly independent states because Canada respected European colonial claims and was not prepared to challenge them.[13]

The problem for the Europeans was that the war had destroyed their industrial capacity and the colonial world offered the raw materials and markets essential to the rebuilding of their economies. They therefore sought to balance the demands for freedom that echoed across the Global South with their needs as industrial nations. The responses were varied and pragmatic. In many cases, wars of independence were fought, and in others the transition was relatively straightforward. The Europeans did not want to see their influence in their former colonial possessions taken up by rivals in Europe, and they were mindful of the global pretensions of the United States. In general, the more powerful the European empires, the more easily Britain was able to accommodate the independence of its colonies. Successful transitions from British rule to a trustworthy indigenous ruling elite took place throughout most of the British Empire. The French were somewhat less successful, notably in Indochina and North Africa, but they soon adapted to the changes and developed a linguistic exclusion zone around many of their former colonies. Smaller states like Belgium and Portugal, whose economies and national prestige were much more dependent on their colonial possessions, fought protracted wars of independence, bankrupting their former colonial possessions on their way out.

Throughout the 1950s much of the non-industrialized world was caught up in struggles for independence occasioned by the collapse and fragmentation of European empires during the Second World War. For Canada, the opening up of the world came as an opportunity that was also a significant challenge for a country with such limited exposure to the rest of the world. Whereas the European powers, even in their decline, had hundreds of years of experience with the less developed regions of the world, Canada was a newcomer on the international stage. Similarly, with its imperial experience in the Philippines, Cuba, Puerto Rico, and throughout Central America in the first half of the twentieth century, the United States had already developed a large and reasonably well-informed bureaucracy to deal with its international affairs. Again, Canadians were new to working and living in other countries because Canada had relied heavily on Britain to represent its interests abroad during the late-nineteenth and early-twentieth centuries. As a result, Canadian government bureaucrats, if they were not British, had few international contacts and few opportunities to develop them because much of the world had been all but closed to Canada and Canadians until 1945.

While Britain welcomed Canadian support to help maintain influence within the growing family of nations that formed the Commonwealth, France did not see Canada as a natural ally in the post-1945 period. Not until the founding of La Francophonie in 1970 did France and Canada develop a formal relationship that was similar to that of Canada and Britain. No Canadian aid was solicited or offered to former French territories because France, unlike Britain, made a more concerted effort to reimpose its control over its colonial possessions in Asia and to intensify its control over its colonies in Africa. The invasion and occupation of France by German forces in the Second World War had cut off contact between France and its colonies, giving people in the colonies a taste for independence. The subsequent occupation of those same colonies by various other powers exacerbated the tensions when France renewed its claims at the end of the war. As a result, France had sought to re-establish control over its colonies before it could begin to negotiate independence.

One of the problems faced by all of the industrialized countries of the West, and especially one with such limited international exposure as Canada, was the lack of specialists in various fields of international development. The oldest network of individuals and institutions concerned with development, the Society for International Development (SID), was founded in 1957 in Washington by international development practitioners and policy advisers who recognized the need to draw upon the experience of others to design strategies for dealing with global poverty. Similarly, although universities everywhere had departments and schools with a focus on specific areas of the world, stand-alone programs focused specifically on international development were non-existent. Schools like the Institute for Development Studies in Sussex did not exist in the 1950s and did not start producing graduates until the late 1960s. In Canada, McGill University's Centre for Developing-Area Studies was founded in 1963 and was among the first in Canada to offer academic programs with international development as a focus. This did not deter the Canadians, because universities across the country contained researchers who could be pressed into service as part of the government's desire to provide solutions to the problems of development. And, since development problems were considered largely to be the result of poor countries lacking infrastructure and modern technologies, Canadian scientists were the first to be asked to lend their expertise to the task at hand.

There was nothing unusual about focusing on technical fixes and scientific solutions, but, given the lack of scientific and technical capacity in poorer countries, this solution had two important effects on future development initiatives. The first was the training of individuals and often the creation of educational programs and facilities by Canadian and other Western educators. The second was the reliance on Western experts with Western experience to look for scientific and technical solutions to the problems faced by people living in the Global South. The problem with this type of development assistance was that it did not necessarily lead to independent research and much of the research itself was dependent on Western expertise and support. Moreover, proven Canadian science did not always work in countries with different climates, social structures, and economies. The experts sent to help out were also not often versed in the vast religious, cultural, political, economic, and social differences that existed. With time, it became clear that hard science did not have all the answers, and the social sciences gradually became a major focus of Canada's international development efforts.

One of the keys to building Canadian capacity in international development was the creation of government agencies and the training of civil servants to manage aid. The first big step toward developing a specialized civil service dedicated to development assistance was not taken by the Canadian government until the election of John Diefenbaker in 1957. Unlike Britain, the United States, and France, Canada did not have a sphere of influence from the pre-war years, nor did it have many civil servants with overseas experience, much less experience in foreign assistance to poor countries. Though John Diefenbaker was not particularly interested in foreign development assistance, he is credited with the establishment of the External Aid Office, the precursor to CIDA, in 1960.[14] The person selected to head this new wing of government was Herb Moran, a former British military officer who had served in India but who was then working for the Canadian government.

Moran followed in the footsteps of others, notably Nik Cavell, who was born in England, joined the Indian Army in 1913, and saw Great War service in Mesopotamia and on the Indian frontier. Cavell became the director of the International Economic and Technical Division of the Department of Trade and Commerce when it was formed in September 1951. Accord-ing to David Morrison, he was known as someone whose "forte was pro-motion rather than management." Cavell was also one of the few civil ser-vants initially involved with the Colombo Plan who had experience in a poor country.[15] Although it is true that it would have been difficult to find someone without a military background to do the job in the period imme-diately after the Second World War, it is also a historical fact that former military officers profoundly shaped Canada's Official Development Assis-tance.[16] People with a military background were brought in for the simple fact that it was assumed they knew how to put things in order and were good at solving big problems. Thus, they treated development as a military campaign that could be won using military planning and precision as a means of achieving set objectives. Indeed, the discourse on international development in the 1950s and '60s is often described as a military opera-tion in which Western experts were portrayed as soldiers in a war against poverty. This was made clear by Major-General Brock Chisholm in 1951 when he spoke about "defeating" disease and by Nik Cavell, who a few months later described the Colombo Plan as an "operation."[17] For these two lead-ing Canadian figures in the history of international development, the problem was clear. The world was engaged in a struggle to overcome the ravages of poverty and the threat of communism, and action was needed.

Military men with international experience like Cavell, Chisholm, and Moran were soon joined by others who had missionary experience in Canada and abroad.[18] The missionaries were educators, health specialists, and other skilled individuals who had faith in progress and were enthused by the social gospel movement of the late-nineteenth and early-twentieth centuries. They applied Christian principles to social problems in the hope of alleviating poverty. By mid-century, many thousands of Canadians had ventured abroad to work as missionaries within the British Empire and beyond. According to one source, "In proportion to its size and resources, the churches of Canada sponsored more missionaries at home and abroad than any other nation in Christendom," and in the absence of formal diplomatic relations with the rest of the world, the missionary movement was Canada's de-facto foreign policy.[19] Moreover, in line with the history of the Catholic Church in Latin America before the 1960s, Catherine LeGrand's research suggests that "foreign missionaries" were generally assigned to "outlying areas of particularly poor and difficult urban bar-rios," the kind of places where locally born priests did not want to serve.[20]

By the time that Vatican II and the advent of liberation theology in the 1960s served to sensitize the Catholic Church to the plight of the poor, many Canadians had been front-line missionaries in some of the poorest regions of the world. Who better for the Canadian government to turn to for advice on the social aspects of development than Canadian missionaries who had served abroad?

A good example of a missionary-turned-international-development specialist is Jacques Amyot, who worked for IDRC in the 1970s. Amyot was born in northern Alberta to francophone parents who sent him to Valleyfield, Quebec, for an education. He became a Jesuit priest and was working as a missionary in China at the time of the Revolution in 1949. He lived in China from 1947 to 1952 and was then sent by the Jesuit Order to the University of Chicago to study social anthropology. His graduate research took him to the Philippines, but when he graduated in 1961 he was sent to Thailand, where he worked at Chulalongkorn University. Amyot was responsible for establishing the departments of anthropology and sociology, and he started the Institute of Social Studies in 1969 to advance research at the university. In 1974, he left Thailand and the Jesuit Order and hoped to obtain funding from CIDA to conduct research on resettlement in the Mekong Delta. He returned to Ottawa for meetings but found that CIDA was a dead end. Amyot then went to IDRC, where he was first offered a Pearson Fellowship and then was asked to be IDRC's representative in Southeast Asia. Thus, Jacques Amyot, the former Jesuit, became an IDRC program officer living in Singapore, bringing his years of experience in Asia to the organization.

Although Amyot's participation in Canada's Official Development Assistance was late in coming, he is a good example of the kind of person who was attracted to Canadian aid work. They were individuals who made sacrifices to assist fellow human beings, and in the 1950s and 1960s, with independence movements and radical politics changing the nature of the developing world, Canadian missionaries were active participants in events throughout the Global South. During the same period, the Catholic Church was undergoing fundamental change, and returning priests, nuns, and lay missionaries were engaged in the politics of the Second Vatican Council (1962–65). It is not surprising, therefore, that in Canada the Catholic Church founded its own foreign assistance organization, Development and Peace, at the Conférence des Évêques Catholiques du Canada in 1967.[21]

Canadian missionary presence abroad increased throughout the 1950s and 1960s. A number of church-affiliated development-orientated organizations came into being in the postwar era. For example, Operation Crossroads Africa, an organization founded in 1958, spread north to Canada in 1959 with the support of the United Church of Canada and became Canadian Crossroads International.[22] Crossroads joined a number of other fledgling non-governmental organizations (NGOs), mostly branches of American or British associations that emerged in Canada in the postwar period.[23] These organizations may have predated the Second World War, but the modern term "non-governmental organization" has its origins in the post-1945 world. The United Nations Charter provided for the Economic and Social Council to "make suitable arrangements for consultation with non-governmental organizations" with international organizations and national organizations. This consultative role for organizations was not only focused on questions of development but was an important step toward providing a foundation for the legitimization of NGOs around the world. The NGOs of the period were concerned with the ravages of war in Europe and were not yet focused on poor countries in the South. Once the plight of Europe had been dealt with, NGOs began looking south for places to continue their work. In Canada, one of the pre-eminent NGOs in the field of development was the Unitarian Service Committee.

Lotta Hitschmanova, the founder and former head of the Unitarian Service Committee, is the best example of the combination of influence of military organization and Christian mission in a Canadian NGO. Hitschmanova was a refugee from Czechoslovakia who fled the Nazi advance and arrived in Canada in 1942. She founded the Unitarian Service Committee (USC) of Canada in 1945. Her assistance work, like that of her adopted country, focused initially on relief and reconstruction in war-ravaged Europe. Then, in parallel with Canada's efforts to assist the poor in other parts of the world, Dr. Hitschmanova pointed the Unitarian Service Committee in its current direction of international development assistance. Wearing a trademark army nurse's uniform with a military-style hat, and working tirelessly with missionary zeal to raise funds for the USC, she became a household name in Canada. The USC was joined by similar organizations in the late 1950s and early '60s to form the foundation of Canada's NGO community. Together these organizations came to form a training ground for the new civil service that came into being with the formation of the External Aid Office.

A final step toward the completion of a foundation for the expansion of Canada's international development efforts came with the United Nations declaration of the 1960s as the Development Decade, following John F. Kennedy's suggestion to that effect during his September 1961 address to the UN General Assembly. The UN called upon member states to take action to reduce the inequity between the rich and poor of the world. In general, the resolution followed the trajectory for international development established in the previous decade. The focus was to be on industrialization, the development of agriculture, national planning, and the fight against illiteracy, hunger, and disease, the promotion of vocational and technical training, an increase in the flow of public and private capital to developing countries, an increase in export earnings, and the utilization of resources from the disarmament of both the East and the West for the purpose of economic and social development.[24]

In many ways, Canada was ahead of the game when the UN made its declaration. The External Aid Office was already established, a number of initiatives involving the refining and expansion of Canada's Official Development Assistance program were under way, and, most importantly, the period of postwar prosperity enjoyed by Canada was beginning to result in bigger budgets and new opportunities at home and abroad. Moreover, the country had accumulated an enormous amount of prestige at the international level for its contributions to the world during and after the war. The 1960s was therefore a time for Canada to collect on the dividends it had accrued since 1945, and it is with this general backdrop that Canada developed the strategy for international development that is still with us today. A number of other milestones would be reached over the next fifty years, but the foundation for Canada's participation in international development efforts was cast.

In June 1957, John Diefenbaker defeated Louis St. Laurent's government, of which Pearson was a part. Diefenbaker took a slight interest in foreign development assistance, but his government established the External Aid Office in 1960. At the same time, the old Organisation for European Economic Co-operation (OEEC) was turned into the new Organisation for Economic Co-operation and Development (OECD), the club of European and North American industrialized economies, and it set up the Development Assistant Committee (DAC), which oversaw each members' foreign aid contributions. Canada did not do well in the DAC or in its own aid programs. Indeed, the DAC complained in 1962 that rich Canada was devoting only 0.27 per cent of its GNP to the aid file, one of the lowest per-centages among OECD countries. Ironically, Canadian aid as a percentage of gross national product is not much higher today than it was then.

Nevertheless, a major turning point in the evolution of Canada's ODA programming came in April 1963, when Lester Pearson was elected as prime minister. While ODA did not immediately capture his attention, he was interested in increasing Canada's contribution to international development and was well aware of Canada's profile among the nations of the world. Pearson had been around government for a long time — indeed, since the 1920s. He had been a deputy minister of foreign affairs in the 1940s and the minister of foreign affairs from 1948 to 1957. It was in the latter capacity that he had encouraged the Canadian cabinet to support the Commonwealth's Colombo Plan of 1950, which was intended as a bulwark against the spread of communism in Asia but was also of some assistance to those countries targeted for help in their development. The bulk of Canadian assistance went to India, with Pakistan and Ceylon receiving far smaller amounts. Of course, Jawaharlal Nehru, India's prime minister from independence until 1964, was an enormously attractive global figure, and Canada's high commissioner in Delhi for five years, Escott Reid, was an admirer of his. A close friend of Pearson's, Reid encouraged Ottawa to invest whatever dollars it could into the country, the world's largest democracy. Out of that, among other things, came the pro-vision of a CANDU nuclear reactor, constructed over the period from 1956 to 1961.

During Pearson's tenure as prime minister, the External Aid Office was transformed into CIDA, which was tasked with allocating the bulk of Canada's ODA. Along with the new organization came a new appointment to a top civil service position in Ottawa. Maurice Strong was lured from the private sector to transform the External Aid Office into CIDA, and he became the new agency's first president. Strong was born in Manitoba in 1929, and by the time he arrived in Ottawa three and half decades later he had led an extremely interesting life. He left home as a teenager, joined the Merchant Marine and travelled abroad, and then worked in northern Canada in Inuit communities for the Hudson's Bay Company, followed by a stint in the mailroom at the United Nations. He then became a highly successful entrepreneur who by the age of thirty was a self-made million-aire. His entrepreneurial and managerial talents had attracted the notice of the prime minister, and in 1966 he was tapped for the job.

Coming as he did from the private sector, Strong could not understand why CIDA did not have a research arm. In his previous world, most large corporations did. Why should government be different? Accordingly, he began to develop a plan for the creation of a new kind of international development institution, and he proposed to Pearson that some sort of research organization was necessary. This would be a new method of delivering assistance, in that it would solve economic and social problems through the development and use of technologies appropriate to the needs of developing countries. Strong and others in Ottawa worked toward developing what was to become a new and uniquely Canadian means of delivering development assistance.

In 1970 the International Development Research Centre opened its doors. CIDA, always criticized and never able to live up to the expectations of those who see development as a matter of fixing problems with tried and tested methods, may be considered a mainstream development agency, but IDRC is anything but. Though often seen as competitors, CIDA and IDRC have different mandates and are subject to different domestic and international pressures. They often collaborate, but they are also independent of each other, and this is how IDRC was envisioned to function in the Canadian aid family.

Maurice Strong's ability to convince the government of Canada to support the idea of a new, research-oriented institution was aided by the success of the Pearson Commission on International Development. After stepping down as prime minister, Pearson was asked by the president of the World Bank, Robert McNamara, to head an investigation into the effectiveness of the World Bank's development assistance during the first twenty years of its existence. Working out of an office in the CIDA headquarters provided by his friend Strong, Pearson produced a report entitled "Partners in Development." Commonly known as the Pearson Report, the document was delivered in September 1969 and offered a number of recommendations on the future of development assistance. Not surprisingly, IDRC, which came into existence in May of the following year, would follow up on the report's suggestion that Canada should direct some of its international development assistance to research into the problems of the developing world. It was also not surprising that Lester Pearson was chosen to serve as the first chair of IDRC's board of governors.

In early 1970, Maurice Strong, then still president of CIDA, explained to the Standing Committee on External Affairs and National Defence that

CIDA was responsible for advising the Government of Canada in development matters and, consequently, the agency performed the basic research and preparatory work that led to the proposal to create IDRC. Strong explained that developing countries were spending a small fraction of what countries like Canada spend on research and development. He warned that the gap between rich and poor countries would widen if the research and development gap and the education gap widened.

Looking back, it is obvious that IDRC could not have been established during any other part of Canadian history than the late 1960s, when political and economic conditions permitted bold new experiments. While Pierre Trudeau is generally given credit for making IDRC a reality, the honour should more correctly go to Lester Pearson, Canada's prime minister from April 1963 until April 1968. The establishment of IDRC was a part of a period of activism in Canadian politics such as has not been seen since, and it resulted in, among other things, the Canada Pension Plan, public health care, unemployment insurance, new social services, a new flag, and changes to Canada's immigration act that would make this country into one of the most multicultural in the world. It was an impressive and unparalleled display of policy interventions in the best sense of the phrase.

What may appear today as a straightforward proposition was in the 1960s a radical idea in the field of international development. Prior to the creation of IDRC, no governmental or non-governmental organization anywhere had as its primary focus the development of the scientific and technological capacities of developing countries. After consulting with development experts around the world, taking suggestions from various interest groups in Canada and abroad, and after lining up support in Ottawa, IDRC was created through an Act of Parliament. The act marked a new departure for Canada and Canadians along the road of international development. Attempts have been made to replicate IDRC elsewhere in the world, but no other government has succeeded in creating an institution quite like it. Chapter Two deals in depth with the characteristics that have ensured that IDRC remains distinct from other aid organizations, but its exceptional governing structure is worth mentioning here.

IDRC is unique in that it is a Crown corporation governed by an international board of governors. Ten members plus the chair of the board are Canadians appointed by the federal government, and ten are non-Canadian experts on development from around the world. No other country in the world has an official foreign aid agency whose decisions are made, in large part, by foreigners. Crown-corporation status means that IDRC is not bound by the same constraints as CIDA or other federal government departments. IDRC can and does go wherever it is mandated to work, and it does not have to ask permission from the government of the day to work in a given country. This is particularly important at times when Canada and the international community collectively turn their backs on a country or a people, such as it did in South Africa under apartheid or, more recently, in Palestine after the recent electoral success of Hamas. IDRC is free to investigate and report on any development-related subject and, with few exceptions, is not obliged to follow the Canadian government's agenda. IDRC is like all of the major Canadian scholarly research funding agencies combined: it is the Social Sciences and Humanities Research Council, the Natural Sciences and Engineering Research Council, and the Canadian Institutes of Health Research for the developing world.

However, unlike Canadian research funding agencies, IDRC must often begin by assisting researchers from the Global South in developing proposals for funding that will appeal to international funding agencies. For researchers unfamiliar with the expectations and demands of Western funding institutions like the World Bank, the Ford Foundation, and CIDA, the preparation of winning research proposals can be daunting. Therefore, an important role for IDRC is to assist researchers from poor countries in preparing project proposals and, where capacity is lacking, to provide assistance with the training necessary to make them competitive. IDRC helps researchers become established and considers its work complete when an individual or project is able to move on to other sources of support for research.

Since its inception in 1970, IDRC has supported about 13,000 projects, which means funding for an average of 250 researchers or groups per year. Of course, these figures vary over time and in different regions of the globe, but today IDRC operates in about 100 countries connected by six regional offices — in Montevideo, Cairo, Singapore, New Delhi, Dakar, and Nairobi — which serve as hubs for regions and for programming. In addition to being governed by an international board, the individuals employed by IDRC, in Ottawa and around the world, do not have to be Canadians, and several of the top management positions are held by non-Canadians. Persons occupying positions requiring expertise in international development are hired regardless of their nationality. Also, the regional offices are Canadian offices transplanted abroad. Canadian values and practices govern the workplace, and IDRC is often cited by those familiar with it as having a different kind of approach to development and a different kind of environment in which to discuss the challenges of development.

On a financial level, IDRC, which manages a fraction of Canada's already small contribution to international development, is almost negligible in the global theatre. At present, IDRC receives approximately $130 million per year from the Canadian government. This amount is set at 3 per cent of CIDA's budget appropriation. IDRC can easily boast playing a role in international development that is far more significant than the resources at its disposal would suggest. This is because IDRC is a model of accountability, it has enjoyed a stable yet progressive administration, its employees are among the best in the business, and it has an international reputation that is second to none. IDRC is Canada's 3-per-cent solution to the problems of the developing world and, judging by its success over the past four decades, an increase in the strength of this solution would obviously result in a more significant contribution on the part of Canadians to international development. If it were a business, IDRC would be a highly successful enterprise. However, IDRC is not a business. It is a Crown corporation without a strong constituency in Canada, and it is therefore vulnerable to the whims of the Canadian government. For this reason, IDRC works hard to maintain a reputation in Canada and around the world that is beyond reproach.

This book is, in some ways, a call for more effort on the part of Canada and Canadians in reaching the United Nations Millennium Development Goals of spending 0.7 per cent of our gross national income on development assistance by 2015. The fact is, 1 billion people now live in slums, 1.5 billion live without electricity, almost 1 billion people are chronically malnourished, 1 billion have inadequate access to water, and 2.5 billion lack basic sanitation. Of course, many of these people suffer from multiple inadequacies, but the fact remains that about 3 billion people on this planet now live on less than two dollars a day. Nevertheless, with the global economy shifting as a result of the emergence of the newly dynamic economies of the so-called BRIC countries, the challenges of longterm development have increased. A billion or so people in countries such as Brazil, India, and China are now able to purchase more of everything and, as a consequence, the poorest people on the planet must now compete even more fiercely for their share of the world's resources.

Notes

1 Chisholm, "World Health," The Empire Club of Canada Addresses (Toronto, Ontario: Empire Club Foundation, 1951), 339.
2 For an example of an attempt to demonstrate how one organization stayed "ahead of the curve," see Emmerij, Jolly, and Weiss, *Ahead of the Curve? UN Ideas and Global Challenges.*
3 See Hillmer and Granatstein, *Empire to Umpire,* 287, who state that "IDRC was instituted in 1978 by Trudeau to foster research … (and to provide a job for his former aide, Ivan Head)." A similar omission of the IDRC can be seen in Tomlin, Hillmer, and Hampson, *Canada's International Policies.*
4 Today there are 192 members of the United Nations, the vast majority countries struggling with the challenges of development.
5 Bothwell, *The Penguin History of Canada,* 356–57.
6 Peyton, Lyon, and Ismael, eds., *Canada and the Third World,* xxi.
7 Cavell, "Canada and the Colombo Plan."
8 Bothwell, *The Penguin History of Canada,* 356–57.
9 Hurley, "Ceylon and the Colombo Plan."
10 Cavell, "Canada and the Colombo Plan."
11 Morrison, "The Choice of Bilateral Aid Recipients," 124.
12 Morrison, *Aid and Ebb Tide,* 33.
13 Investments by Canadian corporations like Alcan or missionary activities by groups like the White Fathers were a different matter because they were not considered to be Canadian interference in the political affairs of the European powers.
14 Other government aid organizations established in the period include Germany's Federal Ministry of Economic Cooperation and Development (1961), l'Agence Française de Développement (officially dating back to 1941, but a pivotal change occurred in 1958 with the creation of the Caisse centrale de coopération économique which focused on newly independent states) and the Norwegian Agency for Development Cooperation (1952).
15 Morrison, *Aid and Ebb Tide,* 31.
16 Another Canadian of note from the period who had a military background was Hugh Keenleyside, ambassador to Mexico in the mid-1940s and the director general of the United Nations' Technical Assistance Administration from 1950 to 1958. See Hugh Keenleyside, "Ten Ways to Escape the Death of the World," *Maclean's,* September 3, 1966: 24a–24c and 24f. Major-General Brock Chisholm, became the first Executive Secretary of the World Health Organization, from 1948 to 1953.
17 Chisholm, "World Health."
18 Nik Cavell was followed by Orville Ault as director of the International Economic and Technical Division of the Department of Trade and Commerce. During the Second World War Ault was head of the Educational Services Overseas and a student at the Imperial Defence College in London, England.
19 Austin and Scott, Introduction, *Canadian Missionaries, Indigenous Peoples,* 4.

20 See Catherine LeGrand for interesting perspectives on Quebec missionaries in Latin America. "L'axe missionnaire catholique entre le Québec et l'Amérique latine: Une exploration préliminaire."

21 See Jean-Guy Vaillancourt for a full discussion of the Catholic left in Quebec during the 1960s and '70s. "Les groupes socio-politiques progressistes dans le Catholicisme québécois contemporain," 277.

22 Crossroads Africa was founded by an African American minister, the Rev. James H. Robinson, who served as minister of Harlem's Presbyterian Church of the Master. Crossroads Africa was called the "progenitor of the Peace Corps" by President John F. Kennedy.

23 Smillie and Helmich, *Non-Governmental Organizations and Governments*, 103.

24 Jolly, *UN Contributions to Development Thinking and Practice*, 87.

CHAPTER TWO

IDRC: Forty Years of Research for Development

Bruce Muirhead

The International Development Research Centre (IDRC) is a product of a certain time, place, and philosophy paralleling what was happening domestically in Canada with the very activist agenda pursued by the government of Prime Minister Lester B. Pearson. It reflected a confidence in government and that "development" remained possible, both views of which were to come under increasing fire into the mid-1970s. Its mandate was also unique; that came with support for funding research for development in the South where the researcher was not merely the vessel into which Northern projects would be poured, but the expert who would actually determine the program of work. The Office of the Auditor General put it well when it noted, following a comprehensive audit of IDRC undertaken in 1982, that "The Centre's approach to research aid is based on the premise that the best people to decide what the developing countries really need are the people of those countries, and that research aimed at meeting those needs is best carried out by scientists of the developing world."[1] The *IDRC Act* established IDRC at arm's length from government, which provided it with a certain independence to plough its own furrow, and which imbued the organization with certain features absent from most other official development agencies.[2]

Beginning with four divisions (Agriculture, Food and Nutrition Sciences; Information Sciences; Health Sciences, and Social Sciences) and a very small budget, IDRC committed itself to funding applied research in the way noted above. Division-based program officers would provide expert advice to putative Southern recipients as well as encouraging researchers in innovative and interesting areas to apply. IDRC's focus was resolutely on the Global South, and it eschewed funding Canadian researchers until the early 1980s, despite demands that it do so. That has resulted in a Centre much better known in developing countries than it is in Canada. Throughout the 1970s and into the late 1980s, it added divisions and personnel, at its peak employing more than 600 staff. It also supported regional offices in Africa, Asia, and Latin America, eventually settling on six by 2001. IDRC was also bestowed with an innovative and unique governance system that was to prove remarkable. Established as a Crown corporation, it had the freedom to pursue its own lines of enquiry unfettered by government direction. Its board structure of twenty-one helped: eleven, including the chair, were Canadian, with ten foreign appointments. Others marvelled at this unusual structure for a public corporation. But IDRC was always unusual; it was set up that way. David Hopper, its first president, merely entrenched it.

The Centre Takes Off

Hopper viewed IDRCs first board meeting as crucial. It was here that IDRC's ethos would be established, to carry it through into the future. That was true, and IDRC does owe its organizational and philosophical footprint to David Hopper.[3] As well, the adoption of a unique style of operation was the result of his interpretation of the Centre's broad mandate. Nor were there any to protest that direction; the president's position "within the international scientific and academic community, together with his extensive experience in development via previous associations with the World Bank and the Ford and Rockefeller Foundations" (he had been called "Foundation" Hopper), allowed him a relatively free hand. Maurice Strong, who had pushed hard for Hopper's selection, was absolutely correct; he wanted an iconoclast and also someone who would pull the new organization in the direction which Strong thought appropriate–against prevailing wisdom but with a minimum of tilting needlessly at windmills. With a willing board of governors and the wording of the IDRC Act permitting, this is exactly what happened.

A self-described "field man," Hopper emphasized that he did not want the Centre to become a think tank, but instead he envisioned it would play a vital role in working actively with Southern researchers as they sought to make the lives of their countrymen better. His statement to the October 1970 board meeting, which came to be unofficially known as IDRC's first strategic plan, did inform its activities, and the general sentiment expressed persists to the present. It would not be research active but research supportive. "In the next few months," he began, "our task is to nurture the Centre's internal organizational ethos and its capacity to address the issues of development."[4] He wanted an IDRC that was adaptive, flexible, extremely professional, and hard-working, which he got. That came out of the dedication and commitment of those first employees, supported and pushed by the president with his very firm view of what he wanted to accomplish.

In concert with that, Hopper's deliberative way forward in October 1970 was to suggest that IDRC focus on farm and non-farm people living in rural areas, as these were the global citizens who were most affected by the change from neolithic to modern. This in itself was contentious; not until 1974 was rural development recognized as a central issue at the World Bank and taken up by others following its lead. The Centre was very much ahead of the curve in setting its priorities. Such a focus would provide a "broad umbrella under which the Centre's staff would select ... worthy projects for consideration." A total program of interlocking activities could be set up that would "form the ribs of the umbrella onto which could be sewn the fabric of world advance[!]"

Hopper's Centre would support research in agriculture, forestry, and fisheries; indeed, the whole space of rural life would become IDRC's beat — education, nutrition, local government and administration, social institutions, the rural environment, and the physical health of the rural family. Further, program leaders could address issues like population expansion and the attendant issues of providing gainful employment for rural people by "improving productivity and enhancing opportunities in farm and off-farm occupations, stressing particularly the creation of expanded labour absorption potentials within the frame of a dynamic rural village, small town, and larger growth centre in an effort to reduce the flow of people into the cities." While the latter proved impossible to accomplish over the next four decades, IDRC did develop, fund, and implement programs like small- and medium-sized enterprises policy in the South which did address many of the issues laid out. Importantly, Hopper also talked of the Centre's "philosophy of approach" to projects that would establish the welcome accorded to it among Southern peoples. Over the next forty years, a unique IDRC perspective was established which became one of its identifiable features of *funding* research in the South and eschewing research imperialism — what advertisers might call its brand.[5]

By 1977 IDRC punched, as the old adage has it, above its weight in the international arena, exerting an influence, for example, on the Ford Foundation, which added non-Americans to its board, while the Australian Agricultural Centre was structurally affected by its operations, and the Swedish SAREC was constructed on the IDRC model. From the beginning, IDRC had focused on the support of direct funding for researchers from less developed countries (LDCs), putting the onus on them and their institutions to develop and articulate projects. That was a fundamental part of the Centre's uniqueness. But perhaps most importantly from a government perspective, the Centre seemed to be good value for the money. One reason for that, treasury board secretariat suggested, was "the quality of [its] staff [which] unquestionably contributed to its high state of efficiency."[6]

The early days were also "'passionate and hot' and hardly bureaucratic at all," as John Woolston, the director of Information Sciences, remembered. Program Officers (POs) had an immense amount of freedom to go out and investigate what could be done in co-operation with Southern researchers. While there was accountability, to both the board and senior management, they were also very much on their own. POs were not unlike early pilots — they flew "by the seat of their pants."[7] Roving program officers also contributed to the betterment of IDRC; if they saw something innovative and interesting in one place, they would tell of it in another. Still, that early exhilaration could not last forever; as the Centre grew, procedures became more complex and reports longer. When Ivan Head took over in 1978 as president following Hopper's departure for the World Bank, it marked the passage of IDRC from relative freedom to a more constrained operation.

Ivan Head Takes Over

As the new president got his feet under him, division directors rehearsed their situations; for the most part, it was "steady as she goes." Joseph Hulse of Agriculture, Food and Nutrition Sciences (AFNS) led off, as perhaps reflected the order of importance of IDRC at that time. Continued areas of emphasis included marginal lands, multiple cropping systems, use of wastes and by-products, aquaculture, post-production systems, and small forestry initiatives, the areas in which some of the 380 projects the Centre had managed to 1978 could be found. There was quite a diversity of content, given that AFNS was supporting projects in so many different socioeconomic and agro-climatic environments; the crop science program, for example, was taking place in 46 different countries, fisheries in 19, animal sciences in 19, and forestry in 18. Hulse and his division continued to concentrate their priorities on the well-being of the rural poor, which had been Hopper's primary focus, and within that general concentration they had been particularly concerned with the semi-arid tropics, in particular, the Sahel, then ravaged by a horrible drought.

Finally, AFNS was also embarking on a new approach to development–farming systems research, which marked a breakthrough in the conceptualization of agricultural research. This was a necessity, or so many of the division's program officers believed, because there had been very serious shortcomings in earlier attempts to introduce new technologies to farmers in developing countries. Farming systems was an attempt to incorporate a multidisciplinary focus into agricultural research. By the 1980s, most Centre-supported agronomy projects were using a farming systems research methodology, despite the fact that "it was considered to take 'a great deal of time to organize.'"[8] IDRC began support for this approach early; the first project was funded in 1979 through the International Rice Research Institute. It moved beyond the traditional commodities approach and began to reflect the reality of small farmers in Africa, Asia, and Latin America.

Health Sciences focus of activities included fertility regulation methods, tropical diseases, rural health care, and rural water and sanitation. IDRC continued to subsidize research in Southern countries in this area where more immediate results might be obtained from developed country laboratories but where LDC training would have been negligible.[9] Since 1970, the division had been involved in fertility regulation, investigating new methods in technology, clinical trials, safety measures against contraceptives in use, and some training as part of the grants program. As well, what the division's director had called social obstetrics had been a focus during the last decade. This examined maternal problems during pregnancy, issues with mother and child immediately following birth, and any that had occurred during the child's first year.

The division's primary emphasis, however, remained centred on the question of health care delivery, a very difficult problem given that health ministry budgets in the South were lamentably small; this was simply not a priority for most LDC governments with very limited resources. IDRC had invested much coin in funding research in the area of auxiliary health personnel—those not officially trained but capable of improving health outcomes. Indeed, the director then felt that enough had been done in this area and the emphasis should now be on implementation. Most ministries of health in LDCs did not have the personnel to carry orders from the top to the bottom, or communication in the other direction, nor any adequate supervision for auxiliary and paramedical personnel. These might sit around for five months out of every six with nothing to do because they did not have the necessary tools, such as drugs, to do anything with. Health Sciences was also funding workshops in Africa in which potential trainers had been selected from various countries and taught the new technologies and methods of health preservation. They then returned to their regions to close the circle.

For its part, Information Sciences continued to make all data it could available to Southern researchers through systems like AGRIS that IDRC personnel had helped develop; it "now contained more information from developing countries than any other file on agricultural information being produced either commercially or in the public sector."[10] The example provided by AGRIS had been a Centre priority: the development of bibliographic information systems in those subject areas where IDRC-funded researchers were active. For social sciences, the broad outlines of the past seven years remained in place. For example, to cite only two areas, education with a concentration on the elementary level was prioritized, while the largest project IDRC had undertaken to date, science and technology policy instruments, now needed a period of consolidation and dissemination.

Training had also come to be perceived as vitally important for the developing Centre. By the early 1980s, about ten per cent of all program support was directed toward it, and indicators suggested that that would increase. Indeed, as all divisions began to consider putting more resources into Africa, the training aspect became more important, given that the institutional base in large swathes of the continent was embryonic. As was generally conceded at the Centre, African countries were most in need of "building an indigenous research and planning capacity."[11] Such a shift, to sub-Saharan Africa, had major implications for Centre program officers as those countries were less capable of generating results; additional pressure was then placed on frontline officers, who would trek through the continent looking for business. IDRC would also have to help to strengthen institutions "and projects [would] need to be less ambitious and last longer."[12] Moreover, impact might have to play second fiddle to enhancement, at least for a while; the research base in the region was at a relatively rudimentary level. While all countries in the region had established universities (if sometimes not very good ones), the emphasis at all of them was in teaching to train students to the graduate level, not research. Few universities had developed post-graduate programs, and funds for research were very scarce. Given this situation, a bright student had to travel to Europe, North America, or the Eastern bloc for training and, once there, often chose not to return to the sponsoring country. The worsening economic condition that characterized the late 1970s and early 1980s only made this more difficult—both for the return of students and because it resulted in the reduction of research funding that was provided by national governments to universities.

This new determination changed the focus of some of the divisions, at least. The issue of entering more forcefully into underrepresented areas was raised in the context of determining broad strategic direction. For example, at the October 1985 board meeting, it was pointed out that many new research partners needed a degree of coaching: "training in research planning, administration, and management has been neglected and is actually non-existent in some regions. This results in...the absence of long-term research goals."[13] Despite those hurdles to appropriate project development and supervision, IDRC put its money where its mouth was; by 1988, it was directing 30 per cent of its appropriation to African institutions, up from 24 per cent in 1986.[14]

As IDRC evolved its funding focus so, too, did its existing divisions. For example, AFNS had changed dramatically. By the mid-1980s, the division was championing some new approaches like pest or rangeland management and community-based participatory methods. As well, in keeping with the Centre's new emphasis, the policy implications of the work were identified at the very beginning of the project development process instead of as an afterthought. Similarly, interdivisional co-operation was more obvious than it had been.[15] That reflected board deliberations which had focused on "the convergence of various disciplines and areas to cope with major problems which are, by their nature, interdisciplinary."[16] Finally, the Centre also explicitly funded work in urban areas; in many ways the growing slums that dotted the area around large cities needed more assistance than did rural regions.

Clearly, as the 1990s approached, the Centre made a number of refinements to its programming and culture. The clarification of its mission and objectives was accomplished by increased emphasis throughout on coherence among its programs, and on the end results of its activities. As well, interdivisional co-operation was a greater priority and some Centre-wide programs had been created. Further, Health Sciences and Social Sciences were more community focused, prepared to support research on an interdisciplinary and interdivisional basis. Similarly, revisions to the strategic plan had made the regional perspective more prominent in planning at both the divisional and corporate levels. AFNS was restructuring in order to better reflect its concerns about the sustainability of agricultural production, resource conservation, and rehabilitation, and pesticides and pest management. It was certainly ahead of most other agencies as it would be years before most would begin to consider these issues. In short, the new divisional focus had shifted from an emphasis on increased agricultural production to one where access to food and other basic needs for the individual took priority.[17] In practical terms, this meant increased emphasis was given in project planning and design to social and economic considerations, to the reduction of poverty, to rural employment and income generation, and to nutrition, all within the renewable natural resource and utilization system.

Concern that increases in agricultural productivity in the past had sometimes been at the expense of the stability and sustainability of the productive resource base also prompted the division to pay much more attention to issues of environmental conservation and rehabilitation and natural resource management in general. Similarly, concerns about health and ecological effects associated with the use of toxic agricultural chemicals meant increased emphasis on finding less hazardous pest management methods. Ecological and health concerns were then integrated into AFNS's overall program, and a program officer position was created specifically to promote programming in the area of the environment and sustainable and safe agricultural production systems.

Health Sciences had also reorganized itself in the latter part of the decade. It had noted, for example, that the division's "activities tend to be discipline-bound and focus on only a few of the target population's symptoms of ill health. Few programs or projects follow a holistic approach and fewer examine causal factors that are not biomedical... [but] behavioural health conditions and those related to social and economic circumstances are of increasing concern in developing countries."[18] Its decision was to promote a more holistic approach to programming in what would eventually become something like the much-vaunted Ecohealth program initiative. By 1987, the division had shifted its focus to, among other things, "develop policies, practices and technologies to improve the physical environment of communities and the physical and social environment of individuals."[19] The programs that emerged dealt with people and their communities, including health and the community, health systems, and health and the environment.

Also considered was the use of technologies, the transmission of communicable disease, methods to promote participatory research, women and children in health promotion, health education and strategies to improve the nutrition of women and children. Further, through its "Health and the Community" program, the division would undertake funding for projects focusing on the physical and biological elements in the environment that affected the health of the poor, and those were almost too numerous to count. A 1988 document quoted approvingly from an expert in the field who had noted that "Health is just one element in the total development picture; accordingly, health problems cannot be tackled in isolation from the other elements. In other words, the attack on the problems of health should be mounted as an integral part of a broad frontal attack directed against the multifarious forms of poverty. There can be no hope for a significant and lasting improvement in health in the absence of a simultaneous improvement in all other sectors."[20] Health was not the absence of disease, nor could it be achieved by controlling disease. Rather, "Numerous genetic, social, cultural, environmental, and economic factors interact to produce both health and illness."

Social Sciences had established a new program framework that included economic policy, population, education and society, and regional development. Information Sciences had turned its attention to a new strategic plan, as well, that would include studies of broad issues such as the utilization of information services and products, the refinement of geographical strategies, and the assessment of newer information technologies. Community-level information services remained a priority, and the division was refining its processes designed to allow it to respond more effectively to local initiatives in disparate parts of the world. However, the focus on Africa would be maintained, especially as the division's special strategy for supporting information activities for the continent was entering its second year.

All of this activity pointed to IDRC's redefined approach to development research that included increased interdivisional co-operation, enhanced capacity-building, dissemination of research results, and regional perspectives. Divisions had made an effort to coalesce around several development themes, and a number of Centre-wide initiatives had been mooted. These focused on particular development problems and were representative of the overall trend in IDRC to pay more attention to regionally focused issues and the ultimate outcome which its research support pursued. Further, Agriculture, Food and Nutrition Sciences, Engineering and Environmental Sciences, Health Sciences, and Social Sciences, through the restructuring that had taken place, gave particular attention to the need for adding a broader interdisciplinary focus to their work.

Keith Bezanson and the Renovation of the Centre

Ivan Head's term ended in mid-March 1991, and he could look back on thirteen eventful years.[21] However, as its twentieth birthday came and went, IDRC operated in a completely different global environment to that which had been present at its creation or even as Head had assumed office; an increasing world population, crippling debt in many LDCs, holes in the ozone, the old Soviet Union and eastern Europe plunging into chaos as that empire dissolved, narcotics consumption up, and the first Gulf War just over.[22] As suggested by that list, world happiness remained a distant goal. That was the situation as Keith Bezanson took control, and his Centre would develop a new strategic plan, *Empowerment through Knowledge*, that reflected a rather different road IDRC would have to travel to remain effective.

The document was written primarily by the president and was an attempt "to translate the Centre's mission into a clear program framework that [would] guide and inform the detailed decisions to be made in consultation with [IDRC's] research partners and that will permit an assessment of [its] progress."[23] To accomplish that required a number of things: "a new perspective on development and IDRC's place in it; a sharper program focus; a restructuring of programs to maximize the impact of available resources; greater efficiency in program execution and administration; perseverance in effort; and, flexibility and agility in changing circumstances." Further, the document correctly demanded the whole notion of development be rethought; the underlying conception of the practice as linear was no longer valid. *Empowerment* in its title captured the essence of what development should be. It also reiterated the underlying bedrock of Centre philosophy that "development" could not and should not be imposed upon a society from outside; it "should mean above all giving people the power, that is, the adequate knowledge and capacity, to decide what is best for them and to act accordingly in fulfilling their own destinies." Much of the early 1990s was spent changing direction and practice, most of which was "captured under the rubric of Empowerment through Knowledge (EtK). This EtK mantra was that there was a process of discussion within the Centre but it was very activist, driven by [Bezanson], partly because of his perception of this need to change and change urgently or there was no more IDRC."[24] He was certainly keen on changing the basic thrust of the Centre, away from what it had been since its inception, a science and technology organization, to a more social sciences one. AFNS had been disbanded in mid-1991, which was a key indicator of the new wind blowing through the organization.[25]

However, no sooner was *EtK* written than the Centre was blown sideways by the hurricane of deficit reduction in Ottawa. There were various schemes mooted to change it into a departmental corporation, or even to wind it down, but none of that happened. Instead, it was made the implementing agency that oversaw Agenda 21, Canada's commitments made during the United Nations Conference on Environment and Development held in Rio de Janeiro in June 1992. Agenda 21 was a 600-plus-page document that had emerged as a consensus from UNCED and which consisted of forty chapters organized across four broad categories: social and economic dimensions; conservation and management of resources; strengthening the role of major groups; and means of implementation. It was also a successor to the landmark 1972 Stockholm Conference on the Human Environment which had first put environment on the international agenda. As IDRC official Terry Smutlyo has said, "Rio was a milestone in redefining ourselves as an Agenda 21 agency... It was a chaotic period in terms of program structure. All sorts of things were happening. There was no coherent central focus to our programming. [Still] everybody had to be a player in the new world."[26]

That was the case, and at the October 1992 board meeting a number of papers were presented for consideration that attempted to make some sense of Rio and its aftermath, primarily focusing on integrating environment into policy-making. Four themes were taken up: a program of research and training in economics and the environment; national sustainable development plans; strengthening local management for sustainable development, and building capacity in environmental research and policy. Further, the Centre proposed that it fund a program of research that concentrated on technology for sustainable and equitable development, given its proven track record in supporting research and technology development in several key areas of clean technology, such as water quality management, remote sensing, biological agricultural inputs, and industrial waste management.[27] As well, information for sustainable and equitable development was proposed, a program that recognized the role of information as a powerful resource to support development.[28] Food systems under stress were also tackled. In the South, population growth was generally outstripping food production. Again, the Centre had had much experience with aspects of the issue. The program would address stress in different parts of the world: areas undergoing desertification, especially in Africa, fragile highland regions in Latin America, Asia and Africa, and rapidly expanding urban areas, in particular in Africa.[29]

Beset by adverse forces, IDRC was evolving quickly from its old structure, an evolution that sped up considerably in 1995, with a significant cut to its programming budget. The Liberals had taken office in late 1992 and, faced with a massive and growing deficit, had taken the axe to federal spending. Clearly, the Centre was "at a crossroads" and would have to devise a strategy that would help in the troubled years ahead.[30] As it had made a unique contribution to development since its creation, it would have to engage in a new type of uniqueness for its future, what Maureen O'Neil was to later call "start[ing] its own experiment."[31] Over the next year, that occurred as it took steps towards issue-based programming, away from silos based on disciplinary programs. It began with a development problem, drew in the relevant disciplines, and linked scientists more effectively in order to learn from each other.[32] Further, policy-makers and civil society were engaged at the outset. That continued a long-term process that had worked for greater effectiveness through enhanced focus and greater multidisciplinarity.

In the face of a massive budget crunch in late June 1995, it was decided that the Centre must get rid of its divisions.[33] Four program divisions were thereby merged into a single Programs Branch, effective August 1. The priority-setting exercises that IDRC had undertaken through an intensive consultation in Ottawa and the regions had yielded some fruit. The main criteria that staff had been asked to consider when evaluating priorities were development pay-off, potential for revenue diversification, and the likely visibility of the "product" and IDRC's contribution. On that basis, the projects proposed for funding in the 1995–96 fiscal year were fitted into clusters with each cluster representing a separate set of issues in which it was judged that the Centre could make a difference.

All projects were now developed under five sustainable and equitable themes: food systems under stress; integrating environmental, social, and economic policies; technology, environment, and society; biodiversity, and information and communication. It was noted that "As IDRC moves into a more interdisciplinary mode, it is expected that information projects will play a greater role in linking, enriching, and demonstrating the potential of all its projects. IDRC will fund projects in health with reference to policy integration and to ecosystem health." However, most Centre funding would now go to program initiatives (PIs), developed with Southern researchers to respond to particular sets of issues. PIs were managed by a team of program staff with, usually, three to five core members, and almost all PI teams included both regional and Ottawa-based program staff.[34]

All that took some getting used to. As the former director-general of environment and natural resources, Anne Whyte, put the new condition, "decisionmaking in the PI teams was extremely difficult because it was kind of a committee approach to things—that has costs and benefits. It's more participatory and therefore it is very much more difficult to get any kind of decision coming out."[35] The shift was also inevitable, or so she thought: "It had partly to do with the fact that the Centre got smaller. If you are bigger you can have these interdisciplinary teams stay within divisions and they are working just fine, but when you reduce your resources and you have to get smaller, then what do you do?" Clearly, the change was "radical and traumatic," yet possessed of "path-breaking potential."[36] It was also an attempt "to change the grammar of development" in the sense of tackling problems in a more integrated way.[37]

It was also accomplished in about five days as the divisions were blown apart and the structure that had sustained IDRC since its establishment was no more; then the scramble among Centre staff to secure a position began. Chaos is a word that can be used to describe the effect. One IDRC staffer later wrote that "it can be observed that many institutions have downsized; some have restructured their operations; and a few have tried to reorient their thinking towards a new paradigm. *Very few had done all three at the same time.*" Yet that was what the Centre accomplished—a remarkable institutional innovation that would, over time, contribute to better results. Bezanson told staff that "We are moving into new territory… and will need high levels of tolerance as we try new mechanisms and structures. We will need to accept a degree of ambiguity because it will simply not be possible to lay down all the new 'rules of the game' *a priori* with great precision."[38] New territory was almost an understatement. IDRC's way of going about its business was unrecognizable when compared with earlier years. Despite the excitement and the challenge, it was difficult. "The easy years," Bezanson wistfully told the board, "are part of what now seems like ancient history. There are no easy years now." He might have talking about himself with that sentence.

As he began to think about leaving the Centre, he oversaw the process that developed the *Corporate Program Framework to the Year 2000*. Adopted by the board in October 1996, it defined IDRC's objectives for the period as: "To foster and support the production and application of research results leading to policies and technologies that enhance the lives of people in the developing regions; and, to mobilize and strengthen the indigenous research capacity in the countries of those regions, particularly capacity for policies and technologies for more healthy and prosperous societies, food security, biodiversity, and access to information.[39] It also offered up six themes that constituted the programming framework under which the Centre would concentrate its resources, including food security, equity in natural resource uses, biodiversity conservation, sustainable employment, strategies and policies for healthy societies, and information and communication. Under those themes the Centre funded fifteen program initiatives.[40] It had been a long road with many a winding turn, and Bezanson had had enough; on April 16, 1997, he left.

A Return to Zen
The new president, Maureen O'Neil, moved into his old office one day later. Her job was to calm IDRC waters, roiled by the massive change that had taken place in two short years. Part of that meant addressing issues raised by program initiatives. Their introduction, as suggested above, had involved much trial, error, compromise, and debate, and had very much altered the intellectual constructs that had guided the Centre since its

founding. Indeed, it represented a foundational change in the *way* it went about its business and in the *thinking* about how it did so, although not so much in the output of that business, funding research for development. The number of program initiatives was capped at twelve, and there were three program areas under which all PIs fell, which included environment and natural resource management (ENRM), information and communications technologies for development (ICT4D), and social and economic equity (SEE).[41]

Each of these mirrored a particular strength of the organization — for example, with ENRM, the Centre, a leader in support of research on the management of natural resources in all regions in which it operated, assisted researchers on focusing projects on community-based alternatives to traditional top-down natural resource management in rural areas, as well as on studies of national and regional policies that expanded the space for local management.[42] SEE supported work in areas like governance in sub-Saharan Africa (SSA), peace-building and reconstruction in southern Africa, Central America, and the Middle East. It also supported research on three sets of stressors that had implications for human and ecosystem health: mining, urbanization, and intensive agriculture. In the case of ICT4D, the Centre supported far-reaching programming designed to help recipients participate in the twenty-first century communication revolution.

Through this consideration, IDRC's mission remained empowerment through knowledge while retaining those principles — sustainable and equitable development — that had come out of the UN Conference on Environment and Development in 1992; those would undergird all of its programming.[43] Indeed, they remained a cornerstone of the Centre's belief "that equitable and sustainable human activity depended on men and women's control of their own social and economic progress, on equitable access to knowledge of all kinds, and on an indigenous capacity to generate and apply knowledge."[44]

Increasingly, PIs focused on sub-Saharan Africa as an area in desperate need of the sort of programming that IDRC could deliver. As IDRC found its way forward, programs including sustainable employment emphasized small, medium, and micro-enterprises, innovation and technology, and also investigated the role of women in small business. Trade, employment, and competitiveness had a large portfolio of projects in the region, while the themes of food security and equity in natural resource management were also active in sub-Saharan Africa, designed to help communities enhance the equitable, sustainable, and productive use of land and water resources to improve the quality of life of impoverished farmers. As well, the Centre was interested in bringing information and communication technologies to the continent. For example, it led the way with Acacia, an international effort that represented a major program initiative, "Communities and the Information Society in Africa," in order to empower sub-Saharan communities with the ability to apply new information and communication technologies to their own social and economic development. IDRC had laid out its concerns about the dangers of ICT marginalization in Africa, which had been flagged by leading African researchers during the mid-1990s. Ultimately, Acacia became one the of the most "African-owned" of ICTs for development on the continent, receiving strong backing from participants as well as those governments involved in the four-country ministerial-level Maputo Declaration: Mozambique, Senegal, South Africa, and Uganda. It was also fortuitous that it had the support of the then-minister of foreign affairs, Lloyd Axworthy; one of his priorities was the development of a global information strategy and Africa, he thought, was the perfect place to begin.

And so it seemed it was given the success of the program: "Mobile phones [were] everywhere [by the early 2000s], a part of the reality of African development. Ten years ago it would have been impossible to imagine ICTs being used in schools, in medicine, and in trade. And [in 2001], Phase III of Acacia [was] trying to create a research network [for Africans] to do research in ICT4D."[45] Indeed, 2003 was the first year in which there were more mobile subscribers than land lines in the world; by 2005, about 80 per cent of all telephones on the African continent were mobiles, holding tremendous potential for innovative approaches to health care delivery, from continuing medical information to demographic surveillance to patient monitoring. They were "changing the livelihoods of women in Africa as well as changing the relationships between the sexes. ICTs were having an impact on economic growth, and they had a hand in improving services with government, its accountability and transparency, as well as enhancing communication between administrations and their constituencies.[46]

That meshed nicely with another IDRC program area, social and economic equity, and one of its broad trends that focused on the changing role of the state as governments recognized the inadequacy of their past responses to governance and human security concerns. The Centre in this case was a "catalytic organization, keeping things moving, an organization which inspired confidence and credibility."[47] Out of this project emerged a cutting-edge program initiative, Information and Communication Technologies for Development (ICT4D), which has also been enormously successful, and which has enriched peoples' lives the developing world over.

As the millennium came and went, the range of issues that demanded attention included a host of things not even conceived of a few years earlier, like new transformative technologies including genomics, genetic engineering, and nanotechnology. IDRC was also keen to support research on the economic, environmental, ethical, legal, and social issues surrounding their development and use, as well as to enhance research on questions of governance, public understanding, access, and benefits associated with new transformative technologies in and for the South.[48] That meant increasing engagement with Canada's granting councils — the Natural Sciences and Engineering Research Council, the Social Sciences and Humanities Research Council, and the Canadian Institutes for Health Research. The result is a series of international research chairs, funded 50/50 by IDRC and its granting council partners.

As well, it would fund research in science and technology innovation policies that were directed toward poverty alleviation, increasing equity in science and technology policy discussions in low and middle income countries. The new program area soon proved its worth; IPS became instrumental in supporting science and technology within the framework of the New Economic Partnership for Africa's Development (NEPAD). In September 2005, at the second science and technology ministerial conference held in Dakar, Senegal, ministers attending had adopted an ambitious new consolidated action plan on science and technology for Africa; IDRC's PI, Innovation, Policy, and Science, was instrumental in supporting the core secretariat for NEPAD's science and technology effort, as well as key research activities carried out by the secretariat, for which the Centre had been singled out by the chair of the minister's conference for its support of science and technology.[49]

The other program areas remained largely unchanged.[50] Environment and Natural Resource Management remained focused on helping countries find feasible and sustainable approaches to enhance water and food security, human health, and natural resources management, building their foundations on democratic participation, good governance, and social equity. An important component of the program was to strengthen the linkages between research, policy, and its implementation in order to ensure that its findings were translated into policy. Social and Economic Policy focused on "public policies that can lead to poverty reduction and enhanced social equity," by which it hoped to achieve policy change in three ways: by strengthening long-term capacities to carry out, manage, and disseminate research; by supporting policy-relevant research and analysis on issues of immediate policy concern, and by assisting researchers and civil society organizations in the facilitation of public accountability by informing debates on key policy issues.

What of the Future?

O'Neil was a very successful president. Importantly, she had traction in official Ottawa and was universally admired for her savvy and intelligence, factors of considerable weight. As the vice-president, programs, Rohinton Medhora, remembers, "She knew how to situate things for IDRC."[51] She continued the IDRC tradition of being ahead of the curve in conceiving of its program areas and projects, as well as being a listening organization. Sometimes the former came from the latter, a very unusual development in the world of international assistance. But it was quintessentially IDRC. Under her presidency, IDRC came to reflect twenty-first-century issues, like the effects of new communication technologies on development or those of bio- and nano-technologies. As had been the case since its inception, O'Neil's IDRC framed its programming as a reflection of the intelligence, competencies, and capability to be found in the South.

And what of its future? Can IDRC remain a creative, innovative, ahead of the curve, and listening organization? Indeed, is there a role for the Centre in 2010? Arguably, the need for IDRC is greater now than at almost any time in its history. The plethora of challenges the world confronts, from climate change, to alterations in forms of global governance, to future directions of national innovation and science policy reviews, confound the development process. How does one include gender in a project that investigates agriculture in Yemen? What about the continuing role of information and communication technologies in development in less advantaged parts of the world? How will desertification affect certain parts of the world and deforestation others? There are thousands of questions like these that the Centre has the expertise to investigate, if it has the resources.

Clearly, as the world changes, IDRC's research for development mandate allows those most affected to interrogate their own situations through questions that they devise, a policy that goes back to Hopper's conception of what this kind of organization should do. IDRC had led by example over the past forty years, and a number of critics and organizations are now coming around to its perspective, even if they have not heard of the Centre. In *The White Man's Burden: Why the West's Efforts to Aid the Rest Have Done So Much Ill and So Little Good*, William Easterly, an unremitting and influential critic of development as it is now conceived, writes about this problem using words strikingly reminiscent of IDRC practices: "The core problem...is that few Western aid programs ever seek feedback from their consumers, the world's poor. Aid bureaucrats seldom feel accountable to anyone other than their rich-country principals... On the basis of this analysis, [his] advice to Western donors is that they should stop thinking of themselves as Planners and begin thinking of themselves instead as 'Searchers.' They should investigate what is in demand in impoverished countries, adapt to local conditions, and stress accountability."[52]

The idea seems so simple and obvious that one is left wondering why it has not gotten greater traction in development organizations' strategic plans. It has in IDRC's.

Notes

1 "Comprehensive Audit Report to the Board of Governors of the International Development Research Centre," August 1982. Accessed at http://www.idrc .ca/uploads/user-S/11558266111Comprehensive_Audit_(1982).pdf.

2 IDRC–A, "Canadian Broadcasting Corporation, International Service, Round Table Discussion with members of the IDRC following the conclusion of the first board of governors meeting, held in Ottawa, October 26–28, 1970."

3 Library and Archives Canada, Treasury Board Records (RG 55), Accession 90-91/164, Box 31, file 8068-03, "Evaluation of the International Development Research Centre–Documentation of Phase I–General Review," Program Branch, Treasury Board Secretariat, 30 October 1978. Emphasis not in original.

4 See "Statement to the Inaugural Meeting of the Board of Governors of the International Development Research Centre, 26 October 1970," accessed at https://idlbnc.idrc.ca/dspace/bitstream/123456789/2215/1/Hopper18.pdf. Much of the ensuing discussion comes from this document.

5 IDRC–A, William Found, "Participatory Research and Development: An Assessment of IDRC's Experience and Prospects," Evaluation #295, 30 June 1995, 1. In his evaluation, Found points out that the World Bank came around to the merits of participatory research by the mid-1990s. CIDA produced a study of the advantages of PR in 1994. It is not, however, suitable in all cases of development.

6 Library and Archives Canada, Treasury Board Records (RG 55), Accession 90-91/164, Box 31, file 8068-03, "Evaluation of the International Development Research Centre – Documentation of Phase I – General Review," Program Branch, Treasury Board Secretariat, 30 October 1978.

7 Woolston interview.

8 Eva Rathgeber, "Turning Failure into Success: The Deconstruction of IDRC Development Discourse, 1970–2000," Evaluation #479, September 2001, 37.

9 IDRC–A, Meeting of the Board of Governors, B of G Notes (22), 3/80, 82.

10 IDRC–A, Meeting of the Board, March 1978, John Woolston. AGRIS was an Agricultural Information System database where researchers from around the world could post information about research results. Researchers in other parts of the world could then access the information.

11 IDRC–A, Meeting of the Board of Governors, B of G (28) 3/83, 68.

12 IDRC, "In-Depth Review of the Agriculture, Food and Nutrition Sciences Division," submitted to the Ad Hoc Committee of the Board, September 1985, xvi. Accessed at https://idl-bnc.idrc.ca/dspace/bitstream/123456789/6233/1/68607.pdf on 5 November 2008.

13 IDRC–A, Meeting of the Board of Governors, BG (33) 10/85, 96.

14 Program and Policy Review IX, 48–49.

15 IDRC, "In-Depth Review of the Agriculture, Food and Nutrition Sciences Division," xiv.

16 IDRC–A, Meeting of the Board of Governors, B.G. (35) 10/86, 16.

17 For a discussion of this, see IDRC–A, Revised 1989–90 Program of Work and Budget, January 1989, 29–32.

18 IDRC–A, "Health Sciences Division Statement," October 1988, 1.

19 "Health Sciences Division Statement," 12.

20 L. Hendretta, "Health and Development: Review of Policy Options at the Grassroots Level," in W. Lathem, ed., The Future of Academic Community Medicine in Developing Countries (New York: Praeger, 1979), 59, as quoted in "Health Sciences Division Statement," 5.

21 Hardie interview.

22 IDRC–A, Ivan Head to Board of Governors, "Towards 2000: A Strategic Framework for IDRC," 18 February 1991, BG 46/3, i.

23 IDRC, Empowerment Through Knowledge: The Strategy of the International Development Research Centre (Ottawa: IDRC, 1991) 7. Much of the following text comes from this document.

24 Interview with Brian Davy as done by Martin Kreuser, 28 June 2004, Ottawa, ON.

25 Interview with Bryan Davy, 13 August 2008, Ottawa, ON.

26 Interview with Terry Smutylo as done by Martin Kreuser, 14 June 2004, Ottawa, ON.

27 IDRC–A, BG 49/20, "Technology for Sustainable and Equitable Development: Policy Options and Institutional Frameworks," October 1992.

28 IDRC–A, BG 49/21, "Information for Sustainable and Equitable Development," October 1992.

29 IDRC–A, BG 49/25, "Food Systems under Stress," October 1992.

30 IDRC–A, EC 93/20, "Preparation of Program of Work and Budget for 1995–96: Discussion of Issues by the Executive Committee," January 1995.

31 IDRC–A, "Introduction by Maureen O'Neil, Corporate Strategy and Program Framework, 2000–2005," September 1999.

32 IDRC–A, *Program of Work and Budget, 1996–97*, March 1996, 29. Many of the following paragraphs come from this document.

33 IDRC–A, Executive Committee Meeting, June 22 and 23, 1995, "Completing the Transition: Strategic Adjustments for IDRC, 1995," 19 June 1995.

34 IDRC–A, *PWB, 1996–97*, 30.

35 Interview with Anne Whyte as done by Martin Kreuser, 6 August 2004.

36 Hardie, "The Program Initiative System in IDRC, 3.

37 IDRC–A, KAB to All Staff, 26 June 1995.

38 IDRC–A, KAB to All Staff, 31 July 1995.

39 IDRC–A, BG 59/14, *Program of Work and Budget, 1997–98*, March 1997, 35.

40 IDRC–A, "Briefing Note for the Minister of Foreign Affairs, the Honourable Lloyd Axworthy," 28 January 1998. For the fifteen program initiatives see BG 59/14, *Program of Work and Budget, 1997–98*, 36–42.

41 IDRC–A, BOG 2004 (03) 16, Brent Herbert-Copley, "PI External Reviews: Synthesis Report, Social and Economic Equity Program Area," March 2004, 3.

42 IDRC–A, BOG 2000 (03) 05, *Program of Work and Budget, 2000–2001*, 46.

43 IDRC–A, BG 99 (03) 19, "Corporate Strategy and Program Framework, 2000–2005," Discussion Draft, March 1999.

44 IDRC–A, BG 99 (10) 13, "Introduction by Maureen O'Neil, Corporate Strategy and Program Framework, 2000–2005," 15 September 1999.

45 Interview with Alioune Camara, Dakar, Senegal, 18 May 2007.

46 IDRC–A, BOG 2005 (10) 41, "Acacia Prospectus Development–Status Report, October 2005," 21 October 2005.

47 IDRC–A, Meeting of the Board of Governors, 31 March–1 April 2005, 4. The characterization of IDRC in this way had occurred in India, but it applies equally here.

48 IDRC–A, Meeting of the Board of Governors, 31 March–1 April, n.d., 22.

49 IDRC–A, President's Report to the Board of Governors for the period 1 June–30 September 2005, 19 October 2005, 5–6.

50 For the Environment and Natural Resource Management prospectus, see BOG 2005 (10) 09, for Social and Economic Policy prospectus, see BOG (10) 06, and for the ICT4D prospectus, see BOG 2005 (10) 07.

51 Interview with Rohinton Medhora, 6 August 2009, Ottawa.

52 Review article, Joshua Kurlantzick, "Planners & Seekers: William Easterly, *The White Man's Burden: Why the West's Efforts to Aid the Rest Have Done So Much Ill and So Little Good*," *Commentary Magazine*, June 2006, accessed at www.nyu.edu/fas/institute/dri/Easterly/File/commentary_plannersandseekers.pdf.

CHAPTER THREE

Development *Dharma* and International Co-operation in a Changing World

Dipak Gyawali

Missionary Calling

In countries of the non-industrialized South, so termed because labels such as "underdeveloped" or "Third World" are now no longer "politically correct" or relevant after the collapse of the Second (communist) bloc, development has become the new religion of our times. Amorphous though the term can be with incompatible meanings ascribed to it, it maintains hegemony over Southern public policy discourse as an unquestionably desirable goal. No one can be against it in the South and still hope to avoid social or political marginalization. But, as with any proselytizing religion, one finds not only developmental fauna, but also altruistic missionaries and cut-throat competitors, orthodox practitioners and subversive heretics, zealous crusaders and laid back cynics. With few exceptions, the International Development Research Centre (IDRC) being one of the most well known, the development industry is a profit-making venture that does not necessarily develop sustainable international linkages that assure the partnerships that are the foundation of equitable international collaboration.

For someone from the South such as this author, a career in development did not come with a choice: it was not something one "got into" as with the Peace Corps or other voluntary development agencies of the Euro-Americans. While engineers and economists from the South were expected to be doing development, it concerned not just the modern professions of engineering, medicine, economics, or management but was also the very calling of any Southern politician or businessman. They all were in their vocations for the purpose of *bikas, pragati, sampannata* or *sribriddhi* of their communities ("development," "progress," "well-being," and "prosperity," terms in Sanskrit taken into Nepali and other South Asian languages). So hallowed and unquestioned are these terms that, true to the Hindu practice of naming children after the myriad gods of the pantheon, one finds many boys named Bikas or Sampanna and girls named Pragati as well as many names prefixed with "Sri." Any young man or woman with a modern education was expected to "develop" the country: it was their *dharma* to follow and it was also, by default, the *dharma* of those less educated to listen to the modern catechisms and unquestionably allow the development set to ply their trade in the name of *bikas* for one and all. Equity in development ventures would rarely be under consideration when development decisions would be taken, and it would be too late when, many years later, the consequences had to be evaluated; but the actual beneficiaries of development would always be the development set that plied their trademark *dharma*, and the price of such *karma* would be paid by the society as a whole, and by the environment.

The issue thus is not development as understood locally according to prevailing traditions by one of the Sanskrit terms above; its modern character is defined by the practice and politics within and between national and international bureaucracies engaged in the development discourse since the end of the Second World War. Prior to this world remoulding event, foreign aid did not form part of any international intercourse; it comes as a by-product of decolonization of the South.[1] It grew as an institution in response to the fear in the First (Western industrialized) World that the Third (Southern) World might be fatally attracted to the Second (Communist) World. Indeed, I remember growing up in the Nepal of the 1960s where Indians, Euro-Americans, Soviets, and Chinese competed to give aid. By the early 1970s, the Communist bloc had given up in the competition, leaving the field wide open to what eventually became the "Washington Consensus" of privatization and structural adjustment in the

1980s. In a sense,[2] by reifying growth and giving up on the idea of equity, the 1980s and 1990s were weighed down by a sort of fatalism in development tired of trying to "develop" the South and resigned to the idea that the market would somehow magically do it. After the collapse of the Berlin Wall in 1989, the Second World had essentially collapsed into the Third, obviating the need to lure Southerners to face towards the First with blandishments of foreign aid. This heralded the end of the Age of Aid.[3]

By this early decade of the twenty-first century, the development discourse is defined by two poorly acknowledged undercurrents: aid fatigue in the North and the pathology engendered by aid addiction in the South. In much of the aid-giving North, with aid fatigue emerging as a domestic political sore point compounded by the financial crisis of recent times, debates focused on the sustainability of the aid enterprise and have begun to transform into meeting the challenge of climate change. This debate has dragged the aid-receiving South into the fracas as well, even though sustainable development is a concept akin to a multi-armed, multi-headed Hindu deity, and climate change is too far into the future both for the average person trying to survive from month to month in a predominantly informal economy and for the politician trying to survive until the next reshuffle of government. In subsuming within it diverse and sometimes polar opposite ideas — such as inclusive participation of the intended ultimate beneficiaries and fiscal autonomy without subsidy, environmental health and rapid harnessing of potential resources, absence of social disruption with sociopolitical transformation, etc. — the term is also susceptible to very local interpretations in which sustainability of the family as a multi-generational enterprise becomes the prime concern. This is the vast realm of the informal economy. Researchers in India's "hard rock areas" have been rudely surprised when, probing beneath the barely hidden lack of concern regarding the over-pumping of groundwater, they find that a farmer making good money by selling cash crops really does not care whether the water runs out in five years: "With this money, my son is getting an engineering education in Bombay, and in five years we don't need to live here," has been a very rational, if environmentally very unfriendly, response.

The question then becomes: whose risk perception determines sustainability? Is there anything called "unsustainable development"? Indeed, any sensible development has to be sustainable by definition: if it is not, then it should properly be called "mal-development." So how have we landed into this quixotic situation where we end up debating tautologies of sustainable development by perhaps unwittingly sanitizing the discourse on past development malpractices? This essay argues that the answer probably lies in the hijacking of development by certain social solidarities, thereby distorting the instruments of foreign aid. Good or "belle" development is needed everywhere to address problems of health, nutrition, and education and the building of the underlying infrastructure: unsustainable development is mal-development, which should not be considered development at all.

Even some of the most blatant mal-developments can be cloaked in the validating language of development, depending on the political weight of the social solidarity legitimizing its interests through this means. The word sustainability, while conceptually attractive, turns out not to be that simple: tied with the idea of carrying capacity, it implies that there are limits to that capacity that we can know about *a priori*. Unfortunately, complexity and non-linearity are the bane of the natural and social systems we are dealing with. Furthermore, not only the natural system but also most social systems in today's globalized world are not closed but open systems, which makes it difficult to draw boundaries within which a manager can talk definitively of carrying capacities, their limits, and their behaviour, or pass measures to that effect. In a recent study, it was acknowledged that even in remote, seemingly rural Nepal several walking days away from the roadhead, household incomes came from as far away as Malaysia, Britain, or Japan.[4] Put together, these two considerations make sustainable development difficult to operationalize, and its practice is prone to hijacking by the more street-smart solidarities.

Among the many reasons, one that stands out is the mode of doing development through foreign aid. It is through projects that development is implemented by governments and different aid agencies, but projects by their very nature are unsustainable: they have a beginning and they have to come to an end. It is at the handover stage of projects that the questions of sustainability loom large. Unlike projects, however, institutions (not to be confused with organizations, which are a special sub-set) are long-lasting, especially the institution of households in the informal economy. They cognize and strategize to forward their best interests, and the urge to protect them is intrinsic and long-lasting, which is the basis of their sustainability. Unfortunately, the aid industry has not tapped that institutional reservoir of sustainability. Historically, the model of development has been the Marshall Plan promulgated by the victorious Allies of the Second

World War, but the difference between war-shattered Europe and the South are many.

In the former, institutions (banking, insurance, market-favourable laws, market-favouring democratic politics, structures where people with skills in these and many other areas could collectively contribute, etc.) were intact, and all that was needed was the flow of funds to rebuild the bombed physical infrastructure. In the South, institutions of the modern market as well as their elements mentioned above had to be created almost from scratch. This essentially meant that in the former case aid was the healing of a wound, whereas in the latter it was expected to give birth to the organism in the first place. This line of argument highlights the fact that it is not the lack of money but of appropriate institutions that lies at the heart of the problems of underdevelopment in the South. Further below, this essay will argue why the institutional modality followed by the aid industry will not allow proper social carriers to take forward their longer vision of a stable and secure future. It will begin by examining cases of belle and mal-developments, especially in the field of water, energy, and poverty that I have had personal acquaintance with and relate them to the clash between development idealism and practical proceduralism, as well as the resulting cynicism of large aid bureaucracies. Drawing from these cases, this essay will examine the institutional issues surrounding the sustainability debate, indeed of development and international co-operation itself, in the twenty-first century as the Age of Aid winds down.

Encountering Dismal Reality

It was in the hydropower sector that the questioning of the conventional development paradigm occurred in Nepal, and I was caught in the debate from the very outset. In 2011, Nepal will be celebrating 100 years of hydro-electricity in Nepal, she being one of the earliest countries in Asia to produce power in this way, which came in the form of the 500kW Pharping station in southwest Kathmandu valley. The prime motivation for its installation was not to power industry (although eventually it helped power the first goods ferrying ropeway in 1924): it was to light up the palaces of the autocratic feudal Rana *shoguns* of Nepal as a symbol of luxury and the trappings of political power. Because it was brought in by the wrong social carriers for a wrong purpose, growth in hydropower plants never expanded significantly during Rana rule because of a commensurate lack of industrial or commercial and agricultural demand. A second similar-sized power plant, at Sundarijal, came on line only in 1934, again to light the stucco palaces of more Rana offspring; and, despite the fact that the Nepal Himalaya has some of the richest hydropower potential on the planet, thanks to the steep Himalayan inclines and the heavy monsoon rains, power supply grew to only about 300 MW by the end of the 1980s.

While there were development efforts by the Nepali private sector to build power plants and supply electricity from the 1940s until the mid-1970s, the state sidelined them and took the power sector under its fold all through the 1980s until the mid-1990s. This bureaucratic control came about because of the twin impact of Nehruvian socialism in India combined with multilateral development banks intent on pushing big sovereign loans to poor Southern countries. The former was infused with the ethos of electric power being the "commanding heights of the economy" to be controlled by the government, and the latter were flush with petrodollars in the aftermath of the oil crisis of the 1970s. Until 1985, there were two monopoly utilities in Nepal: the Department of Electricity, which built hydropower plants, and the parastatal Nepal Electricity Corporation that operated them and ran the distribution system. In that year, they were merged into one monopoly Nepal Electricity Authority as a precondition for getting multilateral development bank loan for the Marsyangdi Hydroelectric project.

The first multilateral development bank-promoted "large" hydroelectric project in Nepal was the 60MW Kulekhani-1, which was completed in 1981 and still remains the only storage-type plant in the country. However, controversy dogged this project from the start: on a per kW construction cost, this project would have cost almost three times more than what small-scale producers were developing in Nepal, quixotically defying the "economy of scale" principle which should have made it much cheaper. The next project built with foreign aid was the 69MW Marsyangdi, which was even more expensive on the same criterion. However, the third such project, the 201MW Arun-3, estimated to cost $5300/kW, had to be aborted by the World Bank because multi-party democracy had just broken out and activist pressure could not be ignored.[5] The result has been a partial democratization of the power policy terrain, allowing a mix of government, private, and community initiatives that have given the country one-third more electricity at half the cost and half the time than Arun-3 would have. Even more amazingly, a group of Nepali entrepreneurs have built a 4MW hydropower project in the same roadless Arun river valley subsequent to the collapse of Arun-3 at one-third of the cost estimated for Arun-3 using Nepali engineering expertise and financing by Nepali banks in Nepali currency, even when the Maoist insurgency was raging and their construction site was bombed! This reversal of the law of economy of scale deserves to be analyzed for insights if the current mode of foreign aid-dependent international co-operation is to be restructured to cope with the requirements of the twenty-first century and the end of the Age of Aid.

It is interesting to introduce at this point two aid initiatives in Nepal by bilateral development agencies, one Canadian and the other Finnish, that may have started with good intentions but ended up being examples of mal-development. Canadian International Development Agency (CIDA) entered Nepal's hydropower development in the late 1970s in a big way during the tenure as World Bank's vice president of David Hopper. With environmentalism on the rise, Canada's significant capacity to study and design water resources projects were partially idle within Canada. At this juncture CIDA funded a consortium of Canadian consulting companies called Canadian International Water and Energy Consultants (CIWEC) to help the Nepal government identify prospective sites for hydropower and irrigation development. My career in Nepal government's Electricity Department began as the CIWEC project started, and I was seconded to work with Canadian counterparts. A quarter of a century later, in early 2003, I found myself as Nepal's minister of water resources, presiding as chief guest at the formal winding down and closure of this co-operation. It is therefore close observation and reflection spanning over two decades that prompts me to reflect as I do below.

There is general agreement among Nepali water folks that Canada's support through CIWEC helped build significant expertise capacity within the Nepal government and even some outside of it in the private sector. From the late 1970s until about the mid-1980s, Nepalis were privileged to work with some of the best Canadian minds that had grappled with hydropower and irrigation projects in their long careers. They ranged from academics to practitioners, and their collaboration spanned the range from down-to-earth hydrology and geology to high-level policy and strategic international negotiations. It was primarily in the policy-related arena that Nepali officialdom felt that they received the greatest value-addition: most of the water policy people that led the sector through the 1980s and much of the 1990s, even though they may have gained their engineering degrees in Russia or India, found on-the-job training and gained skills in practical aspects of water resource management, as well as the not-taught-in-engineering-schools issues around economics and institutions, by working with Canadian experts in the CIWEC project. Indeed, the founding of Nepal government's Water and Energy Commission (WEC), a much-needed interdepartmental and interdisciplinary body bringing into one policy planning fold the various agencies and subject matters pertaining to water and energy, is the direct result of CIWEC collaboration.

By the mid-1980s, however, this effort started going awry; and it is not clear from whose behaviour the value of this enterprise started dissipating. From the side of the Canadians, it must have been apparent that the construction-focused hydrocracy and project-focused Nepali politicians were not particularly keen on long-term "software" type issues, except perhaps as facilitating big water projects, much as dressings on the cake. If so, why were they wasting their time and Canadian taxpayer money bringing world-class experts to Nepal? To the Nepali hydrocrats, the impression was gaining that the expertise and stature of expatriates proposed to be the counterpart staff at the policy-formulating WEC secretariat were not of the awe-inspiring type that came in the late 1970s and the early 1980s. Also, there was a strange revolving-door set of staff seen between CIWEC and the World Bank and its projects. The matter became painfully clear once the World Bank approved the funding of an approximately fifteen million dollar consultancy study of the mammoth Karnali-Chisapani hydroelectric project in western Nepal on the eponymous river.

This attractive hydro-development site had been a dream of developers since it was identified in the 1960s. It has already seen three major world-class studies funded and conducted by the Japanese, the Norwegians, and the United Nations Development Programme (UNDP), even as the installed capacity of the project kept ballooning from 1800 to 3600 to 4500MW. (The size of a hydropower plant depends upon the kind of Indian power system to which you wish to optimize your peaking hydro capacity and to the manner in which the reservoir waters are to be shared between electricity production, irrigation, flood control, and other uses.) The trouble was that the potential funders of this mega-project would only have faith in a study conducted under their aegis, and hence the need for a new study for the World Bank. In bagging this consultancy, CIWEC expatriates, under the name of Himalayan Power Consortium (HPC), outbid others, including the influential Bechtel Corporation. From then on, CIWEC lost its policy advisor value to Nepali officials and was seen as just another profit-making contractor. Indeed, so little was the trust among Nepalis that the Canadians would look after Nepal's interest on this project and not that of the lower riparian Indians that they readily agreed to a U.S. proposal to separately hire Bechtel to advise the Nepal government and oversee the work of HPC. Of course, behind it also lay what in Nepal is called "donor competition," with each backing its industry champion for possible future work if it came about that such a large hydro project would be undertaken.

The 18-volume report produced by the HPC consortium recommended taking the installed capacity of this mega dam to 10,800MW. The fatal flaw in study, however, lay in the fact that it did not include a study of the macroeconomic impact such a project would have on Nepal's economy, and it also did not study what the irrigation, flood control, and navigation benefits would be in downstream India from this regulatory dam in Nepal that would need to be shared with Nepal equitably if the project were to move ahead. Thus there was little value added from previous studies despite the huge resources spent in this exercise, which became one more set of glossy reports on the shelf. Even more vexing is that, with the huge amount of resources spent in mapping the resources of the Karnali basin by CIWEC, no site less than 500MW was considered for inclusion in the study. Keep in mind that Nepal's entire integrated power system then was of only about 300MW, national demand was growing at no more than 15MW per annum, and the country and its engineers as well as construction contractors had not worked on any project larger than 60MW! This was indeed a strange, large-scale, and export-to-India-only bias for a region where more doable smaller schemes could have helped the poor inhabitants leapfrog into the twentieth century.

This inherent blindness of consultancies towards the existing social realities and fascination with the hyped up benefits of the large scale has vexed and perplexed me a great deal. Canada spent (through CIDA) a lot of development money in Nepal for a quarter of a century in consultancies designed to understand and better plan the country's water resources. Since CIDA terminated its program in 2003 there has been a sense of ephemerality in Nepal, with little in terms of Canadian development ideas that continue on the ground with lives of their own, and even less in terms of institutions, including the WEC secretariat that continues to exist on the sidelines of policymaking. In sharp contrast with expensive consultancies, the far lesser spending in international collaborative research on water management through Canada's IDRC has supported the growth of new ideas and experimentation aimed at improving living conditions. Such a collaboration in ideas, in contrast with one in profit-making ventures, seems to maintain international linkages more sustainably, thus assuring the growth of global camaraderie that lies behind the very notion of international collaboration.

To highlight that point that this contrast between research and consultancy is not just a Canadian phenomenon but one that lies deep at the heart of the global development paradigm, and one which needs to be re-examined in light of the need for more international co-operation in a globalized world against the background of a dying aid industry, this essay will now describe one more case of elegant failure. The Finns, latecomers to development, began to feel a need to flex their international presence in the early 1980s and decided to enter the aid game, with Nepal being a high-profile case.[6] As with CIDA, the development package brought by the Finns included software and hardware; the software side, though much smaller in terms of outlay, shows much better longevity. What is appreciated by many Nepalis is the Finnish help in topographic mapping that has produced the best and most detailed maps of Nepal useful in many different fields of study. The Finns also helped produce the forestry master plan and promoted the much-needed idea of forests not just as an environmental or social resource but also as a sustainable economic one.

Unfortunately, this last idea of developing some sections of Nepal's forests as an economic resource to generate revenue for the state, which was a lacuna in the overall perspective on forest management that has been dominated by conservation and community forestry, suffered a setback. For the Finns, forestry has been a matter of national pride, because their successful management had produced for them the wealth that has allowed the country to leapfrog "from timber export to Nokia." In a fit of missionary zeal, they insisted on the Nepal government privatizing 32,000 ha of prime Tarai forest as part of the aid package. Unlike the coniferous forests of the Scandinavian Taiga, Nepal's hardwood semi-tropical forests are rich in biodiversity and contain within them villages that subsist on forest products, especially fodder for cattle and firewood for domestic cooking. The privatization that the Finns proposed, while perhaps beneficial in the narrow economic sense, would entail significant social costs. Activist protests erupted, and because the Finnish establishment had entrenched itself with the "no privatization, no aid" conditionality, the Finns had to withdraw, and their aid architecture centred on the primary pillar of forestry collapsed.

Not without Hope

It is not that aid projects constitute one dismal history of abject failures: there are outstanding and oftentimes inspiring successes, but these are in most cases outside of the mainstream. Many of them were initiated by heretics who found conventional development approaches meaningless and established big-name aid organizations stifling; I have had personal acquaintance and sometimes deep involvement with many of them. It is a Nepali saying that the beautiful lotus flower only blooms in a muck pond. Despite Nepal's dismal development status, the country can boast of inspiring successes in development, which will be described briefly below. These cases of both mal- and belle developments will be analyzed using Cultural Theory for lessons on what the future of international co-operation should look like.

Rural poverty continues to be a vexing problem in Nepal, and the failure of the "integrated rural development" approach and projects of the 1970s and 1980s inspired by this philosophy that were promoted by both bi- and multi-lateral aid agencies have little to show at the end of it. Furthermore, an analysis of these projects shows that it was precisely in the areas where these Integrated Rural Development Projects (IRDPs), including Canada's Karnali-Bheri Integrated Rural Development Project or K-BIRD (the "bird that never flew"), were implemented with much fanfare that the hotbeds of the Maoist armed rebellion grew and were the most virulent. They became evidence that such insurgencies were not born of poverty but were rather the result of expectations raised but not sustained. However, noteworthy rural development successes such as Madhubasa in east Nepal and Madan Pokhara in west Nepal are still talked about and oftentimes envied by the less developed villages. The former was an almost fairy-tale improvement in the lives of a village of oustees displaced by flood and landslide in the middle hills of Nepal, and it came about due to the collective efforts ignited by a charismatic leader. The latter began as a collective effort of school teachers and other visionaries that, after a decade and more of effort, saw the village completely shifting from poor subsistence agriculture to being a major exporter of vegetables as well as, surprisingly, school teachers to other villages and districts of west

Nepal.[7] In neither of these achievements was there a significant pre-designed input from the Nepal government or foreign aid, except perhaps what the charismatic village leadership was able to successfully capture.

A United Nations Capital Development Fund (UNCDF) and Nepal government development effort of the mid-1980s that came close to failure but was revived and currently runs successfully has been the Marchawar lift irrigation scheme in the southern Tarai district of Nepal that also is the birthplace of Lord Buddha. The project was implemented over an irrigation system on the lower stretch of the Tinau river that the farmers had themselves operated and run for generations; it used to consist of a large "brushwood dam" that needed to be rebuilt every year in the dry irrigation season and was designed to be washed away during the flood season. In the early 1960s, a new modern concrete dam was built upstream with Indian assistance; but, because it was built on an unstable inland delta fan of boulders deposited by the river as it debouched from the Himalayan hills onto the Indo-Gangetic plains, the river bypassed the barrage in the second year after it was built. Thus the old farmers' system had been destroyed but the new one was non-functional. The result was that, with the collapse of the irrigation system, the social system too collapsed; the region becoming a dacoit-infested belt as the people took to any means available to survive.

In the mid-1980s, with the help of the UNCDF, along the traditional development pattern of aid money flowing to the government's department of irrigation to implement it, a lift irrigation system was implemented in the region. While the main structures of the pump house and main canal were implemented within acceptable levels of satisfaction, problems arose with the distribution system where farmers owned quilt-patch pieces of land and where traditionally they irrigated land on a succession system. A very grass roots development non-governmental organization, which I used to chair, was called upon to organize farmers to sort this problem out and to manage the operation of the system as a whole.[8] Thus a descent from hydrocratic hubris to a participatory mode of development saved this project, which is still running, by restoring sustainability.

Another success story was the Bhattedanda Milkway, a goods-carrying cable car used to transport milk to the roadhead without spoiling in the tropical heat. It has helped alleviate the poverty of marginalized farmers in Nepal's southern Kathmandu Valley in a significant way. Initiated in 1994 with the funding help of the European Union (EU) as part of a larger Bagmati Watershed Project (BWP) between 1986 and 1995, the project's second phase between 1998 and 2003 was philosophically enlarged to capture wider aspects of development through integrated management. It was called Bagmati Integrated Watershed Management Project (BIWMP) and strove to come to terms with chronic rural impoverishment in the middle hills of Nepal. Unfortunately, it could not do so because of institutional mismatches and the project was terminated in 2003 despite its contribution to sustainable development.

The milkway was never a part of the development ethos of either Nepal government's ministry of forests managing the BIWMP or the EU as an institution. BIWMP was mainly concerned with high cost (and ultimately washed away) soil erosion prevention with check dams and afforestation. The EU never internalized the ropeway technology or the institutional framework linking market access with rural hill poverty eradication. The ropeway essentially grew out of the unconventional thinking of a few Nepali and European watershed managers and several institutional conditions between 1994 and 1998 that favoured the installation of this new technology.[9] However, the conditions favouring the sustained development of this approach to rural poverty alleviation did not exist then and do not exist now, either within Nepali officialdom or the EU.

There are indicators that make this unconventional watershed management project a model of sustainable development: in its one-and-a-half-year period of operation between 1995 and 1996, unlike in normally marginalized hinterland village areas, it exported one-and-a-half times more milk, vegetables, and other rural products to the cities than it imported urban goods. The project obviated the need for these marginal farmers to boil milk for many hours a day (cutting a lot of trees in the process) to convert it into the thick khuwa paste that could be transported to the market without spoiling, getting less return for all their efforts. The milkway earned money not only for its client farmers but also for itself (even with low milk transportation rates) and was even able to save some of the earnings after paying for the operating cost (something that cannot be said for more prestigious irrigation projects in the country funded by big multilateral donors). These savings came to good use after the withdrawal of the EU when local initiatives had to be taken to revive the ropeway from both institutional and physical collapse.

Because the institutional mechanism had not been correctly designed (the ropeway's beneficiaries were not its operators); because the marginal villagers had to make the quantum leap in technology from operating the unsophisticated boiling of milk on firewood tripods to running precision-engineered mechanical cable cars; and because a competing technology (a gravel road) favoured by truck-owning interests came into being nearby, the milkway could not be sustained and fell into disuse after January 2001. However, a year and a half later, in July 2002, a massive cloudburst washed off a portion of the road (hardly a sustainable hill technology compared to ropeways), leaving the farmers cut off from the milk market. Because their standard of living had increased with their new-found ropeway technology, the farmers were not prepared to go back to their pre-milkway subsistence economy. However, since the EU was in the process of closing the BIWMP, which happened in April 2003, and Nepal's forest ministry was less interested in unconventional ropeways and more in favour of conventional watershed management, no help was forthcoming for the farmers. Even though some Rs 30 million (approximately Eur 3.4 million) had already been allocated for the expansion of the ropeways, it was lying idle for want of a champion social carrier. There were at least six, if not ten, consultancy studies carried out to study the feasibility of Bhattedanda expansion. Even with so many studies, neither the EU nor HMG was able to disburse the allocated money.

The ability of the farmers to access this money was nil, even though they had a crying need to rehabilitate their ropeway and have it carry milk after the road was washed out. They tried all kinds of means and sent delegations to various government agencies and politicians but to no avail: even the allocated EU money could not be released due to bureaucratic red tape, despite a letter from the EU Commissioner Chris Patten to the forest minister. Eventually, the developmentally orphaned farmers decided to do something about it themselves. They used the reserves they had collected from the previous operation and rehabilitated the milkway, which has since carried a million kilograms of goods (more from the village to the city than the other way around) and earned them more than half a million rupees worth of gross income (roughly Eur 57,000). The EU's money allocated for the expansion of the Bhattedanda Milkway, however, remained frozen and was repatriated.

The research organization I was associated with, during the earlier part of period, had grant support from IDRC to conduct research on issues of local water management. This outside-the-box-thinking, innovative milkway attracted our attention as a novel way to save forests, protect water catchment, and alleviate poverty. Although not in the geographical area of our research proper, which was in the southern Tarai, it came onto our radar screen precisely because we were interested in research and not consultancy. We were able to provide the farmers with moral as well as intellectual support for their plans to rehabilitate and subsequently expand the milk-carrying ropeway into deeper hinterlands to benefit even more marginal farmers. The farmers' group eventually did manage to get the ropeway operating again. Not only that, they managed to connect to the nearby community-operated electricity distribution system, switch over from non-renewable, fossil-fuel diesel-generated power (which required about Rs 34,000 per month to run) to renewable hydroelectricity for only Rs 7000 per month. A more participatory success story that is both poverty alleviating and climate friendly would be difficult to find.

Rethinking Collaboration

The end of the Age of Aid has also come with heightened awareness of global warming and the need to cut down on the usage of fossil fuel. More fundamentally, the very methodology on which design and planning of water-related technologies for irrigation, hydropower, flood control, or domestic water supply is facing a crisis of obsolescence without any new methodology on the menu. The epistemic reason lies in the fact that the design of expensive hydro-technical structures such as dams and spillways are based on past hydro-meteorological data that are, through regression analysis, projected into a long time series with the assumption that the future is going to be like the past. If the fundamental danger of climate change is that the future is going to be very different from the past, then this entire methodology of projecting the past, estimating the worst danger that could happen (e.g., a five- or ten-thousand-year flood), and designing water projects accordingly will not have much meaning. It calls for new, even uncomfortable knowledge, not just in hydraulics but also in other fields of study. And uncomfortable knowledge is often very upsetting to the powers that be.

It is bold research that generates uncomfortable knowledge which might be of great use, indeed vitally needed for the largely uncertain environmental and political future that the world entered into as the twentieth century concluded. The question then becomes: what kind of research arrangement will be conducive to generating such knowledge? Cultural Theory (CT), or theory of plural rationalities as it is also called, helps us grope our way around this problem. But before getting into its features, it is important to step back and reflect on what research is and is not, and to specifically distinguish it from more narrowly focussed consultancies that have consumed the bulk of development funding. Development agencies often do not fund research as academics understand it, but have spent a lot of resources on consultancies. Both these activities look similar in that they involve a lot of mental activities, intellectual skills, and preparatory specialist background in particular disciplines. But they differ in fundamental ways.

In a broad sense, researchers begin with the proposition: I don't know the answer but would like to find out, and to do so I do have some methodological skills and a background in problem-solving. Consultancy, on the other hand, says: I know the answers and have the skills, quite often better than anyone else; I can use them to solve whatever problem you may have. Researchers are the originators of their "terms of reference" (the research proposal) which they would try to "sell" to a funding source. In the case of the consultant it is his or her employer that would generate the "terms of reference" and "buy" the skills available in the market at competitive prices. During the course of execution, researchers have the flexibility to interpret the findings as well as surprises that emerge, while consultants are hard-pressed to explain why the unexpected has happened. Research is more often than not openly published and subject to peer review, whereas consultancy reports are the private property of the client, and in some rare cases available as "grey literature."[10] A consultant is often anonymous, hidden behind the name of the firm that can be dissolved or disappear, while researchers are out in the open, ready to take brickbats and bouquets. CIDA consultancies and IDRC research funding can be compared using CT and the teasing out of social solidarities involved in it.

During the Age of Aid, the social sciences have concentrated on addressing bureaucratic hierarchism of the state as the primary vehicle of development, almost a planned revolution from the top, which ensured that the problems to be solved through intellectual effort of research or consultancies was what was the problem for governments. After the collapse of the Berlin Wall, the state was no longer seen as the reliable partner, and the individualism of the market was seen to have the keys to salvation. This pendulum swing from state-bureaucratic centralism to free-market liberalism has not ensured development. What CT calls for is moving beyond monism or dualism in public policy (but avoiding the infinitude problem that is the bane of post-modernist thinking) by focusing on four social solidarities that are found at all scales, from the village to the global arena. Summarizing the latest theoretical writing on CT,[11] its arguments can be briefly encapsulated as follows: the variability of an individual's involvement in social life can be adequately captured using two dimensions of sociality (or discriminators) — transactions symmetrical or asymmetrical and competition fettered or unfettered — which generate four permutations of the ways of organizing.

If one places competition fettered and accountable as the positive direction (right) of the X-axis and that of unfettered and unaccountable towards the left, it indicates the extent to which an individual is incorporated into bounded units. The greater the incorporation (high X), the more is individual choice subject to group determination. If transactions are placed on the Y-axis, what is happening between equals (symmetrical, towards the bottom) or ranked unequals (asymmetrical towards the top), they indicate the extent to which an individual's life is circumscribed by externally imposed prescriptions. The more binding and extensive the scope of the prescriptions (high Y), the less of life is open to individual negotiation; conversely, the less binding (low Y), the more is freedom to network and negotiate possible. In one sense, these two parameters are asking the fundamental questions of philosophy in human life: who am I (X-axis)? And what should I do (Y-axis)? Depending upon a positive or a negative response to these two fundamental questions, the two discriminators together generate four basic ways of organizing (also called four social solidarities): *hierarchism* (high X, high Y), *egalitarianism* communards (high X, low Y), *individualism* (low X, low Y), and the *fatalism* of the conscripted (low X, high Y).

Symmetrical transactions and unfettered competition are the hallmark of the unbound and unranked realm of market individualism where risk-taking is the behavioural norm. It is risk-taking of entrepreneurs that brings forth innovations and new technological as well as management solutions that drive the water and other markets. At the opposite end of the diagonal is the ranked and bounded world of bureaucratic hierarchism where transactions are asymmetrical and competition fettered. Within this management style, risk-managing is the norm with the desired objective being control over the process and outcome. Because much of development debates have remained confined to these two diagonally polar opposite positions, the history of the last half of the twentieth century has resulted in the "market versus government intervention" pendulum swings that bedevils all efforts within the aid industry.

What CT does is to provide the liberty to move away from the political straitjacket of either being a socialist or a free-marketer: one can have some state and some market and, without denying either, something more. By bringing in the other two (often ignored) proclivities to the policy debate — the management styles of symmetrical transactions and fettered competition, which is the world of activist egalitarianism and civic movements, and that of asymmetrical transactions with unfettered competition that results in the fatalised world of conscripts — it provides for a more pluralized policy terrain. In the former, the need for keeping the group boundary intact, as well that of risk avoidance, often leads to alarmism and risk magnification, while in that of the latter, coping passively with whatever risk fate dishes out is the norm.

While the previous two (markets and hierarchies) represented the more stable states, these latter two (communards and the fatalist masses) represent the ephemeral. Indeed, if one examines the nature of civic protests, they arise as a reaction to some perceived danger (whether loss of language, culture, habitat, water rights, or other threats), which, if they have not been sensitively addressed by the powers that be, can bring down governments and the boycott of market products. These groups disappear or lie dormant until catalysed into action by some such provocation from perceived external danger, and hence are seen as less stable a social solidarity than hierarchies and markets. It is also the egalitarian activists who catalyse the fatalist masses, who otherwise are passive and dormant, into some form of reaction. It is for these reasons that the conventional social sciences have mainly considered the world of bureaucratic socialism or that of free market individualism but mostly ignored civic movements and the otherwise passive masses that only react (or more correctly are incited to do so by the other three) during elections and revolutions.

If we leave the passive fatalists aside for a moment and consider only the three active ones (consisting of bureaucratic hierarchism, market individualism, and civic activist egalitarianism), we can think of a three-legged policy stool in which power is contested as it is exercised by the three in their specific ways.[12] Bureaucracies love to exercise power through proceduralism of rules and regulations; market players exercise power through the freedom to network and negotiate; and civic movements exercise their power through critique and moral outrage. It is these proclivities that determine the kind of science that each pursues. Hierarchic science is guided by the ethos of risk management and control; market science springs from risk-taking propensities and is keen on innovation and profit; and civic science prefers risk avoidance and comes infused with a heightened sense of alarm.

CT argues that none of these three propensities can be wished away, nor can they be integrated into one single whole: what should be done is to assure each its voice at the table. Because each defines the problem differently, its built-in institutional filters let though some information that supports its solidarity's cosmology but is blind to others.[13] Hence, in the development debate, it would be wrong to start with the question: what are the facts? Rather, the starting point should be: whose facts? And unless all the solidarities have their seat at the policy table, some "fact" is bound to be left out, and might (and they often do) surface much later as an unpleasant surprise. In the ultimate analysis, this is what participation is all about, not the infinitude of everyone but that of all primary proclivities, that CT identifies as basic.

It is from these perspectives on policy and research that I wish to reflect on the impact of our research on local water management that was supported by IDRC/Ford Foundation funding that has continued even after our research ended;[14] and in that sense they have been very unlike high-priced consultancies funded by CIDA through CIWEC. In that sense, the IDRC support, to borrow from Newton, was akin to being hoisted aloft by giants so that civic science could see farther. What we saw, and more importantly how we communicated what we saw to others and how they reacted to what we said, is really what the "impact" of our research has been all about. It is not easy to quantify since there is an essential non-linearity to it (akin to flapping butterfly wings producing storms halfway around the world), but one can get a general impression from the reactions of others that continue through academia and the political press.

The collegium in the local water management research came together with a vague uneasiness regarding the state of the public discourse on water management. The entrenched positions on the large versus small divide, fascination of the major national water bureaucracies with grandiose plans and their dismissive attitude towards local schemes, as well as the refusal of most knee-jerk social and environmental activists to give credence to doing good science together with good activism were some of the elements of our unease. We were at the border between rational logic and strong emotions and not quite sure how efficacious tools of one would be for those on the other side. Strong feelings are important to move people to do things such as conservation and cleanups, but then so is good science that needs to inform such activism.

For the Nepali team, the restoration of multiparty democracy meant opening up of debates on water projects and policies that were previously settled clandestinely. It included not only projects in Nepal but also those that involved downstream riparian India. Our encounter with IDRC began with one such discourse in May 1992 — the Patna Initiative. It was a meeting organized in the Bihari capital of Patna in east India with support from IDRC that brought together a wide swath of Nepali and Indian academics, officials, journalists, and the political cognoscenti, without the stultifying formality of an official meeting. The free and frank sharing of views encouraged us to organize a follow-up meeting in Kathmandu a year later (the proceedings of which have been published as a special issue of Water Nepal).[15]

This meeting renewed old contacts and brought us together with other like-minded groups. The most important was the celebrated groundwater conference organized by VIKSAT in Ahmedabad that brought to the fore many "filtered out" data seen from perspectives different from that of state groundwater boards. The idea of local water management (a toad's eye view research) with a strong trans-border collaboration component grew in the aftermath of this engagement. Many of us had our concerns, feelings, views, and hunches, but we also had a lot of respect and commitment to science and therefore felt the need to engage in it at the grassroots to understand how water was actually being managed, as opposed to how the state regulations said it should be managed. The IDRC/Ford support for research (and not development consultancy) allowed us to examine in detail what was happening with water in small and what we called "marginalized" basins, and to draw stronger conclusions about the strengths and weaknesses of various management approaches. Our research was immeasurably strengthened by similar insights that our other colleagues from Chennai, Ahmedabad, and Jaipur drew from their work on the topic, and this confidence allowed us to engage in public discourse on water management and to take conventional wisdom head on. It is this public engagement from the perspectives of civic science that was the basis of eventual policy impact to promote alternative development pathways.

The challenges of a globalized world with widening income and opportunity disparities, with conflicts unresolved and conventional modes of governance fraying at the ends, present tremendous challenges for international co-operation that is more required now than ever. There are no blueprints and master plans, and even if there were, finding a consensus on one or more of them would be a formidable problem. What is argued in this essay, with examples from CIDA and IDRC involvement in Nepal's water terrain from divergent perspectives, is fundamentally two things: first, more collaborative research, and less one-way aid and high-priced consultancy advice, should be the mode of problem-solving in the years ahead; and CT would argue that such research needs to speak to all three of the active social solidarities. Market individualism should be able to "data pick" and run off with ideas to innovate; civic egalitarianism must find enough questions to begin a dialogue among contending positions to assuage fears of unacceptable hidden risks, and bureaucratic hierarchism must find answers to their need for regulation. The old Age of Aid is winding down and a new Age of Constructive Global Collaboration is yet to emerge.

Notes

1 Sharma et al., *Aid under Stress.*
2 Gyawali, 1996.
3 Sharma et al., *Aid under Stress.*
4 Desakota Study Team, *Re-imagining the Rural–Urban Continuum.*
5 Gyawali, 1996, ibid.
6 Sharma et al., *Aid under Stress.*
7 Gyawali, Schwank, et al., 1993.
8 Moench, Dixit, and Caspari (eds.), *Rethinking the Mosaic.*
9 Gyawali, Dixit, and Upadhya, *Ropeways in Nepal.*
10 Nepali academia have used the expression *bokshi mantra* (witchcraft's secret incantation) to describe consultancy reports that are not publicly disseminated.
11 Thompson, *Organising and Disorganising,* as well as Thompson, Wildavsky, and Ellis, *Cultural Theory.*
12 Gyawali, *Rivers, Technology and Society.*
13 See Fig. 1 from Gyawali, Allan, et al., *EU-INCO water research from FP4 to FP6,* and Gyawali, *Water and Conflict.*
14 See Moench, Dixit, and Caspari, *Rethinking the Mosaic,* and Desakota Study Team, *Re-imagining the Rural–Urban Continuum.*
15 *Water Nepal* 4, no. 1 (September 1994).

CHAPTER FOUR

The Rebirth of the Argan Tree or, How to Stop the Desert While Giving a Future to Amazigh Women in Morocco

Zoubida Charrouf[1] *and Dominique Guillaume*[2]

Background

Professor Charrouf has been fascinated by the argan tree for more than twenty-five years. This amazing tree is endemic only to the South of Morocco, where it covers an area of almost 8000 square kilometres (2 million acres). Though sometimes irregular, this area, referred to as "the Argan forest," plays a crucial function in southern Morocco, protecting the soil against erosion, fighting the encroachment of the desert, and providing basic necessities of life, such as, food, fuel, and animal fodder, for more than 2 million people on a daily basis. However, because of natural and human factors, the argan forest is, at present, highly endangered. Just after getting a PhD in organic chemistry in the early 1990s, and seeing for herself the decrepitude of the argan forest and hearing the concerns expressed by the local population, Charrouf did not hesitate to apply her scientific knowledge to the cause of protecting the argan forest. Her rescue work began with phytochemical analysis of the argan tree saponins, a type of second-ary metabolite presenting multiple physiological activities. Because the results obtained on argan tree saponins were slow to concretize, Charrouf decided to work on argan oil. At that time, argan oil was exclusively pre-pared at home by hand-pressing the kernels of the argan fruit. The oil was poor in quality and difficult to obtain in large quantities. Nevertheless, Charrouf quickly uncovered the oil's incredible potential as a commodity. Consequently, she decided to rationalize each step of the oil's preparatory process, improving them where possible, and this led to the design of a semi-mechanized process which yielded high-quality oil. In 1996 she decided to implement her methodology and created her first co-operative run by two basic principles: the co-operative would have to be exclusively operated by women, as women are the traditional makers of argan oil, and the income of the co-operative would have to be returned to women. This action would establish the involvement of the local population in tree pro-tection, while at the same time providing women with a monthly income. In addition, literacy programs were offered to the women working in the co-operative. At present, more than 120 co-operatives (twenty of them directly founded by Charrouf) have been established in southern Morocco, mostly in remote rural zones. In total, roughly 4000 women work in these co-operatives, producing high-quality argan oil that can be found on the shelves of gourmet stores in Europe, Japan, and North America. Charrouf is currently working on designing scientific methods to ascertain the qual-ity of argan oil, and to detect if it has been contaminated by cheap oils.

During the early days of her work on saponin, Charrouf met Professor D. Guillaume, an expert in the raising awareness of potential uses and ben-efits of natural products. Charrouf's enthusiasm swiftly convinced him to work by her side on the phytochemistry of the argan tree. This collabora-tive work survived the saponin program's discontinuation, and the two researchers are still currently actively working on methods of determining argan oil quality. Their collaboration has been very fruitful, and over the past 13 years, Charrouf and Guillaume have co-authored more than 25 scientific articles together.

Introduction: The Argan Tree and the Argan Forest

Located at the northwestern corner of Africa, Morocco is bounded by the Mediterranean Sea to the north, and the Atlantic Ocean to the west. On its eastern and southeastern sides, Morocco is a rather mountainous country;

THE REBIRTH OF THE ARGAN TREE 73

the three main mountains ranges, from north to south, are the Medium, High, and Anti-Atlas, respectively. Between the Anti-Atlas and the Atlantic Ocean, southeast of Essaouira and north of Guelmin, to the edge of the Sahara Desert is the Souss plain. For miles outside the cities of Agadir, Essaouira, and Taroudant, argan trees grow along the rocky and dusty hills in broken lines, covering a large part of the Souss plain. This tree (*Argania spinosa* (L.) Skeels) is endemic only to this part of Morocco, where it covers 7907.5 square kilometres (1,976,879 acres). Nationally, the argan tree is second in coverage only to the cork oak tree.

The argan tree itself is a slow-growing spiny tree that varies in size, from short and shrub-like, all the way up to a towering seven to ten metres high. It is an evergreen whose trunk grows gnarly with age, and whose leaves are quite small, approximately one inch long and a quarter of an inch wide, on average. When it blooms, its flowers are small, yellowish and aromatic.

The argan tree is unique for a number of reasons. It is a Tertiary relic species, and it is the only species of the tropical family *Sapotaceae* remaining in the subtropical zone. It can live for up to 150 to 200 years and is particularly resistant to the arid conditions of southern Morocco; its highly spread root system, in addition to enabling it to survive, also protects the soil against wind and water erosion. The argan tree can grow at sea level (along the Atlantic Ocean) as well as in mountainous locations, up to 1,500 m (5,000 ft.) above sea level, though it cannot survive in cold weather. The argan tree can survive for months simply by using water provided by atmospheric moisture. In the case of a long drought it drops its leaves, but it quickly grows them back when water returns. Consequently, in southern Morocco, the argan tree is considered the last barrier against the advance of the desert, a frightening and often irreversible phenomenon that slowly corrupts the agrarian system in all the sub-Saharan parts of Africa. Because the argan forest constitutes a unique ecosystem, and as such deserves a specific consideration, in 1998, UNESCO declared it a Biosphere Reserve site.

Over two million people make their living either directly or indirectly from the argan forest that has become essential to Amazigh people (the argan forest *natives*). The argan tree provides locals with firewood for heating and cooking, wood for construction, and leaves for feeding cattle (goats or camels). The shade created by its branches protects the crops and gardens, its roots serve to stabilize the soil, and its oil is used for medicinal, cosmetic, and culinary purposes. Not surprisingly, Amazigh people have developed a rural system strongly influenced by, and sometimes even based on, the argan tree. Indeed, a special *dahir* (a traditional rural law accommodating religious and civil customs) has regulated the life in the argan forest since 1925. In short, most of the time, rural dwellers can freely circulate in the largest part of the argan forest, but some restrictions on the use of the tree apply to specifically defined areas or even individual argan trees, mainly during the fruit-picking time.

However, despite these regulations, the fragile equilibrium which maintains the stability of the argan forest has been slowly disrupted over the years. This is due to the cumulative effect of various factors, including a naturally reduced regeneration rate from the seeds, several consecutive arid years of unprecedented severity, the construction of an always increasing number of greenhouses, in order to produce the fresh fruit and vegetables necessary to satisfy the tourist industry which is so essential to Morocco's economy, and finally the overuse of argan tree by-products by the Amazigh people themselves.

Consequently, the argan forest has become increasingly endangered. Not only has its area been decreased by half in the past one hundred years but, during the same period, the forest density has gone from 16 trees per hectare (40 trees per acre) to only 3–5 trees per hectare (8–12 trees per acre). It is generally estimated that 667 hectares (1,500 acres) of argan forest are lost every year, the majority of which become desert, or at least unproductive, land. In this sub-Saharan location, such conditions can become severe in a very short period of time.

Therefore, because of its rather precarious position, a rescue plan for the argan forest became an absolute necessity. Surprisingly, while this idea was rapidly taken up by the urban elite, the rural populations proved much slower to accept it, making the implementation of a preservation program more of a problem. Indeed, in some cases, the argan forest inhabitants did not see the preservation of these trees as a dignified and valuable farming activity, since access to the trees and their products had always been free and unlimited, while in others, they merely considered the forest's decline to be a natural and unavoidable process. Some years ago, most of the Amazigh people considered the presence of argan trees in the landscape in the same way as they viewed that of the Anti-Atlas Mountains: time was eroding them gradually, but the process was natural, unstoppable, and something that just had to be accepted. Such attitudes led us to the conclusion that in highly populated, poorly educated, and arid zones, ecological and economic concerns are inextricably intertwined. It became clear that the sustainable development of the argan forest would only be achieved if the perceived economic value of the argan tree was changed, and if the benefits of any preservation plan put into action were directly advantageous to the local populations. In other words, the necessary active involvement of the local population would only be possible if it were directly linked to rapid financial rewards. This conclusion led to the development of an initial program the aim of which was to identify substances of high economic value in the argan tree, and then develop them. This program was designed to transform the argan tree into a cornucopia that would naturally become valued and protected by the local populations.

Initial Attempts: The Search for New Argan Tree Metabolites

The programme we developed to revitalize the argan forest was based on a very simple idea: if we could identify new properties that were of high economic value (i.e., with potential for industrial, pharmaceutical, or cosmetic uses) in the argan tree, the native populations would perhaps see them in a different light, and be motivated to cultivate more trees in order to access larger quantities of this hypothetical new product. The argan tree's incredible longevity and its ability to survive in adverse conditions (heat, drought, and parasites, for example), and even to regenerate from old or damaged stumps, leant support to our hope of discovering such new properties of high economic value. It could be reasonably expected to find substances presenting phytoprotective properties or having the potential to be used as drugs. Plants which belong to the *Sapotaceae* family are rich in saponins, a class of chemical compounds, some of which have been shown to possess such pharmacological properties as antibacterial, fungicidal, antiviral, cytotoxic, piscidal, molluscidal, insecticidal, antifeedant, anthelmintic, diuretic, anti-inflammatory, anti-ulcer, analgesic, anti-pyretic, hemolytic, among others. The discovery of a single molecule which strongly exhibited any one of these properties would spell the success of this program. Therefore, this class of plant secondary metabolites was what we investigated first. Several saponins were isolated from different parts of the argan tree: its wood, leaves, and fruit. A few of them were known compounds which had been previously isolated from other plants, but most of them were new molecules (which we named arganine A-R) encountered for the first time in a plant, though some of them have been re-isolated from other plants since then. Biological tests proved the worth of our plan to discover new properties, as some of the arganines displayed antibiotic, anti-inflammatory, hypoglycemiant, and antiviral activities. Nevertheless, none of these activities was sufficient to justify the accelerated development of the arganines as a new drug and the subsequent rescue of the argan grove in the near future.

The second type of metabolites we investigated was flavonoids. Flavonoids possess anti-free-radical properties, and so it is claimed that they possess anti-aging properties. Consequently, these molecules are prized in the field of cosmetology. Again, despite the fact that valuable molecules were isolated in the argan tree, particularly the leaves, molecules that are presently industrially produced, the prospect of transforming these molecules into a real economic output is so remote that this approach, by itself, could not immediately aid in the rescue of the argan forest. At that stage, it became clear to most of those involved that the quest to rescue the argan forest by searching for new metabolites and developing them was indeed possible, but that it was only likely to be achieved at a point when the argan forest would already be so damaged that to rescue it would demand too much financial effort for a developing country. Hence, it was urgent to revisit our initial approach and focus on more immediate solutions. For a few of us the practice of producing argan oil that had been going on for centuries among the Amazigh people naturally imposed itself as the quickest and the most efficient way to protect the argan tree. In order for this approach to be successful, it was necessary to reconsider each step of the oil production and marketing process to turn it into a new derivative of high economic value able to rescue the argan forest, but the most ambitious and uncertain task was the necessity of changing the rural population's outlook on argan oil.

Argan Oil: From Family-Scale Production to Worldwide Distribution

Argan oil is prepared from the fruit of argan trees. The fruit, which ripens between May and September, is the size of a large olive, and can be either oval, round, or spindle-shaped. Their skin, initially greenish-yellow, turns yellow then brown when they fully ripen. The stone of the argan fruit is made up of one to three almond-like kernels.

Argan Oil for the Family

For centuries Amazigh women have prepared edible argan oil. Indeed, in traditional Amazigh society, argan oil preparation is exclusively a woman's task. Each family collects the fruit and stores them, and women prepare small quantities (less than 1 L/35 fluid ounces) of argan oil all the year long, depending on the family's needs. The oil is produced by pressing the slightly roasted kernels of the argan fruit. Argan oil preparation requires eight steps: picking the fruit (the only task that is sometimes performed by men or children), peeling the fruit, cracking the nuts, roasting the kernels, crushing the kernels, mixing the crushed kernels with water, stirring by hand, and finally, collecting the oil.

Traditional fruit collecting is not mechanized, and because only ripe fruit produces good oil, this means that it is necessary to search and collect ripe fruit that has fallen underneath the trees. In the argan grove around each village, the forest is divided into a quasi-private portion (*agdal*) and a communal portion (*azroug*). Access to argan trees is governed by these rules, meaning that if trees growing on the *azroug* are accessible to everyone, those growing on the *agdal* are not. No fences are necessary, as every villager knows from which trees he or she is permitted to collect fruit. However, for the poorest families, that is, those with no *agdal*, fruit collecting is a back-breaking task, often meaning long periods of work, on steep slopes during the hottest period of the day. Fruit collectors, the lucky ones with a donkey cart, need to trudge through the argan forest to find communal trees whose fruit has not yet been collected. On average, 60–100 kg (140–250 lbs.) of fresh fruit are necessary to prepare 1 L of oil, and it can take a single person anywhere from one to three days to gather the required amount of fruit.

After it has been collected, the fruit is then air-dried for a few days before it is ready to be peeled. The peel is latex-rich and, once dried, the brown wrinkled peel still sticks to the argan nut. Women use stones to weaken the peel, then remove it manually to get to the argan nut, which is the size of a large olive. Argan peel is frequently given to cattle. Goats are also very fond of argan fruit, and when grass is scarce they do not hesitate to climb into the trees to eat the fruit. Later, they regurgitate the "peeled" argan nuts, either underneath another tree or in their stables. Because argan fruit peeling is a long and tedious task, fruit collectors are sometimes tempted to collect the regurgitated fruit which has already been peeled. Not only does this practice raise microbiological concerns, but it also modifies the flavour of the oil. Argan oil prepared, wholly or in part, from regurgitated fruit is of low quality, and is frequently sold to tourists along the roads in plastic bottles.

After they have removed the peel, the women then have to break the argan nuts to obtain the kernels. The nut is oval in shape, and at its widest is about the size of a woman's thumb. To break argan nuts, women use the stones that they used to weaken peel, and, while holding the nuts between two fingers, they precisely hit its apex, breaking it, and in doing so, freeing the precious kernels from their shell. This is a long and painstaking process, and 35–45 kg (77–99 lbs.) of dry fruit yields only about 2–2.5 kg (4.4–5.5 lbs.) of kernels.

To prepare edible argan oil, the kernels have to be roasted over a low fire, for which the argan shells themselves often provide the fuel. The women must continuously stir the kernels during the roasting stage, typically using a sheep shoulder plate or any flat sheep bone to do so. This roasting procedure is necessary to temper the oil's natural bitterness, while at the same time providing it with a unique hazelnut-like flavour.

The roasted kernels are then crushed using a home-made millstone, which is made up of a piece of bedrock and a cone-shaped grinding piece that rotates. The kernels are progressively introduced to the millstone, the result of which is a brownish and viscous liquid, which is gradually mixed with water to produce a kind of dough. The resulting dough is kneaded by hand for several minutes, releasing water-emulsified argan oil. As the water is added, the dough becomes harder and more difficult to knead. Because the process involves so much work, the women always try to obtain as much oil as possible, only stopping kneading when they can release no more drops of emulsified oil from the dough. Regrettably, the remaining dough still consists up to 2 per cent of argan oil. It also contains high levels of proteins and carbohydrates. Such nutritious source is used to feed cattle and goats. The emulsion is then decanted, after which the argan oil is finally ready to be collected. The women will repeat this process as soon as is necessary.

Using this traditional method, it takes a single woman approximately 16–20 hours of work to produce 1L of argan oil. However, women never do this work alone; mothers, daughters, and neighbours work alongside one another, and the long periods needed to prepare argan oil offer an opportunity for women to gather, converse, and sing together.

However, just like the use of regurgitated argan nuts, adding water to the dough raises important concerns. Water is scarce in southern Morocco and, during the dry season, women often use water from collective farm ponds or unregulated pits or from containers that have been stored for extended periods of time. Therefore, the probability of microbiological contamination through the addition of water to the milled kernels is high. Even if clean water is used, the moisture levels of traditionally prepared argan oil reduce its shelf-life, and the addition of salt that is sometimes recommended does not do much to increase it.

In addition to these microbiological drawbacks that could be overcome by the addition of a sterilization process, traditionally prepared argan oil could not be marketed reasonably because it did not keep well, and its taste and quality varied from one batch to another. Clearly, one can understand why the mass production of high-quality argan oil as a method to rescue the forest was not necessarily an obvious solution for everyone!

Argan Oil for Everyone

The idea of marketing argan oil was nevertheless supported by its alleged beneficial properties. Traditionally, argan oil is used by Berber women to reduce skin pimples, acne scars, and chicken pox pustules, and to keep their hair strong and shiny. Edible argan oil is said to be choleretic, to regulate cholesterol and lipaemia, to prevent atherosclerosis, and to have anti-inflammatory properties. Argan oil indeed had an optimum profile to become a prized organic product among G7-country consumers.

In order for this initiative to rescue the argan forest by marketing high-quality argan oil to be successful, it had to satisfy several criteria, both sociological and qualitative. It had to involve and benefit the rural population; that is, it should not result in the poor getting poorer. Also, the argan oil should be produced on a large scale, and should always be of the highest possible quality. The idea of creating women's co-operatives emerged, from the consideration of the first points, together with as many questions. Firstly, because women traditionally prepared argan oil they possessed the knowledge of how to make it, but would they be eager to share it? Secondly, because women run the household, providing them with jobs should increase the household wealth, but would their husbands let them work in a co-operative? And finally, because women run the homes, getting them a job would also reduce the amount of time that the children of the house had to work, but would the men let the children use their extra time to go to school?

Solving the problem of high-quality mass production of argan oil proved much easier. Only fruit with the peel still intact should enter into the argan oil production, as opposed to those which have been "peeled" by animals, and tedious preparative steps should be made easier wherever possible. Because the fruit-picking step was impossible to mechanize, it remained unchanged but would now be financially rewarded. Peeling the fruit could be mechanized using scratching-machines. This would reduce the time needed to peel the fruit and consequently make the idea of using only fruit with peels easier to accept. Though breaking the nuts appeared impossible to improve, the roasting step could be easily standardized by using gas-burners, allowing large amounts of kernels to be roasted constantly. Finally, and most importantly, we could replace hand-mixing with a mechanical press. Such a change would not only eliminate the use of water, and thus the risk of microbiological contamination, but would also allow higher quantities of oil to be extracted from a given quantity of kernels in one-third of the time. For all these steps, progress was slow. Women had to integrate the changes psychologically; we had to convince them that improvement did not imply a rejection of their culture. These were things that could not be rushed. But time is money and money is scarce in southern Morocco. The early support of the International Development Research Centre (IDRC), the first organization to believe in this program, has been essential in stimulating the work on argan oil extraction and the study of its preservation.

While some people initially doubted the quality of the pressed argan oil, chemical studies clearly proved it to be of high quality. The chemical composition of its major elements is identical to traditionally and strictly prepared argan oil. The composition of the minor, but frequently physiologically relevant, elements of press-argan oil was found to be more reproducible. In both traditional and press-extracted argan oil, unsaturated fatty acids (oleic and linoleic acid) comprise 8 per cent of the fatty acid composition; the 2 per cent remaining is made up of saturated fatty acids (stearic and palmitic acid). Furthermore, the shelf life of argan oil could now be extended to several months, just like other pressed edible oils. High-quality argan oil could now be prepared on a large scale; it was ready to conquer the world, if there were organizations that were able to do it.

The Women's Co-operatives

In 1996, after having evaluated the technical feasibility of these improvements in the laboratory, we opened the first women's co-operative in Tamanar, between Essaouira and Agadir. Women were not necessarily easily convinced to work for a co-operative. To increase the co-operative's chances of success, it had been decided that to be a member some rules had to be followed. First, the oil should exclusively be prepared in the co-operative and not at home, to make sure that the oil was prepared from fruit with peels. Next, each woman should provide a certain amount of fruit (with peels) per month to the co-operative and would get paid for it. It was decided that the price of the fruit would be 20 per cent above the market price, in order to encourage women to work for the co-operative, and to make the population realize that fruit collection was a job in itself. Women willing to prepare argan oil in the co-operative would also have to participate in the nut-cracking process and would get paid according to the number of kernels they produced. The argan oil would be sold through the co-operative and the profits shared among the members. Each woman working for the co-operative would also receive free literacy classes. For women who were already literate, we offered courses in oil-extraction technology, legal constitution of the co-operatives, food safety, and management development. In addition to these courses, more general programs dealing with health, civic and religious responsibilities, environment, or micro-projects were also available and drew in a number of women.

The first weeks of this co-operative were quite chaotic; women would come one day but not return the following days. Suspicious husbands would show up unexpectedly. Nevertheless, after a few weeks, a group of sixteen women began to come to the co-operative on a regular daily basis and, with the first paycheque at the end of the first month, suspicion totally disappeared. For the first time ever, these sixteen women were getting paid for their work. They were finally convinced that this co-operative project was not a hoax. Six months after its opening, the Tamanar co-operative had produced 500L (110 gal.) of high-quality argan oil.

The oil produced by the mechanical presses was a success, but the success of this first woman's co-operative was not marked simply by this material production. More important were the changes we observed in the women's behaviour. Indeed, for all of these women, working in a co-operative was their first experience with paid employment; their status changed from housewives to working women. The development of each woman's self-esteem after a few months is likely the most spectacular, though unexpected, result of this co-operative. In Amazigh society, a woman had always been dependent on someone else: first her parents, then her husband. The income they received from their work in the co-operative gave them a measure of independence. Now they had the ability to buy things for their household or themselves, by themselves. With more money at home, the children no longer had to work, and women had enough money to send their daughters to elementary school. The future of Amazigh women was changing. Once the tears of joy evoked by the first paycheque were forgotten, the co-operatives also helped women achieve a real social status. Women realized that they were now full and active members of the village micro-society. From modern society's standpoint, not much had changed, but for these women, the recognition that the activity that they had been doing for hundreds of years was a valuable one helped them to see themselves as valuable persons. Gaining skills in reading and mathematics allowed the women to be able to discuss the household economy, and also that of the co-operative. Their self-esteem growing, women previously considered very quiet or very shy began to dare to speak in public, express their views on the future of the village, even to confront men! And so, more and more women came to the co-operative, and more and more people came to buy argan oil.

Time had come to open another co-operative in a new location. After Tamanar came Tidzi, in the province of Essaouira, followed by, Tiout, in the province of Taroudant, Ait Baha in the province of Chatouka Ait Baha, and many more. At present, 130 women's co-operatives operate in the argan forest, some of which have received international awards, such as the co-operative in Amal that received in a special jury award from the Slow Food Association in October 2001.

However, this success did not always come smoothly. In the village, men were still suspicious. They now had to share their power with women; the equilibrium was changing too fast. The co-operative was a success and growing, and now the small building used by the co-operative was getting too small. But, the men were now asking themselves whether allowing the co-operative to move to another building would also mean giving more power to these women. Was it safer to stop this co-operative before it became too big?

As is often the case, help came from abroad in the beginning. Morocco had always been considered a sun-and-sand vacation destination by tour operators, but these operators now started to include the co-operatives in their guided tour. This new contact not only increased the co-operative income, but it also enabled them to sensitize a larger and often eco-friendly audience to the argan forest cause. Shortly after this, the first television crews began to visit the co-operatives. All major German, French,

British, and American TV networks started to inform the public of the need to protect the argan forest, and of the success of the women's co-operatives. There was even an article in *National Geographic* on the argan forest. The argan oil/argan forest rescue initiative was now expanding far beyond the borders of Morocco; it became an international cause. At the same time, international organizations, both public and private, became aware of the argan oil co-operative project. The early involvement of the IDRC had demonstrated that this project was serious and worth financing, but now that the success of the first co-operatives had proven that there was a market for high-quality argan oil, these organizations were not so shy about participating in the argan-forest project. In 2002, Prince Albert II of Monaco came to Tiout (population 1000) to inaugurate a woman co-operative founded by the Principality of Monaco.

Closer to home, His Majesty Mohammed VI of Morocco, visited exhibits aimed at promoting the argan forest, to which women working in the co-operatives were also invited. Just three short years prior to this, some of these women had been illiterate; now His Majesty Mohammed VI had heard of their work and was showing interest in it. Saving the argan forest was an important project, and they were an integral part of it. Though its original purpose was to give a future to the argan forest, this project has also given a future to Berber women. This has been its real success.

Argan Forest Rescue and Argan Oil Production: Two Works Still in Progress

Preservation of the argan forest is, without question, a necessary cause. This concept is now widely accepted among the rural populations, and several communities have even hired wardens to protect valuable parts of the forest. In addition to these measures, national as well as international argan tree plantation programs are currently in progress in Morocco. Once again, IDRC was a pivotal partner for the success of the replantation programs and, just as in the case of the co-operatives, its early support allowed for the possibility of many other initiatives.

Though increasing the number of argan trees was one of the initial pledges of the co-operative initiative, not all co-operatives are at the level of advancement for the replantation program. However, the Commissariat for Water and Forests is currently making a significant contribution to this cause, and the area of the replanted zones reached 7.7 square miles (2,000 ha) in 2008, with a density of 200 trees per ha (80 trees per acre).

Nevertheless, the success of replantation is made difficult by the dearth of knowledge about how to cultivate a tree, which we only began to study scientifically a few years ago. It seems now accepted that the symbiotic relationship between fungus and argan tree root is necessary for the tree's proper development. Because such fungi are not always found in the soil, this could explain some failure in the past. We must also consider that for some of the native people in the argan forest, planting new trees is motivated exclusively by the desire to produce more fruit, and thus more oil, rather than by the desire to preserve the forest. This is important because the argan tree exists under different genotypes, which is why the fruit can be round, oval, or spindle-shaped. However, the fruit shape is not the only difference between the trees; for some types, the argan nut is much tougher than for others. Since the breaking of the argan nuts is still not mechanized, the idea of replanting argan trees producing easy-to-break nuts has also emerged. While such a position is understandable economically, from species conservation and genotypic standpoints such a proposal could have very dramatic effects, such as impoverishing the global genetic stock of the argan forest. Therefore, caution is necessary, and even though the goal of increasing the argan tree's economic value was one of the foundations of the project, this goal should not lead to the genetic reduction of a species.

Argan oil is, without a doubt, changing the economy of southern Morocco and is likely to positively impact the economy of Morocco as a whole. The region of Essaouira alone produces more than 2,000 tons of oil every year. In addition to women's co-operatives, small and sometimes quite large businesses have appeared. Argan oil massages are offered in every tourist hot spot, and argan oil is now known as the "world's most expensive oil." Some subtropical countries are already trying to grow their own argan trees in order to produce argan oil.

To certify the geographic identity of argan oil and products made from argan oil, the Moroccan government is currently applying for a Geographical Indication. Such an indication that would permit the the name "Argan Oil" or "Argan" to be used only for products coming from southern Morocco and produced according to established standards would bring several advantages to the argan oil producers in the argan forest. The Geographical Indication would increase the value of the rural areas of the argan forest by increasing the value of the marketed product, which would, in turn, generate more revenue for the producers, together with providing a larger export market. The increased profits would enable improvement in the equipment required to produce high-quality oil. The Geographical Indication should also help in organizing the marketing of argan oil by providing a more direct access to more profitable markets than the local market. A new type of organizational structure could be created by which the co-operatives would be Professional Associations which protect the interests of their members, negotiate with other producers, and work at improving the image of argan oil. These professional associations would also work at defining the standards used for the production and marketing of argan oil.

Additionally, a Geographic Indication could add value to the argan forest through the development of eco-tourism, with the opening of tasting centres, restaurants, rental accommodation, or tours of the co-operatives. Already, more than a hundred tourists visit the Tamanar co-operative every day. It is expected that more co-operatives will be formed, resulting in the improvement of women's standard of living, greater assistance for vulnerable and marginalized women, and improvement of the women's level of independence, helping them to make decisions for themselves, to manage their money, and to invest in their future and that of their children.

But, even in the argan grove, all the argan oil producers do not necessary adhere to the initial commitments that governed the co-operative creation. It becomes very tempting to sell cheap corn oil as expensive argan oil to gullible tourists. It is still also tempting to use the nuts which have been regurgitated by animals, eliminating the long and slow peeling process from the production of oil. If consumers are eager to pay up to $20 for 100 mL (3.5 fl. oz.) of cosmetic argan oil, disappointed consumers could also rapidly leave the market and undo all these years of work. Consequently, research to develop methods of certifying argan oil quality and to detect its contamination is still necessary. Scientifically proving the alleged pharmacological properties of argan oil is also an important issue. This work requires also a great deal of funding, far more than what co-operatives for women can generate, so progress is slow. The argan tree has been waiting for two geological eras to be recognized and valued. Patience is also one of its virtues.

Notes

1 Laboratoire de Chimie des Plantes de Synthèse Bioorganique, Faculté des Sciences, Université Mohammed V-Agdal, BP1014, Rabat, Morocco.
2 Université de Reims Champagne Ardenne, Pôle santé, 51 rue Cognacq Jay, 51100 Reims, France.

CHAPTER FIVE

Under Fire: Doing Research in Warlike Conditions

Rita Giacaman, Yoke Rabaia, and Viet Nguyen-Gillham

Historical and Contextual Overview

Palestinians have been living in protracted conflict for almost one hundred years, with varying degrees of exposure to violence and security threats and with periods of extreme Israeli military brutality. Warlike conditions are not only part of daily life; they have become normalized to some extent as a matter of survival and resilience.[1] The carnage of the Gaza Strip beginning December 27, 2008, is only one the many periods when Palestinian civilians were exposed to extreme and extraordinary Israeli military brutality. Described as a war crime,[2, 3, 4] the massacre and atrocities committed by the Israeli army on the destitute Gaza Strip have been the most ferocious onslaught since the 1948 Arab–Israeli war, when the state of Israel was created on Palestinian land.

During the 22-day Israeli attack of the Gaza Strip, almost 1400 Gazans were killed, mostly civilians, and thousands injured, in addition to the rampant destruction of infrastructure, homes, schools, universities, and mosques. The capacity of the Gaza health care system which needed to respond to an enormous number of casualties had already been severely compromised by the state of siege imposed on Gaza for over a year and a half. Yet, tragically, information on the appalling conditions of the Strip continues to be sanitized by the Western, particularly the U.S., media,[5] who, in most instances end up blaming the victims.

It is impossible to tell the story of who we are, what we do, and why we do what we are doing, without looking back at Palestinian history. Our daily lives, our work in research, our field interventions, and our *raison d'être* are all inextricably tied to the century-old story of injustice towards the Palestinian people, and their resilience, agency, and unyielding hope for positive change. A historical overview is also important because the Palestinian narrative of injustice and the struggle for liberation has largely been ignored in the Western world. An understanding of Palestinian history will prepare the way for an understanding of why we focus on psychosocial health, in particular, on that of young people.

The story begins in 1917, when British Foreign Secretary Lord Balfour stated in a letter to Lord Rothschild, the leader of the British Jewish community, that "His Majesty's government view with favour the establishment in Palestine of a national home for the Jewish people" with the understanding that "nothing shall be done which may prejudice the civil and religious rights of existing non-Jewish communities in Palestine, or the rights and political status enjoyed by Jews in any other country."[6] This statement effectively promised the land on which Palestinians had lived for centuries both to the Palestinian indigenous inhabitants and to mainly European Jews who believed that establishing a Jewish state was the only way to provide protection from European anti-Semitism. The Balfour Declaration led to the beginning of a series of hostilities and wars, and, ultimately, to the ongoing conflict that exists today. Seventy-eight per cent of the Palestine that had existed as a unique social, cultural, and national entity for centuries[7] was transformed into the State of Israel. As documented by the Israeli historian Ilan Pappé,[8] more than three-quarters of the Palestinian population was forcibly dispossessed and expelled from the country between 1947 and 1949, turning them into refugees in neighbouring Arab states.[9] Ironically, anti-Semitism was not a Palestinian creation but a European one, yet the United Nations General Assembly chose to solve its problem by creating a new tragedy, that of Palestinian eviction and dispersion, Israeli military occupation of Palestinian land, and protracted warlike conditions.

The major collective trauma of the 1948 Palestine War is still felt by third-generation refugees, especially those still living in refugee camps.[10]

In 1950, the West Bank was annexed to the Hashemite Kingdom of Jordan, and the Gaza Strip came under Egyptian military administration. About twenty years later, Israel occupied the rest of Palestine (the West Bank, including Palestinian Arab East Jerusalem, and the Gaza Strip), as a result of the 1967 Arab–Israeli war and expelled a further 180,000 Palestinians[11] to neighbouring countries.

Palestinian civil resistance to Israeli military occupation began in the 1970s and increased during the 1980s, through collective and grassroots action, civil disobedience, and physical confrontation. It was during this period that Palestinian social action emerged, which focused on building an infrastructure of health, education, agriculture, and other services independent of the Israeli military government. It was also during this period that the Institute of Community and Public Health at Birzeit University joined this social action — indeed, was part of it — to fulfill people's health needs. From its inception, the Institute was actively engaged in participatory research as a matter of necessity dictated by warlike conditions, and also because, as researchers, we saw ourselves as both academics and social activists struggling for the survival of justice and the nation. We were unaware then that our approach was defined as "participatory research" in Western academic literature; it was simply a rational approach which linked academia to real life, combining research focussed on people's needs with their ongoing experience on the ground. As models were being built, close co-operation was established with various social action groups operating at the time and in partnership with community.

In 1987, after years of mobilizing the population into various forms of self-help and popular resistance initiatives, the first popular uprising (*Intifada*) against Israeli military occupation took place. The Intifada engaged the popular masses, including women and children, who had never before participated in resistance.[12] It also engaged academics in different community-oriented efforts, as they were moved to respond to the emergency situation. This period of the first Intifada was marked by extensive violence resulting in the death, injury, and permanent disablement of many people, most of them young. Schools closed down for several years, and economic activity came to an almost complete halt, as public life was reduced to a state of emergency. These were stressful times that led to an increase in community action, most notably in the area of rehabilitation of disabilities, but also, eventually, in the area of psychosocial health.

It was during this period of the first Intifada that it became clear that Palestinians were suffering because of Israeli military occupation, dispossession, dispersion, life lived in refugee camps, and repeated exposure to violence not just physically but also mentally. Until that time, the mental health of Palestinians affected by war had attracted little attention among Western policymakers and practitioners. This period marked a significant turning point, and since then, greater recognition has been given to the fact that Palestinians have feelings and a psychology, and that they are experiencing mental-health problems as a consequence of war, subjugation, and violation.

Thus, new mental and psychosocial health initiatives began to provide evidence of the negative impact of acute warlike conditions on mental and psychosocial health, particularly among children and youth. However, the main focus of that period was on "trauma," which subsequently became a major concern of international mental health projects and those who funded them. This focus reflected the export of Western cultural trends, with their bias towards the medicalization of distress and the rise of psychological therapies. Terms like "post-traumatic stress," "psychosocial," and "counselling" rapidly became points of reference in a fashionable new realm of humanitarian concern.[13]

In one sense, this "trauma" discourse seemed to offer Palestinians the possibility of highlighting causative factors previously rendered semi-invisible: the socio-political condition of the Palestinian people and the collectively traumatogenic nature of military occupation and violent repression.[14] On the other hand, a medicalized response to trauma risked obscuring the social and political meaning attributed by Palestinians to their collective experiences. Some Palestinian professionals adopted the trauma discourse as a means of drawing international attention to the distress resulting from political oppression. However, treatment in the form of counselling and psychotropic medication offered little in the way of alleviating the ongoing collective trauma. For most Palestinians, one-to-one counselling is an imported and culturally unfamiliar practice. It suggests that the pathological effects of war are located inside a person and can be cured through individual treatment, as if the individual were recovering from an illness rather than suffering from collective political injustice.[15]

In 1991, the "Peace Conference on the Middle East" was convened in Madrid and included Israel, Palestinians, and the Arab states. However, it was a series of secret negotiations in Oslo that eventually brought about mutual recognition between Israel and the Palestine Liberation Organization, and, in 1993, the signing of the Declaration of Principles on Interim Self-Government Arrangements,[16] otherwise known as the Oslo Accords. This declaration led to the handing over of selected spheres of administration, including responsibility for health care provision, to an interim Palestinian National Authority (PNA). This authority was intended to govern parts of the West Bank and Gaza Strip during a transitional period when negotiations of a final peace treaty would be completed.[17] The PNA lacked then, as it does now (2009), control over borders, over the movement of people and goods, and over land and water.[18] With time, it also became evident that the Authority suffered from other shortcomings, including the absence of collective decision-making and integrated planning, and excessive civil service appointments made in compensation for "revolutionary heroism," political support, or both, which has been a major drain on the national budget.[19]

This was the period of so-called peace-building, which followed some thirty years of Israeli military rule in the area. Those thirty years had severe negative ramifications, not only on political and social life, the economy, and infrastructure, but also on the mental health of the general population. Protracted periods of stress, poverty, oppression, and a sense of powerlessness brought about by military rule opened up a space during the Oslo Process period for a public forum on youth violence and psychosocial health. This kind of forum is especially relevant given that more than three-quarters of the Palestinian population is under the age of thirty.

Two contradictory perspectives on Palestinian youth soon emerged. One was held largely, but not solely, by outsiders who saw the young people who took part in the First Uprising as having grown up in conditions of chaos. According to this point of view, these young people were a source of violence that needed to be restrained, even controlled. This particular approach to youth violence was fixated on their "violent" behaviour, with little regard for the context from which this violence emerged. For those who held this perspective, the solution was to get the youth off the streets and back into schools, leaving them with little opportunity for participation or agency. It is not surprising that these young people would take a negative view of such a course of action. The First Uprising not only gave them a taste of participation, it took young people out of a previously disenfranchised state into one of political empowerment.

During this same period, another discourse also began to emerge, one with a more developed understanding of the responses of young people to political violence and hostilities of other kinds. During the post-Oslo years, the space for social and political participation had begun to shrink for everyone, including young people, and this alternative discourse viewed the actions of the Palestinian youth as a response to the violence they had observed and endured through political participation and resistance to occupation. The alternative discourse was accompanied and strengthened by calls from civil institutions to focus on the issue of citizens' rights.

Although concerted local initiatives in psychosocial health interventions took time to emerge, they eventually began to appear, especially among Palestinian non-governmental organizations (NGOs). There were many reasons for this delay including, firstly, the fact that mental health stigma is even stronger than the stigma associated with physical disability, given the elevated social status of the disabled as heroes of the uprising. A second reason was the fact that some forms of violence have always existed as an accepted social phenomenon by some within Palestinian society. Not only was violence against women, children, and young people accepted, it was used by men as an instrument of social control and maintenance of the *status quo*, that is, a patriarchal society in which seniority of age determines power relations. This lack of acknowledgement of violence as a problem inhibited, to some extent, the efforts of those who were attempting to bring the issue of violence against women and children to the fore. Finally, local initiatives were hindered by the distorted perceptions that were disseminated largely, but not solely, by outsiders who were putting forth the image of Palestinian youth, not only as a cause of violence, but also as people who needed to be restrained and even controlled. Underpinning this discourse is the failure to realize that Palestinian youth have been collectively abused by the Israeli army and, for some, by family members at home and educators at school.

However, the development of a vigorous nationalist social activist movement in occupied Palestinian territory during the 1980s had also been instrumental in promoting a strong women's movement, which addresses the problem of violence against women and children, in particular. That period marked a time of active model-building, and the beginning of new initiatives by Palestinian NGOs. Those who were then engaged in this gradual process of institution-building through trial and error accumulated a great amount of knowledge about local needs and experience over time. These popular movements gradually opened a space in which one could raise the question of psychosocial/mental health initiatives as legitimate endeavours.

Other institutions followed suit, either by developing psychosocial/ mental health components within their existing programs, or by establishing new programs to deal with the problems of specific groups, notably women. These initiatives were operating within the framework of a nationalist movement to build Palestinian systems of care outside those controlled by the Israeli military, and to fulfill the needs of Palestinians as a matter of national survival. Yet, despite this, the tension continued between national imperatives on the one hand and the need to address internal social issues on the other. There were some who believed that addressing social problems was disruptive to the process of national liberation, since the national liberation struggle was seen as a priority for action, and addressing social problems at the time was seen as risking to deviate attention and action from this primary imperative.

Thus, the two contradictory notions became conflated over time and narrowed the terms of the debate to either believing that the youth of the first uprising, who grew up in disarray, are a cause of violence within society requiring serious attention, or believing that young people are a product of political and personal violence, and that they have a legitimate right to participate politically in resisting occupation. Despite the efforts of Palestinian civil institutions, which were managing to organize themselves into networks calling for a greater expansion of citizens' rights, including the right to participate in charting their future, there also existed at that time a shrinking of an internally and externally mediated space for public debate and collective agency that impeded the development of these discussions. At that point, contradictory ideas surrounding the agency and participation of youth in political resistance had become irreconcilable, and local debates on the topic, intractable. Eventually, these contradictions led to a state of silence on the subject.

By 1996, in a move initiated by the Palestinian then-Minister of Education in response to what he felt was a need at the time, the Ministry of Education began to launch its counselling program in all public schools. However, due to pressures from donors, the lack of local funds to initiate new programs, and other internal considerations, this program was launched in haste, with minimal, if any, model-building, and with little consideration given to important details that could ensure the success of the program. Such details included, among others, the purpose and method of counselling in the Palestinian context, the human resources and management system needed to implement the project, structural changes within the school system needed to accommodate this new human resource and their project, and the need to develop the means to monitor and evaluate this program. Within the United Nations Relief and Works Agency for Palestine Refugees in the Near East (UNRWA), which caters to the health, educational, and social services needs of about 1.8 million Palestinian refugees of the 1948 war who live in the West Bank and Gaza Strip, the availability of funding played a major role in determining the development of a mental health component within its health program and counselling services in UNRWA schools.

It was during the mid-1990s that the Institute of Community and Public Health (ICPH)/ Birzeit University (BZU) began to pay attention to the psychosocial health of the Palestinians living in the occupied Palestinian territory. A mission statement had been established in the early 1980s linking academic and scientific endeavours to societal development in order to address what seemed to be a rising and pressing need not only for care, but also, perhaps more importantly, for rational and culturally appropriate program and system development. The initial group forming the ICPH conceptualized the university's role as being primarily in the areas of researching communal needs in close participation with communities, model-building, and the provision of training and continuing education schemes.

However, by 1998, Israeli policies of closures and restrictions of the movement of people and goods across borders and within the West Bank and the Gaza Strip were leading to a crisis. The expropriation of land and water sources for the expansion of Israeli settlements and bypass roads, with increased segregation and isolation of Palestinian villages and towns, had negative economic, social, and political consequences, including making it more difficult for villagers to access health services. The absence of any control by the Palestinian Authority over water, land, the environment, or movement within and between the West Bank and the Gaza Strip made a public health approach to health system development difficult, if not impossible.[20] It was also becoming clear that the Palestinian Authority was facing a systemic crisis due to a combination of internally generated problems, serious external political obstacles, and the reduction of donor aid in the area. The gradual collapse of the Oslo Process and the disillusionment of the general population, articulated with other contradictions, led to the eventual explosion of the Second Palestinian Uprising.

In September 2000, the interim political solution provided by the Oslo Accords and represented by the creation of the Palestinian Authority disintegrated with the Second Palestinian Uprising (Intifada), ignited by then-leader of the Israeli Likud party Ariel Sharon's visit to the al-Aqsa Mosque in East Jerusalem. The second intifada was fuelled by widespread discontent with the failure of the Oslo Accords to address accelerating Israeli confiscation and colonization of Palestinian lands in defiance of international law on the one hand, and by the shortcomings of the Palestinian Authority on the other.[21] These developments undermined further an already fragile system of public services, including health services.

Since 2000, life for Palestinians has become much harder, more dangerous, and less secure. A network of hundreds of army checkpoints, curfews, invasions, and detentions, the use of lethal force against civilians, land confiscations, and house demolitions, all allegedly intended to protect Israelis from Palestinian violence, have resulted in ordinary life becoming virtually impossible for everyone, and the collective punishment of the population of the occupied Palestinian territory. Thousands have been disabled or killed by Israeli military action. The erection of the "separation wall" by Israel on West Bank land has led to the separation of families and communities, and limited access to work, school, natural resources such as land, as well as health care and other basic services. All these difficulties have further contributed to the decline in the physical and mental health of the general population, and the increasingly prevailing sense that there is no hope for a secure future.

As a result, acts of resistance, for example stone-throwing by youth, especially around Israeli army checkpoints, began to increase. Enormous and unceasing pressures, and the resolve to respond to violation, combined with desperation, are partly responsible for the increased susceptibility of young people, primarily men, to risky behaviour. Even more noticeably, this pattern of behavioural responses which arises out of specific living conditions is not randomly distributed, but is found in clusters within the population. In the most drastic instances, young men have been driven to put their lives in danger, as seen in cases of those who have died or have been disabled at checkpoints when they attempt to strike back with stones at a phenomenally well-equipped army.

These young people, who were either born or were children during the First Uprising, have grown up with the disappointments of the so-called peace-building period. Since the beginning of the Second Uprising, they have been plunged into and forced to survive in a political quagmire. This generation of Palestinian youth has been deprived and violated on a consistent basis from childhood. Their lifelong experiences have shaped their present worldviews, opinions, and behaviour to such an extent that even life-threatening behaviour is regarded by some of them as dignified, a symbol of their political commitment.

There is no question that, for Palestinian youth, their course of life has changed irrevocably since the beginning of the Second Uprising. During this time, just as the worlds of young people are being turned upside down, many of these same adolescents are reaching a developmental stage when issues of independence may clash with political and cultural expectations. These dynamics have contributed to a sense of internal conflict exacerbating an already vulnerable psychological state. Yet, within the dominant discourse, Palestinians are often cast as passive victims or "suicide bombers" who have lost all sense of morality. The over-representation of young people as either victims or terrorists has ignored or pushed aside questions of how Palestinian youth organize their modes of existence. The realities of their everyday lives, their psychological well-being, and their resilience and strength, receive scant attention from researchers. Despite popular representations in the media that reduce their lives to captions of tragedy and pathos, life for this population is a much more complex and intricate phenomenon.

Intervention Research in Warlike Conditions: From Research to Action

By September 2000 and the beginning of the second Intifada, normal activities were disrupted at the Institute of Community and Public Health, which was then still situated at the old Birzeit University campus in the small town of Birzeit. The gouging of the asphalt surface of the road between Ramallah and Birzeit by the Israeli military, as well as the positioning of an army checkpoint at the Surda crossing on the road towards Birzeit, presented enormous problems when seeking access to our premises. The closing of the Birzeit road coincided with the expansion of Israeli checkpoints prohibiting or delaying access all over the West Bank. As we had also done during the First Uprising, we immediately reverted to emergency operations mode, with faculty and staff working from their homes, or focusing on emergency needs if they were able to reach the institute premises. At the time, we observed symptoms of severe distress among some Birzeit University undergraduates whose lives were suddenly interrupted, such as a girl from the Gaza Strip who dealt with the distress of not being able to reach her family by hitting her head into a wall until she bled. Not only had many of the students lost the ability to reach their homes, but they were also abruptly isolated from their social world at the university. We therefore initiated a study of Birzeit university undergraduates, focusing on mental health in exceptional conditions.

The study sought to highlight the impact of warlike conditions on the lives, perceptions, and aspirations of these students. The study, which covered one-third of the undergraduate population, revealed moderate and severe distress, which was linked to a lack of access to the university life and community, to separation from family and community, to the unavailability of cash for survival, and above all, to exposure to Israeli army violence. Fifty-seven per cent of respondents reported that they knew at least one person who had been injured by the Israeli army, 22 per cent had a friend who had been injured, 11 per cent had had one or more family members injured, and 18 per cent reported that they were injured themselves during a one-month period (October 2000). Students reported high levels of symptoms of psychological distress, with 67 per cent reporting sleep disturbances, 31 per cent nightmares, 52 per cent loss of energy for everyday life, 46 per cent frequent headaches, and 72 per cent inability to concentrate or perform daily tasks. Over 50 per cent reported violent behavioural changes, such as using abusive language to deal with others, fighting and screaming, and throwing and breaking things.

Significant associations were found between some of these symptoms and the distance to the student's family; the farther away, the more symptoms and more exposure to violence, while students living with their families showed significantly fewer symptoms compared to those living away from their family. Overall, the results indicated that students living with their families suffered fewer symptoms of psychological distress than those living in the university hostels or other arrangements. These results indicated that family and communal support is paramount. Reports to the Birzeit University administration led to the establishment of a special counselling/social support program for the latter students.

As Palestinians belonging to an academic institution, we have had to face daunting responsibilities during times of extreme crises. Responsibilities which include ensuring the survival of our family members, protecting our children from violence, providing support to the community as a matter of necessity, maintaining the viability of our team and of scientific and academic work, supporting our students, and maintaining public health research and education in warlike conditions. During this period, we not only worked on research, we also managed to continue teaching our Master of Public Health students who came from all over the West Bank to study, in a non-violent stance against violation. But some of these students — mostly adult medical and health professionals — were also severely affected by events. Some had to travel four to six hours on dirt paths created by communities when a road was blocked or gouged by the Israeli army, braving all elements of dangers just to arrive in class and say, "I am here." Other students used donkeys as a mode of transport across hills and valleys to reach us and study. Others, however, came for emotional support. One student, a medical doctor from the north of the West Bank, appeared one day and told us that he had not come to study that day but to cry and to tell his story. He had been in an ambulance trying to reach the injured and had heard shots. He then felt a splash of liquid hitting the left side of his head. He touched it and discovered that it was blood. He turned around and found his colleague shot dead. All he could do was tell his story, cry until he was exhausted, and then go home.[22]

As conditions worsened, with the increasing frequency of invasions and curfews in the Ramallah District, as well as Israeli army checkpoints, a decision was made to move ICPH premises to Ramallah city to improve access to the workplace, since most of the faculty and researchers were already living in Ramallah city, and to ensure teamwork. The move to Ramallah proved to be an extremely important element in the formula for individual and team survival, as agency provided for hope. A garage was donated for use as temporary premises, we managed to move computers and essential furniture to the garage over dirt roads, and our operations resumed.

By February 2002, Will Boyce from Queen's University visited to discuss the possibility of conducting another study on youth psychosocial mental health covering the Ramallah District. We met in our garage offices to design the study and prepare the proposal, while outside clashes raged between the Israeli army and mostly young Palestinians, complete with tear gas. We were very impressed that Will did not seem to be fazed by these events. We had become used to continuing our work, whatever the conditions outside our closed doors, but we had not expected such determination from a visitor from calm, stable, and orderly Canada. Will Boyce's willingness to venture into the heart of this David and Goliath conflict to discuss research that might benefit Palestinian society in coping with the trauma of occupation was a ray of sunshine.

The PACT program (Palestinian Adolescents Coping with Trauma) was initiated with IDRC's support in 2002. It aimed to investigate the relationship between psychosocial responses and physical effects of exposure to violence and poverty, while also assessing the existing individual and social supports, and the manner in which these supports act as protective elements for adolescent mental health. A mix of focus group discussions with youth and piloting instruments led to the completion of a survey among a representative sample of 3415 high school students in the Ramallah district only, mainly because we could not reach other districts at the time. Supported by Will Boyce and Hana Saab from Queen's University and other colleagues from McMaster and Waterloo Universities, the study demonstrated that both individual and collective exposure to violence (such as exposure in groups or witnessing the violation of others) were associated with negative mental health outcomes, confirming the need to go beyond individual experiences and include the health outcomes of collective violation when analyzing traumatic contexts[23] and planning interventions. The same study also revealed that exposure to humiliation was significantly associated with subjective health complaints.[24] It should be noted here that humiliation is a central tactic of war, often cited by the Israeli and international press as one of the daily experiences that Palestinians must withstand,[25] and as a form of Israeli control over Palestinian lives.

Equally highlighted in this study was the fact that Palestinian girls and boys have different styles of coping with distress. According to cultural norms, boys are given more permission to spend time outside of their homes. This gives them the opportunity to get together with their peers, and it allows them to express their anger by throwing stones at Israeli army vehicles and to participate in marches and demonstrations. While such activities may provide a form of stress relief, they also put the boys in real danger of military strikebacks. Girls, on the other hand, tend to be under much closer family supervision and to spend much more time at home. They reported higher levels of subjective health complaints, such as headaches and depression, as well as more extreme symptoms such as inability to concentrate on daily tasks and studies, and reported having nightmares. By contrast, boys tended to report an increase in aggressive behaviour and the use of abusive language.[26]

The PACT I report recommended that strategies for improving the lives of Palestinian young people should aim for the end of occupation and the misery of life within refugee camps especially. However, more immediate interventions were to focus on the development of systems that would address the needs of severely deprived, yet politicized, adolescents. Such systems should transcend individual-centred treatment and move to the strengthening of care systems based on community support and commitment. More specifically, the report recommended the development of a community model of interventions, the strengthening of youth centres and facilities for young people, the training of youth workers, the promotion of creative counselling on the basis of community support (rather than on the notions of individual pathology and treatment), and the utilization of school resources.[27]

Given these recommendations, the question at that point was which organization or institution was sufficiently community-based to be able to develop such a program. There are a large number of local and international organizations that work on short-term projects with young people, but these are often based in the cities. This means that youth from the villages either have to come to the city to benefit from these projects or their villages have to be targeted for outreach. The first option, coming to the city, is not feasible for many young people in the villages. Not only is transportation expensive, but also Israeli army checkpoints placed at the entrances to cities and villages are major deterrents for the youth population and their families. All too often young men are detained, arrested, beaten, or humiliated as they attempt to cross a checkpoint. Girls too prefer to avoid the long and humiliating periods of waiting at the checkpoints as well as exposure to abusive questions and comments from Israeli soldiers.[28] So the quest remained for an organization that was already active in the villages.

In the early 1990s a rehabilitation program had been established, first in the Gaza Strip, and then a few years later in the West Bank, to support those injured during the first intifada. ICPH had provided conceptual and technical support and training in the initial years, but by the mid-1990s the Community Based Rehabilitation (CBR) program, run by a consortium of NGOs and operated independently, had become well established. At the time of the PACT I study, the CBR program was active in almost 200 West Bank villages. ICPH subsequently contacted the CBR program with an invitation to brainstorm together about the possibility of expanding the CBR mandate to include a psychosocial component. This gave rise to the idea of combining the work with young people with the development of the CBR psychosocial approach. At that point, how exactly this would be organized remained very unclear, both for the CBR program and for the Institute.

Consultation with CBR Workers

After the initial idea of adding a psychosocial component to the CBR program had been discussed between CBR administrators, some CBR workers, and the head of the psychosocial health unit at ICPH, the next step taken was a brainstorming workshop in the fall of 2004. In this workshop, CBR fieldworkers, who mostly came from villages themselves, discussed the various aspects of adding a psychosocial component to their work. There was a consensus among the workers that there had been an increase in psychosocial problems in the community. CBR workers mentioned school dropouts, family disintegration, and people displaying awkward behaviour, as for example the unemployed man who burned his home's furniture in order to qualify for support from the Ministry of Social Affairs so he could pay school fees for his children.

However, opinions differed on whether CBR workers had a role to play in helping to solve these psychosocial problems. Some workers said that since they were already playing a role in solving psychosocial problems within the communities, they welcomed the idea of adding this component formally to their job description. Other workers expressed certain weariness. Not only did they feel that they would need extra training so that they would be able to carry out their responsibilities within the community, they were also worried that this work would add an additional burden to their already heavy workload.

Consultation with International Experts

With the support of Swedish Diakonia and the Norwegian Association of Disabled, the CBR program and the ICPH co-hosted a workshop of international and local consultants on CBR, mental health, and community psychosocial interventions in December 2004. The main discussion revolved around the question of whether the Institute and the CBR program would be able to work together on a social response to the social sufferings brought on by war. At the end of the workshop, the parties agreed that the need to counter the biomedical and individual approaches with a collective and communal approach, while building on the human resources available in the community and fostering the energy of young people towards positive action, warranted this joint initiative. It was with the help of the local and international consultants that ICPH and CBR drew up the various instruments that were to be part of a psychosocial needs assessment. In the meantime, ICPH had submitted a new proposal to IDRC for the funding of a co-operative joint research-to-action project with the CBR program in the north of the West Bank. IDRC reacted positively, and we received funding for PACT II (2005–7).

Needs Assessments, Community Consultations, and Pilot Interventions

The complexity of the ensuing collaboration between the CBR program and the ICPH cannot be underestimated. The process took off with needs assessments in four pilot villages, as needs differ by community and region. ICPH was responsible for the design of the instrument and the analysis of the findings. CBR provided the fieldworkers for the household survey and a co-ordinator. Both teams worked together on training the fieldworkers responsible for carrying out the survey and monitoring the process of the fieldwork. The data analysis indicated that, while the entire population of these four villages suffered from political, economic, and social and psychological stress, there were specific worries about the behaviour and mental health of young people growing up in an increasingly hopeless situation. Under the professional supervision of one of the co-authors of this chapter, Dr. Viet Nguyen-Gillham, who mentored the ICPH mental health researchers, joint CBR and ICPH teams then conducted a series of community consultations in the villages with the triple purpose of communicating the findings of the needs assessment back to the community, receiving feedback from the community, and probing for intervention ideas.

In general, the groups consulted all agreed that the most important problems their communities faced were the Israeli occupation and the poor economy. However, they also agreed that these problems were simply too big for "us" (the community, CBR, and ICPH) to work on. The communities also agreed that they were concerned about their young people, and they mentioned a large range of problems: poor academic performance, boys hanging out in the streets, no after-school activities, boredom, and lack of hope for the future. When challenged with coming up with possible solutions for some of the problems related to the young people, many of the groups had good ideas, such as providing a space for young people to meet and organizing extracurricular activities. But when we asked the groups why such solutions were not being implemented, their answers were usually evasive. It often came down to the fact that nobody in the community was taking responsibility, and that they wanted some external institution to help them.

We must admit that in these consultations we often felt an undercurrent of hope among the villagers that we (CBR and ICPH), as visitors to their villages, would somehow be able to produce financial support for these communities. From the beginning, we had to make it very clear that this would not be the case. We were talking about a different kind of support, whereby we would help the communities to help themselves. Usually the consultations ended with a brainstorm for ideas on how the community could work on some of the problems related to the younger generation. In addition, the consultations also led to an agreement that the CBR program would support the communities in developing a strategy on how to engage with young people for the good of the community.

This research brought us to the next phase in which two newly hired CBR workers would start this work with young people. At this point, neither the CBR program nor ICPH had a clear idea how this project would evolve. As a local institution interested in sustainable development, we were aware of the possibility that village communities may accept projects without too many questions so long as there is a financial incentive.[29] We also recognized the risk involved with a ready-to-be-implemented solution that might lead to merely lip-service participation on the part of the beneficiaries, and where the end of the funding is usually the end of the work. Instead, ICPH felt it was ready to take on the challenge of engaging in the much more difficult process of working together with the CBR program on the design of a youth-oriented model. One of the assumptions underlying the model is the engagement of young people in a way that would benefit and accommodate the interests of the young people themselves, their communities, and the CBR program. A well-documented approach to research in the United States and Canada,[30] for example, is Community-Campus Partnerships for Health, which is a growing movement of academics working together with partners in the community. While this approach may be applied to developing countries, such partnerships have been less well documented in academic literature.

In the meantime, the CBR administration had decided to continue this project with ICPH with the CBR North program, but not CBR South. This decision suited our institute, because travelling to the villages in the north was beginning to take a toll on our mental health team. It had become apparent that it would not be feasible for our three-member team to travel to and work in the south of the West Bank, as well as the north. The trips to the Jenin villages, which before the Israeli closures would have taken one to one and a half hours, sometimes took three or four hours because of the long waiting times at the Israeli army checkpoints. In 2005, especially, we often had to drive through olive groves and on dirt tracks to circumvent closed checkpoints. In one particular instance our van got stuck on a dirt mound, and we all had to descend and help to push the van back on the dirt track again.

After the needs assessments, we had only one year left to work with the CBR program on the pilot interventions. We realized then that, even with a perfect pilot intervention, we would lose an important research opportunity if we could not follow and monitor the process of CBR's implementation of the work with youth. IDRC acknowledged the importance of learning not only from the process of research to action, but also from what we called the two-way process whereby research guided the action, but the action also influenced the research component.

In fact, the pilot interventions whereby the two new CBR workers tried to set up youth groups in four villages were not always successful. We encountered many obstacles and learned a great deal in the process. The main lesson was that the decision of a direct service provider and an academic institution to work together does not necessarily result in immediately successful co-operation between the two partners. One needs to allow for a period of trust to build in such a relationship. In our case the co-operation improved significantly following the pilot period, after more than a year of working together on the intervention. The turning point came after a ten-day evaluation during which an external evaluator and ICPH, with logistical support from CBR, conducted a series of interviews and focus groups with regular CBR workers, the pilot CBR workers, CBR supervisors, and administrators. The evaluation also included visits to youth groups, interviews with parents, and an interview with the agency providing financial support to the CBR program.[31]

It was during and following this evaluation that we learned that the regular CBR workers had questioned why they were not involved in the pilot, that there was confusion about whether this work was "a Birzeit University project" or whether it was really important for the CBR program. We learned that each institution has its own culture and that it is important to be aware of this. The CBR workers also had basic questions about working with young people, some of the most crucial being whether this work would derail their own program or whether they would be neglecting the people with physical disabilities, whom it was their first priority to help.

Evaluation is often done as the final part of a project. We were fortunate to be able to use the evaluation as a *formative* assessment that helped us to plan for the next period. We discussed the results of the assessment in a one-day workshop including ICPH, the CBR program, the consultant who worked with us throughout the ten days of the assessment, Will Boyce of Queen's University, and the regional director of the organization providing funds for the CBR program. The discussion was not easy, and the tension between the Institute's focus on young people and the CBR program's concern about a loss of focus on people with disabilities was obvious. Sometimes, though, an outsider with a more objective stance can be trusted to come up with a workable solution. Will Boyce, who had been listening quietly as the discussions became increasingly heated, was the one who saw that working with young people and putting the interests of people with disabilities first could be combined in Youth as a Strategy.

In PACT III (2007–10), the CBR program has taken the lead in further developing what they still refer to as "the component" (the psychosocial component). Slowly a new term, *the component of Youth as a Strategy*, is coming in use. They have assigned an experienced CBR worker to the role of co-ordinating and supporting the CBR workers who feel ready to start working with young people. Some of the more experienced CBR workers are beginning to work with young people in a way we could not even have dreamt of in PACT II.

In one village, the CBR worker facilitates a group of mostly schoolgirls, along with some university students and unemployed graduates, in the morning. Around noon she meets with a group of boys, mostly university students and unemployed youth. Usually, some of the older girls also attend the boys group. In the half-year that the CBR worker has been working with these groups, the young people have embarked on some amazing initiatives. Together with another organization in the village, they organized a festive evening during the month of Ramadan, and they have designed and handcrafted cards to wish the various organizations and institutions in the village a happy feast. They have also organized a bus trip for people with disabilities, their families, and the members of the groups to a neighbouring village. In their discussions they have raised issues of importance to themselves and the rest of the community, such as the problems faced by young men in raising the capital to buy the gold jewellery men are expected to present to their brides upon their marriage.

The CBR North program has, at the time of this writing, seven CBR fieldworkers facilitating youth groups. Not all are equally successful. Working with young people is new for the CBR workers, and some are not used to taking the ideas of young people seriously. Nor are the young people themselves accustomed to taking an active role in issues that relate to people with disabilities, their community, or even to their own problems or those of their peers. ICPH is still providing support and training to the CBR co-ordinator, while at the same time monitoring those factors which assist and those that impede successful work with young people. Upon the request of the CBR supervisors, we are working with them on the design of a monitoring system and database.

At this time, it is too early to say whether ICPH's careful work with the CBR North program on Youth as a Strategy will help assure all CBR workers that working with young people is beneficial to the CBR program itself. However, the prospects are good, as one of the supervisors gave the following observation of the work in one of the poorest villages in the Jenin district: "We have good examples; look at these four girls with disabilities! They used to sit at home and not come out. They were very shy. Now they belong to this group and participate in community activities."

Working with the CBR North program has enriched the original idea of working on an intervention for young people. With CBR spearheading the initiative, we believe that the work with young people has gained a new momentum. It has evolved into an intervention for and with young people and their communities, including a group that, perhaps more than any other group of young people, needed this opportunity, namely young people with disabilities.

Notes

1 Nguyen-Gillham et al., "Normalizing the Abnormal."
2 Falk, "Israel's War Crimes," *The Nation*, December 29, 2008 http://www.thenation .com/doc/20090112/falk?rel=hp_currently (accessed January 2, 2009).
3 Milne, "Israel's Onslaught on Gaza Is a Crime That Cannot Succeed," *The Guardian*, Tuesday, December 30, 2008, http://www.guardian.co.uk/commentis free/2008/dec/30/israel-and-the-palestinians-middle-east (accessed January 1, 2009).
4 Levy, "The Neighborhood Bully Strikes Again," *Haaretz*, December 29, 2008, http://www.haaretz.com/hasen/spages/1050459.html (accessed December 29, 2008).

5 The Editors, "Cast Lead in the Foundry," *Middle East Report*, December 31, 2008 http://www.merip.org/mero/mero123108b.html (accessed December 31, 2008).

6 Quoted in Khalidi, ed., *From Haven to Conquest*.

7 Rashid Khalidi, *Palestinian Identity*.

8 Pappé, *The Ethnic Cleansing of Palestine*.

9 Kimmerling, "Sociology, Ideology, and Nation-Building."

10 Baker and Shalhoub-Kevorkian, "Effects of Political and Military Trauma on Children."

11 Aruri,"Dialectics of Dispossession," 5.

12 Tamari, "What the Uprising Means."

13 Summerfield, "A Critique of Seven Assumptions behind Psychological Trauma Programmes in War-Affected Areas."

14 Punamaki, "Relationships between Political Violence and Psychological Responses among Palestinian Women."

15 Summerfield, "Effects of War," 1106.

16 United Nations, "Question of Palestine: History," http://www.un.org/Depts/dpa/ngo/history.html (accessed March 20, 2008).

17 United Nations Department of Public Information, "Socio-Economic Achievements of the Palestinian People, 1993–Present: Building a Public Administration under the Palestinian Authority," in *The Question of Palestine and the United Nations*, http://www.un.org/Depts/dpi/palestine/ch9.pdf (accessed December 29, 2007).

18 George Giacaman and Dag Jørund Lønning, eds., *After Oslo*.

19 Shu'aybi and Shikaki, "A Window on the Workings of the PA: An Inside View," 90.

20 Rita Giacaman, H. F. Abdul-Rahim, and L Wick, "Health Sector Reform in the Occupied Palestinian Territory (OPT): Targeting the Forest or the Tree?"

21 Hammami and Hilal, "An Uprising at the Crossroads."

22 Rita Giacaman, "Editorial: Coping with Conflict."

23 Rita Giacaman, H.S. Shannon, et al., "Individual and Collective Exposure to Political Violence."

24 Rita Giacaman, M.E. Abu-Rmeileh, et al., "Humiliation: The Invisible Trauma of War for Palestinian Youth."

25 *Haaretz*, "Humiliation at the Checkpoints," August 8, 2008, http://www.haaretz.com/hasen/pages/ShArt.jhtml?itemNo=315603&contrassID=2&subContrassID=3&sbSubContrassID=0&listSrc=Y (accessed August 8, 2008).

26 Rita Giacaman, H. Saab, et al., "Palestinian Adolescents Coping with Trauma," Birzeit University, November 2004.

27 Ibid.

28 *B'Tselem*, "Beating and Abuse," http://www.btselem.org/english/beating_and_abuse (accessed February 14, 2009). See also, *B'Tselem* "Restrictions on Movement," http://www.btselem.org/English/Freedom_of_Movement (accessed February 14, 2009).

29 Olivier de Sardan, *Anthropology and Development*, 147.

30 *Community–Campus Partnerships for Health*, http://www.ccph.info/ (accessed February 14, 2009).
31 Coleridge, "Palestinian Adolescents Coping with Trauma, Phase II: A Formative Assessment," CBR report, November 2007 http://idl-bnc.idrc.ca/dspace/handle/123456789/37570 (accessed May 10, 2009).

CHAPTER SIX

Informal Waste Recycling and the Landfill in Dakar

Oumar Cissé

Development Problems Targeted by Research

My interest in environmental issues was first piqued during my Masters studies, and I began to question the state of the urban environment, particularly urban solid waste management, when I was the Municipal Engineer for the city of Rufisque, in the Dakar region. During this period, the issue of solid waste management in urban neighbourhoods where the principal method of disposal was a landfill became a major concern with regard to both the health of residents and the general well-being of community. At the same time, questions of injustice, inequality, and poverty became my central preoccupation and marked the beginning of my engagement in civil activism. The combination of this academic/professional route with my motivations as a socially active citizen brought me to the African Institute for Urban Management (IAGU), an NGO specializing in the technical applications of solid waste management and disposal for municipalities.

Through my association with IAGU, research into solid waste management became the focus of my career, and through my contributions to the

field, I have been able to bring together local stakeholders through participative practices. Consequently, my doctoral dissertation for the Faculty of
Urban Planning at the University of Montréal focused on informal recycling of wastes in the city of Dakar. This research eventually led to the publication of *L'argent des déchets. L'économie informelle à Dakar* [The Money
of Wastes: The Informal Economy of Dakar] in 2007.[1] My return to IAGU
in 2004 was marked by a further move in the direction of research on
waste management as development.

Fortunately, Canada's IDRC, IAGU's long-running partner in the
financing of research/action projects on the relationship between poverty
and the environment, launched a funding competition which provided
the opportunity to further investigate this issue. IAGU then submitted a
project that targeted the Mbeubeuss landfill in Dakar, questioning its
impact on the environment, on the health of the bordering communities,
and on the social economy. The emphasis of this project was placed on the
informal economic development of wastes, and the activities of waste
pickers and other informal waste recyclers. As this career path shows, the
informal economy of solid waste recycling in Dakar lies at the centre of my
scientific and professional interests.

The management of solid waste is a major concern in most Sub-Saharan African cities, where 50–75 per cent of municipal budgets is committed to this activity. Local authorities of these urban centres demonstrate a
considerable interest in waste recycling too, but with a bias towards building high-capital facilities for incineration, composting, or methanization,
promoted by Western corporations. As for the informal waste recyclers—
that is, those citizens for whom waste recovery constitutes a way of life— they
are, at best, ignored, but most often they are driven out of areas they
occupy, as though they were thieves or bandits. Waste recovery is a common activity in the larger cities of developing countries, particularly in
Africa. Such is the case in Dakar, where waste pickers can be seen on the
streets and city waste depots, and also in Mbeubeuss, a unique landfill on
the outskirts of the city.

In Dakar, these individuals recover all manner of recyclables, including
bottles, plastics, metals (iron, copper, aluminum), wood, cartons, and even
food waste. This recovery is practised by the waste pickers, the first link in
a chain that is also comprised of resellers, artisan/waste pickers, and specialized wholesalers.

Those Who Play a Role in Waste Recovery

The principal players who engage in this informal waste recovery in Dakar are the waste pickers, the resellers, the specialized wholesalers, and the artisan/waste pickers. In Dakar, waste pickers are the most important group involved in informal waste recovery. Searching garbage cans and garbage dumps, they specialize in the collection of scrap metal, other metals, and plastic products that can be sold. Within this group exists a subgroup of waste pickers/buyers. While they do not search the waste sites themselves, they often receive payment in advance from the resellers for whom their products are destined. They purchase individual items from the individual waste pickers who scour the streets and small dump sites around the city and from households. They purchase small amounts of recyclables, collecting enough to make a trip to the resellers on the outskirts of town viable.

One of the most significant subgroups is made up of the stationary waste pickers of Mbeubeuss Landfill. These are people who work all day at Mbeubeuss dumpsite itself, meeting garbage trucks as they arrive at the dumpsite and sifting through the waste as soon as it is unloaded and before a bulldozer begins to spread and compact it. Given their location and the waste pickers' need for a secure place to store recyclables as they are found, some of these scavengers also run small depots called *pakks,* where people stockpile recyclable materials for safekeeping. In exchange for protecting the assets of individual waste pickers, they are paid a percentage of value of the recyclables they keep safe from theft.

The next group of people in the chain of informal waste-recovery are the resellers. These entrepreneurs buy the recovered material from the waste pickers and are situated in a pakk, which is a compound surrounded by a rudimentary fence made up of recovered materials, such as sheet metal, boxes, or pieces of wood. Between six to fifteen waste pickers usually work for one pakk. Their clients are artisans, who require scrap metal and non-ferrous metals; specialized wholesalers, who require scrap metal, non-ferrous metals, and plastic shoes; traders, who supply markets inland with bags and drums, and micro-entrepreneurs, who package products such as paint thinner, varnish, glue, and grease. The resellers are assisted by waste pickers who are paid to sort, clean, bundle, and otherwise prepare products for sale.

In addition to resellers, specialized wholesalers also take part in informal waste recovery. This group specializes in the resale of one or two types of recyclable products to recycling factories, often in amounts exceeding one tonne. Like the resellers, they often have a pakk at the dumpsite and sometimes also have outlets in public markets, their own transport vehicles (such as trucks), and the means to weigh and store materials. Each whole-saler is tied to a particular recycling factory who buys their "products."

Finally, the artisan-waste pickers buy scrap metal and non-ferrous metal, such as aluminum, from the pakks. For the most part they are met-alworkers who operate small foundries and forges and make various metal products. Some also work with plastics, making, for example, plastic tarps out of the plastic wrappers discarded by local industries.

In Senegalese society, these types of jobs carry with them a low social standing that only gets lower as the occupation comes closer to physical contact with raw garbage. The waste pickers are the most visible partici-pants of the process, and their livelihoods are viewed in Dakar as a means of survival with no relation whatsoever to the protection of the environ-ment, or to the dynamics of the local economy. Waste pickers are also tar-geted by international co-operation projects, especially those focused on combatting urban poverty. Because of informal economic development of waste recycling, the role played by the Mbeubeuss landfill in the econ-omy and in society became the main focus of the action research project described in this paper.

The Mbeubeuss Landfill

In Africa, uncontrolled dumping is characterized by a lack of advanced planning for landfills, a lack of means of collection and treatment of the leachates, the failure to compact and bury garbage, no effort to capture methane gas, and, importantly, the ubiquitous presence of waste pickers.[2] In Dakar, Mbeubeuss receives 500,000 tonnes of waste annually, and most of the activity is uncontrolled.

The Mbeubeuss landfill is a terraced waste disposal site which is not monitored by local authorities. Garbage compaction is done by loaders and heavy machines designed for road work. At the dump entrance, there is a checkpoint with a weigh bridge to measure the tonnage of the waste. This weigh bridge is emptied daily. From this checkpoint runs a road about 2.5 kilometres long. It is built on a garbage base now approximately 6 to 10 metres above the original ground level and overshadows the com-munities of Gouye-gui and Baol. For approximately 200 metres along the road there is a section where composted soil is made use of and sold.

The dump is made up of four centres of activity: the communities of Gouye-gui and Baol, the dumping area, and the soil compost recovery area. Gouye-gui is the closest of these centres to the dump entrance, being about 600 metres way. It brings together about 100 people who work in about 30 pakks constructed from material recovered from the dump. The doors of the pakks are closed with padlocks to secure the recovered material stored inside. At Gouye-gui, they sell bottles, scrap metal, non-ferrous metal, bags, wood, plastic shoes, and many other recovered items. This village specializes in the recovery of industrial waste and plastic cloth. It is not frequented as much by the waste pickers and restorers who have been at the dump for the longest time. These individuals are very active in the Bok Diom, which is an association formed between waste pickers and resellers to defend their interests.

Located deeper inside the dump, Baol carries the name of a region in central Senegal from where most of its inhabitants originally came. Baol exists in the shadow of the road built on a garbage base and which leads to the Grande Côte of the Atlantic Ocean. Here one can find dozens of pakks and sheds laid out at random. This village is inhabited by waste pickers and resellers (many of whom are members of the Bok Diom) and their families. Behind Baol is the beginning of the Niayes, a humid valley region that stretches hundreds of kilometres to the north of Dakar. The Niayes is one of the most important agricultural regions in the country, and it is largely devoted to market gardens and small farms.

Although it has been operating since 1968 without planning or supervision, the Mbeubeuss landfill remains neglected in the scientific community in terms of its impact on the communities located in and around it, and on the environment and the economy of the area in general. Our decision to study the valorization of waste and the challenges to society presented by the Mbeubeuss landfill was influenced by the following factors:

- Previously, no opportunities existed to do in-depth research on these two questions. NGOs like ENDA supported the community of waste pickers for many years, particularly by helping in their organization and the establishment of their associations, by providing health systems, financing revenue-generating activities, and advocating among the authorities on their behalf. The Environment Ministry's main concern about Mbeubeuss was the potential environmental risks associated with it. Thus, during the past twenty years consultants were hired on two occasions to conduct studies of the environmental impact of the garbage dump. However, no integrated, participative, or plural research which would promote complete understanding of these two questions within the context of development in the Dakar region has been conducted to date.

- Research focused on the waste pickers is made difficult by the fact that this community does not want any attention drawn to itself. Most of the waste pickers who work at the Mbeubeuss dump site live in obscurity and, because of the stigma attached to the way they earn a living, they keep their life in the garbage dump a secret from friends and family. Even though they may earn a good living, the waste pickers are very much aware of the stigma that society places on those who work in and with garbage. Thus it is difficult to convince the waste pickers to participate in studies of their communities and lives because they fear exposure and they reject intrusions by outsiders, such as researchers and other professionals, into their workplace and their daily lives.

- Appropriate research tools were not available to properly conduct research on themes of this nature. The participation of diverse communities, collaboration between many fields of research, and co-operation between researchers and decision-makers are essential to make this research effective.

- Finally, the significance of this research has always been debatable due to the limited interest displayed by decision-makers in questions of informal economic development of waste. As a consequence, the risks that the result from this activity, no matter how pertinent or important, may be ignored by the authorities.

Research and Results

The principal objectives of my doctoral research resulted in the publication of *L'argent des déchets*, which confirmed the existence of two general categories of workers (high-end and low-end) within the system of informal waste recovery. The low-end category is comprised of waste pickers, and the high-end category is comprised of resellers and wholesale distributors. The criteria adopted to determine the division of these categories were: the level of investment required to start the activity, the social status associated with the activity, and the amount of training required to do the work. By assigning these criteria, we were able to obtain an indicator of how difficult it was to enter into certain lines of work.

The second major objective of my doctoral research was to evaluate the impact of factors such as access to land, participation to associations, the level of informality, professional experience, and linkages with the modern economy, as well as the impact of individuals holding multiple jobs, on the growth of revenue and investment taking place in the high-range segment of informal economic development of waste recovery.

My research regarding the division of categories has shown that: (1) the more difficult it is to enter into a certain line of work, the higher the income; (2) the activity of waste recovery is easy to enter into; (3) there is no confirmation of the existence of two distinct levels of economic activity, one a survival level and the other a level of growth and advancement; (4) only child waste pickers are confined to the survival level (in terms of revenue); (5) the social status attached to particular activities remains the principal criterion for the determination of the accessibility to that activity. We have thus observed that segmentation depends more on the objectives and the motivation of the individuals involved.

In relation to the factors identified above, my research has demonstrated that in Dakar: (1) it is not possible to form a systematic conclusion that the revenues and investments grow in conjunction with the increase of the index formed by these factors; (2) access to land resources is considered by investigators to be the critical and determining factor in the growth of revenues and investments; (3) participation in associations seems to be important only for resellers and artisans; (4) professional experience and holding multiple jobs does not seem to have an impact on the level of income; (5) the growth of waste pickers' income depends on their age and the possibility of storing the material they find before sale; (6) the feeling of land access security derived from a particular occupation is more relevant than real and legal land security; (7) the women taking part in the informal economic development of waste are not in competition with men, they are not involved in collection in the city centre, do not have a separate site for their activities, and prefer to work in the resale of specific materials in the markets.[3]

My current research takes the form of a research-action project entitled "The Waste of Mbeubeuss: An analysis of the impact and improvement of the condition of life and environment to Diamalaye (Malika)," coordinated by African Institute for Urban Management (IAGU) and financed by IDRC. It consists of evaluating the impact of the Mbeubeuss landfill on the surrounding communities and the waste pickers themselves, and on the agriculture and livestock raised in the area. We are also working towards establishing local policies and pilot projects to reduce, eliminate, and/or correct the negative effects of the dump, and to reinforce the local economy. The overall objective of this research-action project is to develop an understanding of the dump's impact on the environment and the resident populations, and to provide solutions to environmental problems with the object of improving these populations' standard of living. This research-action project has three main stages: (1) participative and interdisciplinary research; (2) the planning and development of pilot actions and local policies; (3) the publication and dissemination of the project's results.

The participative and interdisciplinary research is organized around five main activities: (1) categorizing waste and assessing the flow of people, materials, and resources into the Mbeubeuss dump; (2) determining the state of the environment through analyses of water, soil, and air; (3) studying the socioeconomic dynamics of households in neighbouring communities of Diamalaye and Darou Salam, as well as in the waste pickers' households; (4) raising of poultry and pork; and (5) market gardening.

The research outlined below, conducted by a trans-disciplinary team in connection with local authorities and communities, proves that the dump negatively affects the environment and the quality of life of the populations of Diamalaye and Darou Salam, and of the waste pickers, but, for the waste pickers, it is an important source of revenue.

An average of 3500 persons make their way to the Mbeubeuss dump on a daily basis (33 per cent of whom are waste pickers, resellers, and other buyers of recovered materials), where their activities generate a close to thirteen million francs[4] per day, a significant amount for such a marginalized sector in such a poor country. Mbeubeuss also takes in the all of the garbage thrown out in the region of Dakar, which can be composed of up to 45 per cent fine materials, such as sand and ash, and 20 per cent of which consists of perishables. A large part of the remaining 35 per cent of the waste brought to the dump is recyclable.

In terms of environmental impact, Mbeubeuss is the cause of significant soil contamination. Heavy metals poison the ground within and surrounding the dump up to 50 metres outside its borders. None of wells used for drinking water at Diamalaye and in the landfill is suitable for human consumption due to contamination by metals and pathogenic micro-organisms. Nevertheless, more than two-thirds of the households in Diamalaye rely on this well water for daily consumption. Additionally, the Mbeubeuss landfill is the only source of soil compost in the region, which is frequently used in urban green spaces, increasing the agronomic performance of plants with long growth cycles. However, the levels of heavy metal within the soil compost surpass levels recommended for market use. Despite this fact, this contaminated soil is distributed widely.

The settlements of Diamalaye and Darou Salam targeted by our research are situated on the outskirts of the landfill. They have proven to be poorly integrated into mainstream society, consisting of a marginalized population with very low levels of income. For example, only 38 per cent of all school-age children in Diamalaye attend elementary school, while the net education rate at the national level is 58 per cent. The Mbeubeuss landfill impacts the health of the resident populations, as well as their livestock. Approximately 26 per cent of poultry in the neighbourhoods surrounding the landfill drink well water that is contaminated with mercury. As for the humans, we note a high percentage of ailments that can be attributed to the poor environment people live in. For example, respiratory infections (affecting 14 per cent of the population), intestinal parasites (9.1 per cent), dermatitis (8.4 per cent), and oral infections (8.1 per cent) are the most frequent ailments that affect the residents of the area. Also, 34 per cent of women over 15 years old were found to have gynaecological problems. These health problems have economic impacts as well: we found that the treatment of the diseases which were linked to exposure to contaminated water or soil represent 43 per cent of budgets of health centres in the area, and cost the sick more than thirteen million francs (13 400 000 FCFA) in 2007.[5]

In light of these very significant results, it is clear that the waste of Mbeubeuss constitutes a real and potential threat to the environment, the health of the population, and the growth of the local economies of the nearby urban centres of Malika and Keur Massar, even if these results are only preliminary. The necessity of closing/restructuring and rehabilitating the landfill cannot be emphasized enough; this must be done in order to preserve and revitalize the economic advantages that the landfill provides for the thousands of people, particularly the waste pickers.

Consequently, in line with the initiative which was set in motion by the central authorities and supported by the World Bank for the restructuring of the Mbeubeuss landfill, an initiative strongly inspired by the results of our research, our project plans to test a series of pilot projects, the purpose of which is to revitalize and improve the activities of waste pickers and the conditions they live in, as well as peripheral activities like those of agriculture and pork farmers, and urban gardening and forestry. It also aims to improve the management of solid urban wastes, to preserve the health of the communities of Malika and Darou Salam, and to promote the local economy in these districts.

Overall, participatory research on informal waste recovery and on the impacts of dumpsites has had numerous results. Firstly, the Dakar Metropolitan Government (CADAK) has accepted and integrated informal actors of solid waste management into its official system, particularly at the level of the transfer station facility and the landfill itself, and to formulate a strategic plan for solid waste management, taking into account the results of our research. Second, local authorities and the Environment Ministry are now involving the waste pickers' association in the decision-making process regarding the Mbeubeuss landfill. And finally, there is now a better understanding of the multi-dimensional impact of the Mbeubeuss landfill on the environment, agriculture, poultry, and pork production, and on the economy and health of the communities which surround it.

Today, Senegalese authorities have decided to close the Mbeubeuss landfill and rehabilitate the area it occupies. The results of our research work has been used extensively in the studies done by the Agency of Municipal Development (ADM), APIX and CADAK on processes of redeveloping the Mbeubeuss landfill, particularly those which feature the reintegration of the waste pickers into mainstream society. Our work has also helped to change the minds of Senegalese authorities who initially wanted to simply close Mbeubeuss and open another landfill site elsewhere. We were able to demonstrate the importance of the communities whose economies are dependent on the landfill. Our research has helped to improve relations between the waste pickers and their communities in the landfill and the residents of neighbouring communities who viewed the waste pickers as a problem and only wanted to see the Mbeubeuss closed. It has also brought about a greater acceptance of informal waste recovery as a proper occupation, due largely to a series of news reports about the landfill and the people who live and work there. These reports raised public awareness across the country. Finally, the capacities of Senegalese institutions for education and research, such as the Institute of Health and Development (ISED), the Inter-State School of Veterinary Sciences and Medicine (EISMV) and IFAN, have been significantly strengthened in the fields of participatory and trans-disciplinary research, of research-action, of influencing new policies, and of the development of waste management themes within their programs.

Impact of Research on Women and Families

The research on which I have focused my attention for over a decade, with the support from the IDRC, has permitted me to investigate and understand the place and interests of women in the informal economy of waste management in Dakar. My work has demonstrated that, in contrast to the situation in Asian cities, women involved in this activity are less in competition with men but are more strongly rejected by the general public and confined to a few specific niches of informal waste recovery. My research has also demonstrated that women are a minority within the framework of informal waste recovery, and that they often combine waste recovering with pig farming and hawking in local markets. Their presence in the landfill is very limited, but neither harassment nor discrimination towards them has been observed. However, the preliminary results of our research have shown that women's health is more severely impacted than men's by exposure to the large-scale contamination of the landfill.

Essentially, these preliminary results show significant levels of gynaecological and reproductive health problems in women who regularly frequent the Mbeubeuss landfill. These health problems are probably caused by the heavy metal contamination which exists there. While the results of a long-term study are awaited to confirm these findings, it is obvious that there is a similar impact of heavy metals on the health of the children who frequent the landfill site. Exposure to heavy metals can lead to a significant delay in these children's mental development and foreshadow signs of poisoning. The presence of children in the landfill is common even with the efforts of organizations like the International Labour Organization (ILO) which work to keep them away from the area. Children are more vulnerable to contamination, and they are often the objects of harassment and discrimination, especially when it comes to questions of money. Children are exploited by others in the economy of the landfill because they are less capable of defending themselves.

Our work has also demonstrated that women have a strong presence in the pig farming sector in the area surrounding the Mbeubeuss landfill. Pig farmers, who rely primarily on food wastes collected at the landfill, are confronted with significant production difficulties. The demanding nature of this type of farming, the lack of systems for urine collection and disposal or for regular sanitation and health maintenance of the animals, as well as the difficulty of being located in inhabited areas, are great problems which make these women targets of recrimination by other residents. Through our research, after having confirmed the seriousness of these situations, we are trying to develop measures to improve livestock farming and, as a result, the overall living conditions of these women.

Our work has also shown that the women and their families who live in the area bordering the dump are more affected by the environmental impacts of the landfill. As evidenced by the poor condition of the water that they use for domestic consumption, the pulmonary illnesses and other afflictions that they suffer, and the insecurities that they face on a daily basis, the women of these poor households are especially marginalized by living in proximity to the landfill. Their social position is also made more precarious by their children's trips to the landfill in search of items to sell. In order to help offset some of these difficulties, our present research-action has fostered the construction of public fountains that allow women access to clean, healthy water at a lower cost, and also the establishment of a micro-credit system to reinforce revenue-generating activities for the women.

The Involvement of Communities

The research-action project of the Mbeubeuss puts emphasis on the communities of Diamalaye, the pilot area of the project, on waste pickers, and on the Commune of Malika. This participatory approach began with the preparation of a Concept Note. Along with several colleagues from IAGU, I visited the site not only to gain familiarity with the geographic zone of the project, but also to meet the communities that would be the target of our research. It was through this preliminary exploration that we met M.S., the leader of the Diamalaye district. Over the course of our discussions, we learned that it was he who first settled on the site in 1973, and who founded the community of Diamalaye.

During a second visit with M.S. we met several notable people from the community with whom we were very eager to collaborate in this new IDRC program, an eagerness which we readily expressed to them. These introductions allowed us to exchange ideas and discuss the principal problems that confront the population of Diamalaye, such as the lack of potable water, the insecurity which results from a lack of electricity and the proximity to the landfill, and the lack of any infrastructure like a school system, a health clinic, or a playground. These visits led the Diamalaye district delegate to sign of a letter of support for the project proposed by IAGU.

Upon the selection of our Concept Note by IDRC, one of our first actions was to inform the district delegate. The first meeting was held in the IAGU office and was attended by the community delegate, accompanied by two other notable members of the community, and a representative of the Mbeubeuss landfill waste pickers. The presence of the representatives indicated the community's ready involvement in the process. This final selection took place in December 2005. Therefore, 2006 was devoted to the preparation of the detailed research proposal, which was a long and intense effort.

The development and elaboration of the research proposal began with the establishment of a research team. This team was composed of researchers from diverse institutions and members of the communities targeted by research, including a representative for the women of the community, a representative of the waste pickers from the Bokk Diom Association, a representative of the Diamalaye youth, and a municipal councillor of the Commune of Malika.

To work as a team with members with such diverse backgrounds and with such diverse priorities requires the development of particular skills. This is why, with support from IDRC, we held a three-day workshop on participatory research methods and outcome mapping. The roles of the communities and individuals from them were established during this workshop, and this permitted us to better determine their needs and expectations, as well as the structure of the district, and also to identify the key players involved.

After this workshop took place, a group of researchers were assigned the task of conducting a social diagnosis of the communities at and adjacent to the landfill. This diagnosis took four days to complete, and all the information gathered was given to the community representatives who had attended the workshop. This inclusion of the community representatives also helped us to define their roles; they became known as social facilitators. These four days of discussion with people from different social strata in the communities of Malika and Diamalaye included women, local leaders, and youth associations. Through these discussions we were able to develop participatory communication tools with the different target groups and communities in order to better understand their interests and primary needs.

Beyond their role as facilitators, the social facilitators revealed themselves to be conscientious "researchers" in their own right, but with a different sensitivity to the issues than their counterparts from the academic community. Classic research is too often constrained by a reliance on scientific evidence and a Cartesian logic, but this alternative approach allowed us to focus on community participation as the foundation for all aspects of the study. Consequently, research team meetings yielded fruitful exchanges between academics and members of the community, with the result that a process of ongoing reinforcement of individual capacities was established.

Under this umbrella of participatory action research we established a participatory local committee with 42 representatives from various community-level organizations and associations. Chaired by an elected representative from the Commune of Malika and set up in offices provided by the Commune, the committee serves to facilitate exchanges and share information with the communities about the objectives, approaches, and results of the research. In addition, the committee discusses the management and implementation of the project, as well as sharing information about the consequences of the research on the population, on the various pilot projects being undertaken, and on anything that might have political implications. Targeted community forums have also been held to reach out to the communities or groups who are directly affected by the project and aspects of the research. This was done with the pig farmers, the chicken farmers, the market gardeners, the waste pickers, and the residents of Diamalaye. These forums permitted the researchers to discuss and share their ideas, their research results, and their research interests with the people concerned. Through this dialogue the researchers were also able to listen to community members tell about their concerns and hear what they proposed as solutions to the problems they faced on a daily basis. For example, the researchers learned of the community's ideas about how they thought research could lead to improvements in the working conditions at the landfill.

The research-action project also foresees the establishment of a system for local consultation within the framework of local government and led by local authorities. These local consultations would bring together all the stakeholders, community organizations, and the researchers, along with regional and national public institutions, and international development agencies to share the results of the research and begin developing strategies for the implementation of proposed solutions based on the research.

An office was set up in Malika's Commune to familiarize the residents with the project and facilitate their contact with the researchers. All of the documentation associated with the project is made available through the office. In this type of community involvement, the project co-ordinators and researchers always take the opportunity during municipal council meetings in Malika to outline the research results, to explain the stages of progress on the project, and to propose ideas for new pilot projects and local policies. From the start of the project, along with the institutional launch, we organized a popular forum in Wolof, the primary national language, in order to increase the population's involvement in the life of the project. The recruitment of members of the targeted communities by the researchers represented another opportunity to involve the community in the project. In fact, students living in Diamalaye were hired as interviewers for the socioeconomic investigation previously discussed. The waste pickers themselves participated in the collection of water and soil samples for the environmental aspects of the study and for the purposes of characterizing the waste, and the counting of the flow of materials, trucks, and people into and out of the dumpsite.

Finally, the project built public fountains and connected them to the potable water network in the Diamalaye district water system well before receiving the results of the analyses of underground water which the people were then drinking. This straightforward action, which responded to a strong and repeated demand by the people from the very beginning of the project, enabled us to win over the Diamalaye households and garner their support. In fact, scrupulous compliance to the logical order of the project would have dictated that we waited until the end of the research to take this action. But had we followed this order, we would have merely reinforced the residents' belief in the ineffectiveness of interviews, analyses, and meetings which, according to them, never lead to action, and do not take into account their most pressing needs, but rather only serve the interests of the project's promoters.

The Current Situation and Challenges

Through our work, the waste pickers became more visible, and their situation is better known to the public and the authorities, even though they continue to work in the landfill. Their acknowledgement and integration in the official system of solid waste management, while theoretically accepted, is not yet secure. The major issue at stake in the near future depends on the withdrawal of waste pickers and others active in the land-fill from this contaminated site, and their integration into the formal system of solid waste management.

Integration of informal recovery into the processes of waste transfer is planned. It is necessary, however, to be sure that the waste pickers are the beneficiaries of the system because other groups better known to the decision-makers could circumvent them. Also, it is possible that the utilization of mechanized sorting could result in decreased profits for waste pickers, financially speaking; the design of a system based less on capital or mechanics could be a solution. Additionally, analysis of the advantages of the system must keep track of the savings in the costs of transferring garbage to the environmentally safe landfill site, and calculate the payment of subventions to waste pickers in order to serve them well.

For those who are working towards the installation of waste recovery units in specific locations throughout the city in order to accommodate waste pickers, it is necessary to take into consideration the difficulties they face in accessing land, particularly because of the cost of land in the city. Lots which are unfit for human habitation must be privileged in offering waste pickers a certain amount of security, no matter how precarious, in these sites.

We have also seen the process of recovering and upgrading the landfill at Mbeubeuss has begun, particularly with regard to the pollution that it generates, the local economy it destabilizes, and the health deterioration it causes in the surrounding communities. While this is a positive move, there is always a possibility that a closed dumpsite may reopen in the future. Similar situations have occurred in other countries in the past, and they cannot be ruled out in Senegal. The introduction of new technologies and the building of a sanitary landfill is a solution to ecologically dispose wastes, but it can also deteriorate over the years to a dumpsite, and this would pose again new challenges for waste management in Dakar. General problems of waste management and the difficulties that confront the institutions responsible for the upkeep of the system are a concern for the future. Therefore, there remains a persistent risk of the return to informal waste recovery and all of the challenges to development such an unregulated system presents.

Notes

1 Oumar Cissé, *L'argent des déchets: L'économie informelle à Dakar* (Paris: Karthala, 2007).

2 Jarrod Ball and Oumar Cissé, *Dumpsites Rehabilitation Case Study* (Séminaire international sur les partenariats publics-privés pour la gestion intégrée et durable des déchets solides, Aprosen, Cepod and Institut de la Banque mondiale, Dakar, 26 au 28 juin 2007).

3 Oumar Cissé, *Les facteurs de croissance des activités informelles de valorisation des déchets solides urbains* (Thèse de doctorat, Faculté de l'aménagement, Université de Montréal, 2004).

4 About CAD $32,500.

5 Magazine Vert-Information Environnementale, *Décharge de Mbeubeuss: Bombe écologique ou source de vie* (Edition spéciale N°8, octobre et novembre 2008).

CHAPTER SEVEN

Digital Technologies and Learning: Their Role in Enhancing Social and Economic Development

Clotilde Fonseca

Development as Opportunity and Capacity-Building

The Poor as Bonsais

Realizing the potential of individuals and communities is fundamental to furthering social and economic transformations. Development, as we know, is not simply a matter of bettering one's income or of introducing social or technological change; it demands, above all, the creation of opportunities to overcome inequities in education, health, income, and access to knowledge. Precisely for this reason, Muhamad Yunus, Grameen Bank founder and Nobel Peace Prize laureate, has described poverty as lack of opportunity. "Poor people are like bonsais," he has noted, "they have not had the opportunities to grow into big trees."[1] This is a powerful and useful metaphor, one that allows us to understand complex development processes in very concrete symbolic terms. Generating conditions that stimulate people's personal, educational, and productive capacities is certainly key to attaining social justice and equity conditions. It should come as no surprise, then, that one of the strongest motivations for professional involvement in development projects lies in an interest in removing obstacles and creating the opportunities for empowerment required for "bonsais" to become full-grown and fruitful trees. Dedication to development generally springs from a strong personal vocation and service-oriented attitude. It emerges from the conviction that one's effort can make a difference, and, in many cases, from the belief that knowledge and concerted action can help transform the world around us.

Being able to contribute in meaningful and effective ways, however, is no easy matter. Work in the development sphere requires specialized professional knowledge and skill. It demands the ability to identify those areas of focus in which personal potential, interests, and preparation can adequately support innovative work in the field. This ability is particularly important if the practitioner is interested in making contributions based on research findings or implementation experiences. Acquiring this type of capability requires, among other things, openness and flexibility, the capacity to identify trends and work with specialized professionals and scientists. It also demands the capacity to interact with collaborating individuals, teams, institutions, and communities. Furthermore, it requires intense commitment and dedication to the work chosen; good intentions are far from enough.

Many of us who have joined the development community in this spirit rejoice at the fact that, at one point or time, we had the possibility to find an adequate balance between our professional calling and our actual work. Many of us still celebrate having had the opportunity to make choices and run the risks inevitably associated with career changes, involvement in new fields, and adoption of emerging development trends and innovative approaches. Linking oneself to new initiatives is always challenging. However, it is in opting for "the road less taken," that one is able to connect with people, experiences, and domains which make it possible to make a difference.

Digital Technologies as Enablers
The role of the computer and digital technologies as enablers for capacity-building and talent-development initiatives, particularly those oriented to rural and marginalized urban youth, was the spark that, in my case, led to

a now twenty-year involvement with the Omar Dengo Foundation (ODF) in Costa Rica.[2] The connection between technology and creativity, thinking skills, and job-related competencies was the catalyzing element that allowed me to shift focus away from a promising academic career in the field of literature and aesthetics, and to fully dedicate myself to an organization which fosters the use of digital technologies in order to stimulate people's talent, learning capacity, and productivity. It was also the field that made it possible to strike a balance between an interest in intellectual work and a call for social action and impact.

It must be said, however, that promoting the use of digital technologies for development is much more than a current trend. It is one of the most effective ways to bring about transformations in student involvement and in teachers' views, particularly when these educative and creative interventions are tailored to enrich the minds of young people. It is also a powerful way to stimulate community and economic development by nurturing and empowering small and mid-sized enterprises, and by fostering entrepreneurship and new types of income-generating activities.

Those of us who have worked towards making digital technologies a resource for bringing about change and empowering people are convinced that these technologies have an extraordinary power to draw out human talent. They are a tool that can enhance education and productivity, particularly in the case of the poor and the marginalized. Experience and research have revealed ways in which equity conditions can be nurtured by eliminating barriers that block access to opportunities for development. Obviously, technology alone does not bring about human development. However, well-designed initiatives and applications that use it to stimulate learning, self-efficacy, and productivity can be extraordinary development tools.

The Development Problem

Anyone who has confronted the challenges of poverty and lack of opportunity, and who has attempted to overcome them, will inevitably face the need to use scientific and technical knowledge to address issues and problems, and to find the tools best suited to confront them. Access to knowledge, as well as to knowledge-generating and knowledge-sharing networks, are critical factors for contemporary development efforts. This is particularly so in projects oriented to improve the level and quality of education and to provide people with a better understanding of the individual and collective implications of current technical and social change.

Work in the area of capacity-building is certainly a major challenge, particularly if one takes into consideration that development is a multi-factor and multidimensional process, and that there are few initiatives that can support these change processes across the board. Focusing on the promotion of learning faculties and productive capabilities is an excellent way to foster opportunity in contemporary societies and to stimulate transformations, especially through programs oriented to enrich or reconceptualize capacity-building processes for the young. This is fundamental in the context of the digital and the knowledge economy, since we live at a time in which, as Manuel Castells has so brilliantly stated, "the human mind is for the first time in history a direct productive force and not just a decisive element of the production system."[3]

Contemporary society, as we all know, demands high levels of intellectual and creative work. The power of the mind, its capacity to understand, produce, and innovate is, in itself, an activator of social and economic wealth. Developing the human mind and stimulating human potential, therefore, has to play a fundamental role in poverty reduction and development strategies. This is an issue not only of academic or "intellectual" importance, but also of major practical significance, one that cannot be bypassed by development agencies, governments, or, of course, education systems. Traditional instruction is today far too limited a goal. New and more effective ways of fostering learning have become essential. As the principal from a Costa Rican school once put it, our great challenge is to create "soccer fields for the mind," that is, a learning experience that can actually stimulate and consolidate intellectual and creative functions.

Equity and Learning Opportunities

Common sense and scientific knowledge have shown that improvements in learning opportunities and access to programs that can empower individuals through education is one of the more effective ways to bring about sustainable change. It is a fundamental factor in the attainment of equity and social justice. Fostering the skills necessary to be productive and active members of society is critical today, particularly at a time when knowledge and competence are a prerequisite for most jobs, even in emerging societies. As we know well, underdevelopment is not only a condition but a frame of mind that is closely associated with level of education, capacities, skills, health conditions, and world view. Countries that have made major advancements in overcoming poverty and underdevelopment are known to have succeeded in the creation of strong, widespread, and well-grounded educational initiatives tailored to the enhancement of their people's skills and capabilities. The core element in these efforts has been the capacity to strengthen the knowledge and competence base of individuals and communities through the development of their own potential and through their involvement in the productive world.

New Approaches in Development Theory

It should come as no surprise, therefore, that during the last few decades there have been important changes in expert opinions about development. These changes are the result of a more critical and practical analysis of recent cases of economic growth and socioeconomic change. The analytical review of the specific contexts and conditions in which achievements in development have been attained has shed new light on the understanding of these processes. These new views certainly privilege the role of education, health, and social policies as accelerators of change. They highlight the importance of making education and social programs available to citizens, particularly to the newer generations. Recent accomplishments in development processes, particularly those in some Asia–Pacific countries such as Japan, South Korea, and Singapore, have followed this path with great success and are today a source of important knowledge and food for thought.

These studies have shown, without doubt, that human factors play a fundamental role in development. A recent study conducted by Amartya Sen on contemporary views of development reveals that new development approaches attach major importance to the potential inherent in social investment and human capacity-building. Sen argues that available data show that even if social development cannot generate economic growth in and of itself, available data suggests that it leads to rapid and articulated economic growth, especially when complemented by state policies aimed at promoting economic growth.[4] This revaluation of the importance of "human capital" is today almost universally recognized and has worked to "soften and humanize" the very concept of development. However, as Sen adds, granting importance to human capital does not necessarily imply a good understanding of the real relevance human beings have in all development processes.[5] This is something that needs further attention and in-depth work.

Youth, Learning, and Development Opportunities

In the context of these new tendencies, Nancy Birdsall, former executive vice-president of the Inter-American Development Bank and an important development researcher, has carefully studied the relationship between education, access to development opportunities, and a society's potential to achieve sustainable economic and social growth. As she has clearly stated of Latin America, "if the region's economies are to exploit the efficiency and growth-enhancing effects of more rapid accumulation in education, they will need to give more emphasis to policies that meet the needs of poor children in the design and delivery of education programs."[6] She confirms the idea that access to quality education is a determinant of development, particularly, as we have noted, at a time of widespread expansion of the knowledge economy.

Within this context, education is obviously important, but, as the Omar Dengo Foundation has always held, learning is even more critical. It is important to highlight that, from the point of view of development, the distinction between "education" and "learning" is certainly not simply rhetorical. It is of major importance today, when there is such strong emphasis given to continuous education processes and to the development of a strong learning capacity and knowledge base that will allow individuals, groups, and communities to adapt to the changing nature of today's workplace and socioeconomic context. Providing high-quality learning opportunities at an early age can have consequences and increase opportunities, particularly for the youngest members of groups and communities experiencing poverty or marginalization. Investing in the young is a fundamental development policy that needs to be better understood and more widely applied. It is an essential tool for breaking the vicious cycle of intergenerational transmission of poverty which affects most poor individuals and communities in developing countries. As Nancy Birdsall has noted, investing in education of the young, particularly the poor young, has a powerful impact on development precisely because "inequality of education also obviously reinforces income inequality."[7]

Identifying new and more effective approaches to learning is thus essential to furthering development processes. Grounding these innovations on scientific knowledge about human cognition and learning is, therefore, a priority. It is not only a necessary strategy, but, also, an ethical imperative. Poor and marginalized children need not be deprived of the benefits of recent research in this field. For this very reason, the Omar Dengo

Foundation has systematically established alliances, research programs, and working relationships with key academic institutions and research centres devoted to studies about cognition, learning, and the development of human competencies. The foundation has made it a point to work together with national and international universities to reduce the knowledge gap that exists between high-level research institutions and what goes on in the field, particularly in low-income and limited-opportunity school and community settings. ODF has always been convinced that the integration of up-to-date approaches to cognition and learning are essential elements in making education effective and able to foster new competencies and capabilities, particularly for the new generations of children and youth in the developing world. ODF systematically attempts to apply this knowledge and experience to the design and implementation of its programs.

The Omar Dengo Foundation and Its Contribution to Costa Rica's Development

Impacts and Testimonies from the Field

An analysis of the contributions that the Omar Dengo Foundation has made to Costa Rica's educational, social, and technological development shows that they are undoubtedly based on a capacity-building view of development and on a clear understanding of the ways in which innovative education initiatives can have an impact on the country's social and economic achievements.[8] ODF's initial work in bringing technology to young children and to rural and marginal schools arose from the conviction that a people-centred, humanistic approach to the use of technology for development can help generate new attitudes and capabilities in young children and, in turn, initiate valuable personal, social, and economic benefits even over a generation, particularly when special attention is paid to developing the capacities of those who live in marginalized urban settings or in rural areas.

The testimonies of young people and community members who have profited from Omar Dengo Foundation programs over the years clearly demonstrate this conviction. Students who had their first contact with technology through the joint program that ODF implements with the Costa Rican Ministry of Education point out that early access to technology has, among other things, provided them with a highly meaningful sense of equity and equal opportunity. They indicate that it stimulated their creative capacity and empowered them to use technology in innovative and productive ways. Furthermore, they consider that access to technology has granted them with a significant advantage in life,[9] particularly in the cases of students from poor rural backgrounds who would otherwise not have had the opportunity to use technology at home or in the areas in which they live, particularly at the time when they were growing up.

A research project conducted by ODF's Research Department examines the role that these programs have played in the lives of the children involved in them.[10] A former participant, Fabiana Contreras, who is today a student of computer science and business administration, recalls that, during her childhood, taking part in the National Educational Informatics Program made her feel that "we were all the same, we all had the same capacity" because, despite the fact that she came from a rural town, she had been given the same learning opportunities as other children in more developed areas. As a matter of fact, she points out, precisely because she was able to work with a computer at an early age and in the context of a program that stimulated cognitive capacities, she was able to develop the mathematical and logical abilities that she feels later determined both her choice of career, and her future prospects. On a similar note, Jason González, a systems engineer who today works as technology manager for an international development bank, has indicated that having grown up in a low-income family, he would have never had access to computers or to the technology-mediated innovative learning experiences with which his elementary school most fortunately provided him. As he notes, he would hardly have had the chance to choose a career in information technologies had he not had the fundamental opportunity he was offered by ODF and the Ministry of Education during his school years.

Likewise, Didier Villalobos, a student of business administration, has expressed that working with computers at a young age provided him with great confidence; it made him realize that he had special skills and abilities he could develop. He came to perceive technology as a tool, not as a threat. He also states that, to him, computers became a "means for self development" and a resource that allowed him to relate to others. These statements, as well as many others that ODF has documented throughout its history, obviously reveal that early opportunities to appropriate technology in personally meaningful ways can empower young people and provide them with experiences to develop their self esteem, their sense of value, and of control over their own present. As many of them stated, it also provided them with a sense that they could be in command and build their own future.

Similar experiences have been documented by those who have benefited from training and capacity-building programs that ODF has created for the teachers, parents, and members of the communities in which its education programs are implemented. As ODF s Entrepreneurship and Digital Productivity Area has documented, these initiatives have provided their beneficiaries with practical and personally meaningful experiences that have allowed them to gain command not only over digital productivity tools but also of new personal, social, and economic knowledge and skills. These capacity-building and training programs have been designed to respond to the needs and requirements of the specific participants. Precisely for this reason, beneficiaries from these initiatives have been able to easily apply the knowledge and experience acquired within the course to their own job-related or entrepreneurial activities. They have thus acquired new production and management abilities.

Within this context, courses designed for female micro-entrepreneurs are worthy of notice. Many of them were initially requested to provide women with digital office skills — word processors, spreadsheets, presentation, and publishing applications — that would introduce them to the use of technology to modernize and improve their businesses. In order to respond to this requirement, ODF opted for an integral approach to training and skills development. It designed its courses not only to train women in the use of technology as was frequently the case, but also to allow them to use these technologies as tools for planning, organizing, managing, and marketing their companies and products. The key idea was not teaching them the applications, but developing learning experiences and learning environments that, while being enhanced by these technologies, focused mainly on the development of specific business and human competencies that would really empower them in new ways. This approach, as the results from these initiatives has shown, allowed them to grow professionally in a more integral way, and not simply through the acquisition of technological skills that, as is often the case in these types of courses, are disconnected from the reality of their day-to-day operation. As compared to other initiatives of this nature, this approach focused on the definition of their company's vision and mission, on the development of their business plan, as well as on the establishment of mutual support online communities of learning and exchange. The project allowed the women to create their businesses' identity, their logos, their business cards, brochures, and marketing strategies. They also learned how to navigate the Internet and to use it to promote their own products and services. The ODF turned the "computer-literacy training" that had been initially requested, into a personal and job-related capacity-building process which empowered these women, developing their entrepreneurial, planning, and management skills, allowing them to grow both as human beings and as businesswomen.

In this case, as in all of ODF's projects, the way in which the role of technology was conceived became crucial to further new capabilities that transcend the mere acquisition of technological skills, and became a fundamental tool that made possible new approaches to productivity and management. The testimonies of the women who participated in these training programs, as well as those of the thousands of citizens — both male and female — who have benefited from such programs, reveal how a course of this nature not only provided them with the required technological skills, but also strengthened their understanding of their own business and of the contexts in which they operated. For example, after completing one of these learning sessions, Tatiana Ballestero, a young woman who owns a small candle-making business, expressed very clearly the impact that this experience had on her: "In the past I just used to make the candles. Today, I have a vision and a mission."[11] Carmen Leniz, owner of a souvenir shop, indicates that the course provided her with an opportunity to increase her self-efficacy. She feels that she now "has the strength to look for options even in the context of a crisis."[12] In another case, Ana Quirós, a middle-aged woman who owns a farm in a rural area, reports that, when she started attending the course, her children questioned whether she was not too old to participate in a training program of this nature; however, this did not hold her back. She notes that the experience of the course has allowed her to introduce significant changes in the administration of her farm, an important step, since she is now working in the field of agro-tourism and producing herbal products. As is obvious, technology-mediated forms of personally meaningful experiential and learning-by-doing learning can have important impacts also in adult low-income learners.

ODF: Its Origins, Purpose, and Development Theories

These testimonies are clearly consistent with ODF's views about development and demonstrate the success of the strategies that the institution has historically put forth in trying to empower its beneficiaries, and provide them with the knowledge and skills required to improve their capacities, productivity, and livelihoods. The work that ODF has conducted in this field is certainly the result of a vision of development that has been strongly ingrained in all ODF initiatives, and that is closely tied to its commitment to the democratization of high-quality learning and equity conditions.

ODF came into being in 1987. It was created by a group of Costa Rican intellectuals and entrepreneurs. This initial group of twenty-two professionals accepted the invitation posed by Oscar Arias, then president of the country and Nobel laureate for Peace, to participate in the creation of new opportunities for Costa Rican youth. ODF was created as a private, not-for-profit organization that joined arms with the Ministry of Public Education to bring technology to rural and poor urban schools. From the organization's inception, the initiatives of ODF focused on creating learning environments and technology-enhanced capacity-building opportunities that aimed to renew and transform approaches to education. Their goal was to open up new learning options for the youth, adults, and senior citizens of the communities in less developed areas of the country, which had not previously had access to the computer technology which ODF now provided.

From the beginning ODF was convinced that investing in the young is an extremely powerful and cost-effective way to accelerate development, particularly when programs are designed to stimulate individual and group cognitive skills and productive capabilities. As early as 1987, ODF viewed the role of technology as critical for development; closing the technology gap was always a clear objective. ODF and the Ministry of Public Education chose to do this by progressively expanding the program which was aimed at achieving universal access to technology-mediated new forms of learning. Unlike many other countries that chose to focus their efforts on installing community centres or tele-centres for the poor, Costa Rica chose to link this new development to the education system. The country established a priority in its expansion process, that being the children and communities in less developed areas of the country. By focusing on youth and education, ODF and the Ministry of Public Education collaborated in the establishment of national policies that have guaranteed continuous growth and sustainability over time.

The decision was made to reach the greatest number of youth through the education system and through educational proposals that fostered technological fluency and cognitive capacities simultaneously. For this

reason, ODF founders and collaborators together with Ministry of Education employees assigned to the project devoted time and effort to study the
more advanced technology-in-education projects being implemented in
different countries, particularly in Europe, Canada, and the United States.
They interacted with well-known academic institutions and studied the
research that was then available as well as more recent literature on the
subject. At the end of that process, ODF opted for the educational approach
that focused on using computer programming as a tool to stimulate learning, cognition, creativity, and technological fluency. It was certainly the
most promising approach, but also the most challenging, for its success
depended not only on the provision of technology and the acquisition of
basic computer skills for the job market, as was the tendency at the time,
but also on the highly important human factors, which included intensive
teacher training.

It is interesting to note that even at that early stage of institutional
development, ODF had a clear understanding of the role of technology in
furthering development and in helping transform the educational profile
of the new generations. One could even say that Costa Rica started closing
the digital gap long before the very concept of "digital gap" or "digital
divide" had been formally coined. ODF founders had a visionary insight
and clearly understood the importance that digital technologies would
have for the country's social and economic development. They were convinced that the program they were helping launch would have a fundamental role both in bridging the opportunity gap and in changing the
country's productive capacities.[13]

The great merit of ODF's initial vision — which remains as strong and
vital today — lies in the clear link that it established between the productive
appropriation of digital technologies and the enhancement of human
capacities. This link is something that many analysts and researchers have
stressed, particularly during the last decade. The competitive advantage of
these technologies, as Nicholas Carr has indicated, lies in the value that
individuals and organizations can add to products and services through
innovation and creativity.[14] In this new economy it is crucial to be able to
count on people who have the ability to make creative and productive use
of these modern tools. National policies that contribute to that effect are,
therefore, critical.

The alliance established in 1988 between the Omar Dengo Foundation
and the Costa Rican Ministry of Public Education did precisely that. It

allowed the country to begin preparing new generations through an ambitious program that invested in children's education throughout the country in a progressive and widespread manner. As Amartya Sen has pointed out, introducing technology into education at an early age provides children with a powerful resource to overcome poverty in today's "skill-intensive society." He is convinced that this is the right policy direction to take, particularly because, due to the specific characteristics of this new economy, the rich tend to benefit more.[15] As we have indicated, this is exactly the area in which ODF has been working. It is the field to which ODF's researchers and practitioners have devoted their major effort, and in which it has attained most of its important achievements for over two decades. As Duncan Campbell, an information and communication technologies expert from the International Labour Organization (ILO), has stated, "these technologies can allow countries to bypass the sequential movement of industrial upgrading, provided that they have the appropriate skills. That is the critical ingredient in being able to participate in a higher value-added niche in global value chains with information and communication technologies. Costa Rica has been a country that has been successful in doing just that."[16]

Over the years, ODF's programs and beneficiaries have diversified significantly. The initial focus on educational informatics, computer programming, and cognition and learning led to educational innovation including the fields of robotics and learning through design. It also made way for developments in creativity, digital productivity, and entrepreneurship, as well as for the evolution of new areas such as citizenship, deliberation capacities, democratic participation, and e-government. Within this context, ODF has developed a great variety of programs, projects, and services that have been implemented mostly in Costa Rica, but also in other countries in Central and South America.

ODF's philosophy and pedagogical approach, however, have remained the same. As is obvious, the work and the developments it conducts today have evolved and consolidated over time, and, in many instances, have also been enriched by the alliances that ODF has cultivated with different universities and research institutes around the world. ODF has had longstanding academic, research, and project development initiatives with institutions such as the Media Lab at Massachusetts Institute of Technology (MIT), Project Zero at the Harvard Graduate School of Education, the Children and Democracy Task Force at the Harvard School of Public

Health, the Center for the Improvement of the Teaching of Math and Engineering at Stevens Institute of Technology, to name only a few. Likewise, it has worked with the research divisions of different technology companies to try out new products or to explore new applications for their new developments.

The Omar Dengo Foundation has obtained important experience and know-how throughout more than twenty years of work in the development field. During this time, it has created unique project design and implementation approaches as well as teaching and learning methodologies that are based on state-of-the-art knowledge of cognitive and learning theories as well as specialized expertise in the areas of entrepreneurship, innovation, and the use of digital technology. The institution has been able to constantly update and improve its initiatives through academic and research alliances, and through collaborative projects with universities, research centres, and corporations, both national and international. Additionally, ODF promotes a knowledge-sharing culture which has made it possible to decant valuable experience from one area in order to use it in another for the enhancement, enrichment, or design of projects.

From Educational Informatics to Entrepreneurship and Citizen Participation

A good example of this type of development is Lanz@, a project conceived by the Omar Dengo Foundation in 2006 to stimulate entrepreneurship, citizen participation capacities, digital productivity, and technology fluency skills in five Central American communities. This initiative was designed to respond to the needs of institutions, communities, and individuals that are conscious about the importance of gaining command over digital resources in order to improve employability and income generation, particularly in the case of low-income citizens. The project was co-designed and implemented with the collaboration of local organizations in five countries: Nicaragua, Honduras, El Salvador, Guatemala, and Costa Rica. The project was conceived as a participatory design and development initiative. It involved intensive knowledge-sharing, collaborative design, and joint implementation.

The experience of each of the participating organizations was very important in the definition of the strategies, approaches, and materials to be used. Thanks to these contributions, the project was able to respond more effectively to the requirements of the individuals and communities to which it was directed. Special attention was given to the social, cultural, and ethnic contexts in which the project was to be developed. Precisely for this reason, participating organizations were carefully selected. They were chosen based on their experience in servicing diverse cultural and income groups. Experience in dealing with poor urban and rural populations was explicitly sought. Some of the institutions selected were private, not-for-profit organizations. Others were public entities. Enlace Quiché, for example, worked with rural communities in the Quiché in Northern Guatemala. Red de Desarrollo Sostenible implemented the initiative in the Olancho region, in Northern Honduras. In El Salvador, the initiative was oriented to the promotion of small and medium enterprises in the urban area of Nahuizalco. In Nicaragua, it was Casa de los Tres Mundos that led the project and worked with cultural entrepreneurship initiatives in the city of Granada.

The project addressed three different development areas oriented to the attainment of specific skills and competencies chosen to stimulate entrepreneurship, technology fluency, and employability, as well as pro-social attitudes and capabilities. Each of these areas involved a capacity-building proposal and a set of materials specifically designed to support meaningful learning experiences in the fields of: (1) business skills and enhanced digital productivity; (2) entrepreneurship and employability; (3) deliberation capacities and democratic participation.

In the design and implementation of these learning experiences careful attention was given to the needs of the participants and to the contexts in which they operate. The learning approach and methodology used were based on the analysis of context and of the needs of the participants. These, in turn, were the result of the interactions undertaken by ODF experts and the counterpart country teams. Emphasis on technology fluency was a fundamental concern. This was not, however, a techno-centric project. Understanding and gaining command over issues associated to management, cost, marketing, and public relations and alliances, to name only a few, were critical, and were systematically linked to the integration of technology to all of these processes.

The experiences reported by project participants are worth noting. They reveal the different ways in which Lanz@ contributed to their empowerment, efficacy, and productivity. For example, Carlos Tenorio, a micro-entrepreneur from Honduras, pointed out that prior to his involvement in this project, he had no real understanding of the cost of human resources within his small business. As a result of this initiative, he recognized the need to keep track of costs associated to this element. He points out, "I used to pay them [people working in his business] from my general income. Today I keep track of my costs separately and take them into account in my analysis. Therefore, I now have more precise costs for my business." Likewise, Jakelin Hernández, from Guatemala, states that she "learned to establish a business and to explore the different functions that are needed to make it successful." As these two participants indicate, the project helped them gain entrepreneurial and employability skills. Many participants also reported that this initiative provided them with the opportunity to develop competencies that have also contributed to their personal and professional development. Lisbeth Valle, from Nicaragua, expressed it clearly: "I even learned to speak in public, which is something very important to be able to express our decisions. I also learned to listen to the opinions of others and about the importance of respect."

As indicated, the project also placed special emphasis on the development of pro-social vision and work oriented to foster social involvement and democratic values. It paid attention to the understanding of citizen rights and responsibilities. It allowed participants to explore new roles as active members of their communities. Comments by project beneficiaries reflect this clearly. A young girl from Nicaragua expressed her views in very powerful terms: "In the past I used to see the dirty brook when I went through there and just covered my nose to avoid the smell. Now it hurts me to see so much contamination and I feel that I have to do something about it. I now understand I am a member of this community, and that I have the right and the obligation to collaborate in helping solve its problems." Likewise, Maria, a young girl from Santa María Real in Honduras, expressed her new vision and attitude in very eloquent terms after having participated in the establishment of a local library in her community: "the most beautiful thing about this library is that, every time we come in here, we will remember that we helped install it precisely because we felt we had a great lack in not having one."

Lessons Learned from the Implementation of Lanz@

Providing youth with opportunities to deal with issues of productivity and entrepreneurship in virtual contexts constitutes a very effective resource for learning. It can become a valuable strategy to prepare new generations for insertion in contemporary job markets. Online coordination through email and instant messaging systems proved to be an excellent way to obtain input as well as to provide support and advice over large distances. Simulations and technology-mediated learning experiences were of great value to develop the competencies and skills that young people need. Innovative learning interactions and methods proved to be useful and effective for the participants involved, including those who are older, with limited educational backgrounds, and from low income levels. In general, these approaches generated excitement, commitment, and more effective learning. Likewise, strengthening of the concept and practice of citizenship and development pro-social attitudes and values turned out to be extremely important for the individuals and communities involved. The project confirmed that the development of business competencies is clearly strengthened by access to human development understood in more ample terms. Strengthening one leads to the strengthening of the other.

The project also revealed that organizations have great need in locating resources and donors that can allow them to escalate projects or to expand their impact once they have identified valuable or innovative initiatives. As a matter of fact, several of the organizations asked ODF for support in finding additional resources to continue the work. They did not always seem to have the fundraising or resource-mobilization skills required to profit further from the experience. Even if many ideas on how to apply the experience in other contexts and to other populations came up, additional time and effort were needed to find new partners and funding that would allow them to amplify and apply the positive results already obtained.

In general, participating organizations had high levels of commitment to the project. They were able to work with good professional attitude and autonomy. Project leaders were willing to walk the extra mile to guarantee the attainment of project goals. Clear and pertinent communication strategies and schemes were also fundamental. This was essential considering the fact that part of the exchanges took place online or through virtual media. Though project leaders could not always allocate the amounts of time required for online interactions — they had other demanding day-to-day organizational responsibilities to tend to — the fact is that having met personally during face-to-face working sessions made virtual communication processes easier. Initial personal interaction provided an opportunity to establish trust and rapport.

Lanz@ was also a good example of South–South co-operation. As is frequently the case, many countries, governments, and organizations are conscious of the importance of improving employability, entrepreneur-ship, and technological competencies in their economies. However, they do not always have available the methodologies or the human and finan-cial resources to undertake these activities in effective ways. Projects of this nature can be a useful tool to bridge the knowledge and experience gap and to strengthen or enrich the capacities of local professionals or groups. The willingness of some donors to support this type of exchange is worthy of notice. In the case of Lanz@, the contribution of IDRC was critical in making this possible. The project also benefited from support provided to ODF by the Swiss Agency for Development Cooperation (SDC), the Inter-American Development Bank (IADB), and the Central American Eco-nomic Integration Bank. These organizations, together with the Omar Dengo Foundation, proved that South-South co-operation can be success-fully articulated, and that innovative approaches to learning and to the integration of technology to development can be undertaken with great effectiveness in different types of communities and cultural environments provided that carefully designed interventions are put in place.

Results of the Implementation Process

The local organizations participating in the project have shown clear inter-est in diversifying and scaling up the achievements obtained through the implementation of Lanz@. Many of them have started to look for new funding partners in order to support the application of these experiences to other contexts. To name only a few, the youth entrepreneurship pro-posal — Lanz@ — is being considered for inclusion in the national techni-cal education curriculum of El Salvador. The National Commission of Micro and Small Entrepreneurs is also trying to obtain funds from Deutsche Gesellschaft für Technische Zusammenarbeit (GTZ) to extend this initia-tive to the Sonsonate community. In Guatemala, there is an interest in intro-ducing Lanz@ to youth programs led by CARE and the Taiwan Coopera-tion Program. Likewise, Enlace Quiché has already introduced the Lanz@ business and entrepreneurship programs to the portfolio of courses it implements in Guatemala. They are also trying to adapt in order to develop entrepreneurship in the field of tourism within the Quiche region.

In Honduras, the Sustainable Development Network (RDS) has decided to make Tecnomype part of the training program that they offer together with the municipalities in the Olancho Region. The Riecken Foundation has also expressed an interest in developing a Tecnomype program nationally. A group of Honduran high school teachers who participated in the Cade program are trying to make it a part of the national curriculum. In Nicaragua, Casa de los Tres Mundos plans to continue offering Tecnomype courses. They also plan to offer it to entrepreneurs in the tourism industry. In El Salvador, the Comisión Nacional de la Micro y Peque a Empresa (CONAMYPE) has already budgeted for the implementation of six Tecnomype training programs that they will offer to carpenters and artisans in the Nahuizalco municipality.

ODF's Impact in Costa Rica's Development

Though the country's transformation is the product of multiple strategies and investments, ODF's contribution to Costa Rica's educational and technological development has been widely recognized in different forms and at different moments. These distinctions very clearly demonstrate the importance that the country gives to the institution's work, and the recognition that different international actors have given to several of its innovations and developments. It must be noted that as early as 1987, the very nature of the endeavour being undertaken led to a "Declaration of Public Interest" that was issued through an executive decree of the Costa Rican government. Furthermore, in 2001, the Costa Rican Congress issued a law which confirmed the public interest in the Educational Informatics Program jointly implemented by ODF and the Ministry of Public Education. This law also authorized Costa Rican public institutions to transfer funds or make donations to ODF to aid in carrying out this important national initiative. This law has made it possible for the Ministry of Education to regularly provide funds, through the national budget, for the expansion and consolidation of the joint program.

The issue of determining the actual impact of the program, particularly educational impact and impact on equity conditions, however, is also a specialized topic that ODF has considered with great care. Though the realities of implementing such large-scale and complex projects generally make it difficult to find the time and the resources to document and to analyze impacts from a research point of view, ODF has always paid special attention to this matter. One of the great problems that ODF has generally encountered in this process has been the difficulty of finding instruments which may capture the types of changes it was trying to promote and, specifically, to identify those changes that were not initially considered, but that inevitably arise within this type of development project.

Identification of Impact and Elements for Project Design

For more than two decades — the 1980s and 1990s — international co-operation agencies, multilateral banks, and even governments held a very conservative and almost linear view of development, particularly when the introduction of technology projects in education systems was discussed. The argument was that if countries had not attained certain levels of development and still had problems of literacy or poverty, they should refrain from investing in new technology. Why should technology take precedence over good drinking water, textbooks, or food production? Unlike industrialized nations that were never questioned about these investments, poor countries had to solve their major problems first before they were allowed to even consider tools that could have strong catalytic effects in development processes, such as the use of technology for learning.

What is more, these agencies, banks, and governments would repeatedly indicate that there was no real scientific data to prove that technology-in-education programs had an effect in major educational indicators such as dropout rates or improvements in the results of standardized tests. Particularly during the late 1980s and early 1990s, many countries were not able to find financial support for their technology-in-education initiatives. Furthermore, some of the countries that were able to make investments of this nature were constantly asked to deliver "data" that proved the "concrete" impact that these projects were having. Quite frequently, the results identified were described as "anecdotal" and without full scientific grounding.

On many occasions, ODF was confronted by this type of argument and this type of judgement. Researchers working in the field clearly perceived that important things were going on, but they had difficulty grasping them and expressing them in the traditional research formulations that these institutions were demanding. It must be noted that researchers and practitioners were clearly identifying results, but they did not have the research frameworks and tools to be able to capture them with clarity and precision. The usual ways of measuring educational value were obviously inadequate when it came to demonstrating the impact of the new tools. How or why should one try to record the innovative impacts of technology in terms of improvements in standardized tests, for example, if the objective of the technology programs was not oriented to having this type of effect?

In view of this problem, and of the difficulties the institution itself encountered when identifying innovative research tools and resources to capture the effects of its programs, ODF set out to develop an analytical framework and impact identification methodology that would make it possible to examine with more precision and care what was going on in terms of contributions to equity and capacity-building in projects that used digital technologies with this specific intention. The project was conceived as a series of thinking frameworks and sets of questions that attempt to capture "what is going on" and the value it has in removing the obstacles in the promotion of equity conditions.

The result of this research project, which was conducted with the support of IDRC, was published in 2006 in the book *Educación y tecnologías digitales: Cómo valorar su impacto social y sus contribuciones a la equidad* (Education and Digital Technologies: How to Evaluate Their Social Impact and Their Contributions to Equity). This work has become a valuable tool, not only for designing and implementing evaluations and research instruments, but also as an element to help in the design of this type of program, since it provides the researcher or practitioner with valuable thinking and design frameworks. Within this context, the evaluation of impact is understood as the capacity to generate value judgements that are based on a clear understanding of what is evaluated, the criteria used to define its value and impact, and the intention of the person or organization conducting the evaluation, that is, the definition of knowledge-generation processes, the introduction of accountability or betterment procedures.[17] This production has been used intensely within ODF. It has also been a useful tool for other organizations with similar needs in other parts of the world.

New Directions: Where This Work Is Leading and Why

Throughout its history, ODF has created important programs in Costa Rica that have been not only successful and sustainable but have provided learning experiences that have allowed the institution to grow, consolidate, and expand its activities to other countries in Central and South America. The institution has a strong culture of project systematization and knowledge management, as well as a strong team of practitioners and researchers who are constantly reflecting about their implementation experiences, introducing improvements, or scaling up initiatives.

ODF has always made it a point to study the evolution of technology in order to identify new resources which can be used to further enhance its projects and consolidate the attainment of its goals. It also carefully monitors social and economic trends in order to better understand the directions in which it needs to orient its programs and developments. Within this context, ODF has been working diligently to develop technology-in-education standards for both students and teachers, so as to strengthen and consolidate the learning experiences it offers the participants in the Educational Informatics Program. This is one of the important lines of research in which it has been working and which it wants to consolidate further.

ODF is also conducting research on "one-to-one" (one computer, one child) approaches to the use of technology in schools, at home, and within communities. This research and development initiative constitutes the continuation of a research project of ODF which aims to provide one computer for all children attending rural multi-grade schools in the country. The main purpose of this research initiative is to develop learning environments and pedagogical approaches that can support teacher training processes and curriculum-related activities within this new, technologically enhanced and intense learning context.

ODF is also working towards the development of a sound e-learning proposal and platform that may respond adequately and help facilitate the conceptual and pedagogical approach it uses in all of its programs. The Foundation is convinced that we need to move from technology-mediated distance instruction to the creation of new learning environments and experiences. Knowing that this is a worthy though challenging task, ODF has established links with partner organizations in South Korea and Finland, and hopes to be able to learn from their approaches to education and civic participation, so as to enrich and expand its experience in this field.

Conscious of the fact that much is said about the knowledge economy, and little is being done in Latin America to try to better understand the educational implications associated with the development of the skills and competencies required by the new generations to be active participants in this new age, ODF is in the process of looking for partners and alliances in order to develop a research initiative in the area of new literacies for the knowledge economy. This work would include the establishment of a conceptual framework to better understand what is required, as well as the development of the pedagogical strategies and learning contexts that may help support these developments, specifically in the Latin American region.

ODF is also expanding its work in the development of new learning environments for entrepreneurs. It is currently preparing to extend Labor@, its technology-enhanced practice firm model, to all technical high schools in the country, and is working on a research proposal and searching for partner organizations that can help track and monitor the impact that this project is having in stimulating entrepreneurial activities among Costa Rican youth.

The Role of "Angel Investors" in Stimulating Innovation and Social Change

It is important to emphasize that, in the case of the Omar Dengo Foundation, the design and implementation of initiatives such as Lanz@ or the creation of a methodology to establish the impact of technology projects oriented to the improvement of equity conditions has been possible thanks to the existence of seed money or research and development funds that make it possible for organizations in the South to find support for innovative projects. Being able to obtain this type of financial assistance is critical in order to foster their creative and productive capacity of organizations that have valuable knowledge and experience. In a certain sense, these funding partners play the role of an "angel investor" who is willing to run the risks inevitably associated with innovation because they consider the idea has the potential to make important contributions, and to generate good return on investment. Clearly, we are not talking about financial return on investment, but rather about the potential to create new knowledge, to contribute a new solution to a development problem, or to generate a new approach that is scalable or adds value.

As we all know, investors decide whether to support an initiative based on the potential and value of the idea, as well as on the track record, competencies, and skills of its proponents. Institutions which support innovation, particularly those that play this role for organizations in the development world, are essential. They add dynamism and potential for productivity to the field and allow organizations in the South to set their own entrepreneurial capacities in motion, and make use of their knowledge and experience to generate new ways of thinking, new approaches, new services, and new products.

In the case of the Omar Dengo Foundation, several organizations have played this fundamental role. Among them is the International Development Research Centre from Canada, which specifically allocates resources to stimulate research and knowledge creation in developing countries. As is well known, IDRC has played this important role in supporting local researchers, practitioners, and developers in order to strengthen their professional capacities, and to allow them to become involved in knowl-edge-generation activities, as well as in the application of that knowledge to innovative development contexts. Some of the ODF's more innovative initiatives have counted on this support.

Likewise, ODF has received this type of support from the Swiss Agency for Development and Cooperation (SDC), particularly in the creation of the Innov@ Institute on Learning and Technology, an initiative that pro-vided ODF with critical research, development, and training facilities for its work in Costa Rica. Work with IDRC and SDC has also allowed ODF to implement innovative co-design and co-implementation project-development approaches in other countries in the region. At the national level, Fundación CR-USA has also made important contributions as an "angel investor."

This type of support and collaboration needs to be highlighted as being of critical importance for development. On the one hand, it provides space and opportunity to innovate and add value, and, on the other, it consti-tutes an important incentive for innovative researchers and practitioners who decide to remain in the development field precisely for the opportu-nity to continue adding value, generating knowledge and exploring new lines of work. This is of particular importance in fields in which basic research intersects with practical applications, as is the case in ODF, namely the relationship between cognitive science and the application of this new knowledge to education and learning initiatives.

Marshall McLuhan has rightly said that we move towards the future with our eyes set on the past. We tend to observe the future through the rear-view mirror. Undoubtedly, the rear-view mirror in the automobile is an excellent metaphor to describe the tendency that as Paul Levinson, one of McLuhan's most important analysts and commentators, indicates, has a distracting effect that does not allow us to perceive clearly what is criti-cal about these new developments.[18] As is evident, this unwanted but widespread tendency imposes limitations on the ways in which we come to understand new developments, and on the way we can profit from them. What is more, it frequently leads to reductionist views, uses and applica-tions which, in turn, produce a loss of great opportunities for social trans-formation and economic development.

This is undoubtedly one of the great contemporary challenges, partic-ularly for those individuals and organizations interested in making the best use of the research findings, knowledge, and technological resources available today. The great challenge is, therefore, bridging the gap between traditional views about development and in-depth and effective social innovation. Understanding the critical activators of social, technological, and economic development is, therefore, key. Contributing to the empowerment of the poor, to the creation of opportunities that generate equity and access to social mobility is essential in promoting human and economic growth. Investing in the young and stimulating their intellectual and productive capacity has become a powerful development strategy. It is also a clear ethical responsibility. Digital technologies and their application to learning are today, no doubt, a powerful tool to help us move in this direction.

Notes

1 Statement made during the "ICT for Poverty Reduction: When, Where and How" forum organized by IDRC and Harvard University, Boston, MA, September 19–20, 2003.

2 For a more detailed description of the Omar Dengo Foundation's work see its website, http://www.fod.ac.cr.

3 Castells, *La sociedad de la Red*, 43.

4 Sen, "Teorías de desarrollo a principios del Siglo XXI," 3–9.

5 Ibid., 12.

6 Birdsall, "Education: People's Asset."

7 Ibid.

8 For a closer analysis of the relationship between education and social policy in the case of the use of technology to foster change in Costa Rica, see Clotilde Fonesca, "Informática educative en Costa Rica: hacia un uso innovador de la computadora en la escuela."

9 Fundación Omar Dengo, *Testimonies: Impact of the National Educational Informatics Program from the Point of View of its Beneficiaries*, research project conducted by the Research Department of the Omar Dengo Foundation, 2004.

10 The following statements and observations have been extracted from *Testimonies*, a 2004 video produced as a result of a research project conducted by ODF's Research Department to identify the impact of the Costa Rican Educational Informatics Program from the point of view of its beneficiaries.

11 Fundación Omar Dengo, "Construir el futuro." This is a short video produced by the Omar Dengo Foundation which describes the experience and impact of the "Emprendedor@ Project: Supporting Women Microentrepreneurs" training program that uses information technologies and tools to promote entrepreneurship and increased productivity. This project was financed by the Inter-American Development Bank.

12 Ibid.

13 For further reference on this matter see Clotilde Fonseca, *Computadoras en la escuela pública costarricense*, 7–9.
14 Carr, "IT Doesn't Matter."
15 Comments made during the "ICT for Poverty Reduction: When, Where and How" seminar.
16 "Leapfrogging in Costa Rica," a video news release production of the International Labour Organization of the United Nations for its 2001 World Employment Report.
17 Fundación Omar Dengo, *Educación y Tecnologías Digitales*, 31.
18 Levinson, *Digital McLuhan*, 15–16.

CHAPTER EIGHT

Past, Present, and Future of Biological Control of Malaria with Community Participation in Peru

Palmira Ventosilla

Background

Recently I met with friends of mine from high school who told me I should be proud to be a researcher, especially coming from a class of only 42. My friend Pilar reminded me that since childhood I have been like a researcher. During the 1974 earthquake in Lima, she remembers that everybody else ran, but I was on the floor listening to the noises, and told her that "the sound was as if thousands of horses were galloping past."

It is my personal conviction that all children have thousands of questions, and each child has the ability to be a researcher; it only depends on where and by whom they are educated. In my case, I studied biology in Lima at the Universidad Ricardo Palma (1976–81). At the time, this university was not internationally recognized. While studying there, I decided to look for training, and during my eighth cycle I began training in the private laboratory of Dr. Hector Colichón. Dr. Colichón only accepted applicants who had completed their studies at one of two nationally and internationally recognized universities: Universidad Nacional Mayor de San Marcos, where he used to work as a teacher and researcher, and the Universidad Peruana Cayetano Heredia (UPCH). However, he made an exception for me, and, after I had taken and passed a test, I worked and trained for one year in this Peruvian researcher's lab. Following this year, I was contracted to work in the laboratories run by his sons. Then, in 1980, I was put in charge of the Microbiological Laboratory of the Instituto Farmacológico S.A. (IFASA). In 1981, I began to work as head of the Microbiology Lab at Laboratorio Microbiológico S.A.(LMB), and in 1982 I was contracted to work at the Diagnostic Laboratory Immunology Cantella Colichon-SA (1981–87), in the area of microbiology, where I implemented and improved new methods of diagnosing pathogens in humans and animals. In 1984, I wrote my thesis, entitled "Isolation of *Streptocuccus. faecalis* Subsp *zymgenes* as indicator of fecal contamination in non-renewable water in the street food expended." This thesis was funded by the Centers for Disease Control and Prevention (CDC), but to receive the donation of reagents and media I had to be in a national research centre, so I was introduced to the Peruvian National Institute of Health (NIH) by a letter from the CDC and I was hired in 1984 as researcher.

In 1985, Dr. Hugo Lumbreras, who was Director of the Institute of Tropical Medicine Alexander von Humboldt of UPCH, requested my transfer, after which I worked as researcher for both institutions with one salary. My main goal as a researcher is to develop suitable technologies for rural communities and areas of endemic tropical diseases. As a child, I saw a great deal of poverty in rural areas while travelling with my family or with the Girl Scouts, and I believe that keys to escaping poverty are education and changing people's attitudes about succeeding in life. Individuals have to be given hope that there is a brighter future and the means to achieve their goals.

Malaria in the Peruvian Context

Malaria is caused by the *Plasmodium* spp. Parasite, which is transmitted by infected *Anopheles* spp. mosquitoes. Malaria affects more than 24 million people annually in 109 countries in Africa, Asia, and Latin America.[1] Malaria kills some 2.7 million more people annually than AIDS. In South America, Peru is one of the countries in which malaria is a serious public health problem.[2] The incidence increases in tandem with the El Niño phenomenon, such as in 1998, when 212,642 cases of malaria were reported, 36.26 per cent (77,108 cases) of which corresponded to malaria caused by *P. falciparum*.[3] An important factor in the variability of malaria incidence is the number and seasonality of cases in previous periods.[4] Reports from the Ministry of Health show the variation in the number of cases from 1940 to 2008. In 2008 there were 38,498 malaria cases, with 4,488 due to *P. falciparum*.[5]

Malaria is present in many places in the rainforest of Peru, such as the Departments of Loreto, Ucayali, San Martin, Amazonas, in the forests of Cajamarca, Junín, Cusco, and Apurímac. Along the coast malaria is endemic in Piura and Tumbes.[6]

The main vectors along the northern coast of the Peru are: *Anopheles* (Nyssorhynchus) *albimanus*, *An.* (Anopheles) *calderoni*, and *An.* (Anopheles) *pseudopunctipennis*. In the jungle the vectors are: *An.* (Nyssorhynchus) *darlingi*, *An.* (Nyssorhynchus) *nuñeztovari*, *An.* (Nyssorhynchus) *albitarsis*, *An.* (Nyssorhynchus) *oswaldoi*, *An.* (Nyssorhynchus) *triannulatus*, *An.* (Nyssorhynchus) *aquasalis*, *An.* (Nyssorhynchus) *evansae*,[8] *An. Braziliensis, and An. rondoni.*

Like most countries, Peru has an active program for controlling malaria,[9] yellow fever, and dengue. The main tools of this program are chemical insecticides, nets, and repellents, and patients are diagnosed and treated for free. Unfortunately, since the beginning of the 1970s, resistance to insecticides has increased in different endemic areas around the world. Fifty-one species of *Anopheles* species have presented signs of resistance to DDT, as well as multiple resistances to organochlorates, organophosphates, and carbamate compounds.[10] Peruvian data on resistance showed that *An. albimanus* was resistant to pyrethroids (alphacipermethrin, cifluthrin, deltamethrin, lambdacialothrin, and cipermethrin) at the doses of 0.1 per cent.[11] Temephos (Abate®) is an important mosquito larvicide that has been used since the 1960s; the first resistance report was shown in a population of *Aedes nigromaculis* in California, and, from then on, resistance has been detected in 20 species of mosquitoes in different parts of the world.[12]

In Peru, the application of insecticides is not very well stratified to be effective and the insecticides themselves are so expensive that they are not always readily available when needed. An alternative method of controlling the vectors is the use of specific entomopathogens.[13] One of them is the *Bacillus thuringiensis* Subsp. *israelensis*, serotype H-14 (Bti).[14] This naturally occurring bacterium is harmless to humans and animals but can kill mosquitoes in the larval stage, before they emerge from ponds as adult mosquitoes. Ideally, use of Bti could cut the transmission cycle of tropical diseases (malaria, dengue, yellow fever, etc.). Bti has been used to control vectors in many countries, including Indonesia, India, Nigeria, Israel, China, Germany, and the United States, using commercial formulations. Other countries like Colombia,[15] Brazil,[16] and Taiwan[17] have isolated their native Bti and are carrying out investigations to determine if they can use them to replace Bti-H14.

In Peru, commercially produced Bti has been evaluated. Bti has also been produced using local alternatives (whole coconut,[18] yucca, and asparaguses)[19] and has been applied in natural breeding sites of *An. albimanus, An. pseudopunctipennis,* and *Culex quinquefaciatus* along the coast of the Peru, and in natural hatcheries of *An. darlingi* in the forest of Peru (Iquitos, Loreto).[20] In order to better understand the present and future of the biological control of the malaria vector I took my research to the community of Salitral, which is located in a district in Peru's humid, semi-tropical northern coast.

Biological Control of Malaria

Community Biological Control of Malaria Using Coconuts in the District of Salitral, Province of Sullana, Department Piura, Peru (1989–2002)

During the course of my research, my team and I developed an inexpensive, environmentally friendly alternative to pesticides, which can be used to control mosquitoes in the fight against malaria. This was an interdisciplinary project with a research team made up of specialists in anthropology, sociology, epidemiology, microbiology, education, and entomology. The main goal of the project was to develop, evaluate, and promote community-based techniques for malaria vector control using the biolarvicide Bti[21] produced in ripe *Cocus nucifera* (coconuts).[22] The coconuts have multiple roles, acting as a fermenting agent, a medium for producing bacterial cultures, in addition to being a storage container. This biotechnological method has been transferred from university to the community, as we have been teaching people how to use coconuts as a natural incubator for Bti production. In Salitral, a rural district along the northern coast of Peru, the Bti-coconut technology is the centrepiece of a community-based malaria control program, which was funded by the IDRC.

Salitral is an ideal location for the incubation and spread of malaria. It is located in the Province of Sullana, Department of Piura, at 80° 37′ W and 4°52′ S. Piura is in the equatorial dry forest and in a coastal eco-region;[23] its annual temperatures fluctuate between 16 and 37 °C. The warmest temperatures are registered during summer (December–April). The mean annual precipitation is 73 mm, but the "monsoon" rains may accrue due to the El Niño phenomenon.

In order to transfer the program to the communities, we implemented an educational intervention in the villages of Salitral aimed at schools and families. The project involved 17 fieldworkers, 50 schools with their Direc-tors, teachers, and students, and local community organizations. We con-ducted initial situational diagnoses with reference to specific subgroups in the community, using specific educational methodologies. One year after the intervention, we conducted evaluation and renewal activities. The coconut-Bti technology was successfully transferred to the community and continues to function independent of university or Ministry of Health participation.

1. Sociological Studies

Before we began the intervention, in July of 1992, we carried out an ethno-graphic study and a quantitative survey of families in three rural commu-nities and one urban one, which consisted of a random sample of 36 fam-ily units (203 family members). We also carried out a field study which sought to identify the community's knowledge and perception of malaria in order to design appropriate educational strategies and tools to be used in the educational intervention. The educational program sought to inte-grate the schools into the malaria effort, and to transfer knowledge to the families of the pupils as a means of involving the community as whole in biological control of vectors.

2. Biological Studies

The Bti-kits for inoculation in the field were designed and prepared at the Institute of Tropical Medicine Alexander von Humboldt, and then sent to the schools. The preparation involved activating the preserved Bti strain and preparing swabs with about 10^3–10^4 spores each, which were then sealed in sterile plastic bags, subject to appropriate quality control.[24] Bti-kits contain one swab with Bti, one swab with 40 mg of sodium glutamate, a small piece of cotton, and instructions for individual coconut inoculation.

3. Educational Proposal

The educational intervention consisted of four phases:

    Phase 1: Social studies and raising awareness (1992–93)

    Phase 2: Intervention in schools (1994–95)

    Phase 3: Intervention in the Community (July 1994 to April 1996)

    Phase 4: Evaluation at three periods:

        • Short term (1993–95)

        • Medium term (1998–2003)

        • Long term (2003–4)

The development and application of the educational proposal was divided into three phases. Phase 1, raising awareness, took place from 1992–93. A malaria awareness campaign was aimed at the communities of Salitral in order to introduce them to the concept. A workshop was held with members of the local youth group of the Municipal Library, Asociación Bibliotecaria Municipal Salitreña (ABIMSA), to prepare the design and organization of this campaign. The workshop covered the basic aspects of malaria transmission and control and specific training in survey techniques. Eight members of the group participated as fieldworkers in the survey process.

Phase 2, intervention in the schools, took place from 1994–95. During this phase, we worked with directors, teachers, and students in the fifth and sixth years of primary school in two of the communities to develop an educational module. The educational materials consisted of a cartoon booklet, a board game, a teacher's guide on how to use the above material, and additional methodologies for teaching the fundamentals of malaria transmission and control, along with a practical introduction to biological control using Bti.

In Phase 2 we conducted a three-day workshop with 45 school directors and teachers from the district of Salitral and a neighbouring school district to introduce them to this material. We presented preliminary versions of all the educational materials, which were critically evaluated by the local teachers before the final version was developed.

After we developed the final version, the project educator and the teachers introduced the principles of the educational module to the students. The children were given concrete assignments to be carried out in their homes and the community during this period. We evaluated 50 participating students and selected 15 to lead the "malaria control brigades" in each school. These "brigades" applied Bti during the summer months

(January–April) and designed field experiments in which they treated ponds with inoculated coconuts.

Phase 3, intervention in the community, took place from July 1994 to April 1996. The religious group, "Wedding at Cana," a recognized and respected organization in the local area, was selected as a reference group in order to facilitate the production and application of Bti. We developed and implemented teaching tools, which included participant discussions, large flip charts, models, demonstrations, pictures, photographs, lectures, slides, and video, which we showed in the field using VCR-TV modules.

In addition to these teaching methods described above, we also carried out practical training procedures, using natural mosquito-breeding places in the valley of the Chira river in Piura. The participating 98 families produced Bti in coconuts using Bti-kits and distributed them in ponds totalling an area of 197.3 m². Other ponds, which covered a total of 298.6 m², were used as controls.

Three stages were planned for progressive distribution of the information and training to other persons of the community: (1) researchers trained promoters, who then, in turn, trained pilot household groups; (2) the promoters and other trained members of the community then trained new household groups, and finally, (3) the researcher and promoters provided follow-up supervision and technical back-up. The training activities were also supplemented by frequent communications, distribution of additional materials, posters, educational calendars, etc.

Phase 4 of this process was evaluation. We divided the project in to three periods and carried out the evaluations accordingly:

Short Term (1993–95): During this period we first evaluated the effects of the educational interventions. In addition, we evaluated the efficacy of the results obtained by the students and villagers with respect to the insertion of Bti into the coconuts, the distribution of the Bti-coconuts to the ponds, the performance of regular and reliable larval counts, and the achievement of reduction of the larval populations.

Medium Term (1998–2003): In this period, we evaluated the communities' knowledge of and attitudes towards malaria and prevention, annually and in the year following the final intervention. The social sciences research team performed the evaluation through the use of standard survey methods.

Long Term (2003–4): During this period, we conducted a knowledge, attitudes, and practices (KAP) survey in the Salitral district, using the Querecotillo district as a control.

Results

Phase 1: Social Studies and Raising Awareness (1992–93)

The results of the ethnographic study and quantitative family survey of the three rural and one urban community within the project were as follows:

Socioeconomic Characteristics

(a) Community organization

The only relatively permanent organizations in the area were the parent–teacher associations in Miraflores and Cabo Verde Alto, and a health committee in Miraflores. In Salitral, there was the religious group Wedding at Cana and the cultural youth organization, ABIMSA. Both of these groups were selected as reference groups.

(b) Education

Schooling is considered a prime necessity for people, and dropout rates are low. The distribution of education levels among the family members studied breaks down as follows: preschool 11%, illiterate 8%, incomplete primary 39%, primary 9%, incomplete secondary 19%, secondary 8%, higher 6%.

(c) Labour organization

Agricultural plots are cultivated directly by the family. Women perform a complementary role in agricultural tasks, and children participate in domestic and agricultural chores from an early age. Following is a break-down of the occupational status of the family members in the survey: pre-schooler 11%, student 39%, farmer 16%, worker 9%, artisan 1%, trader 3%, employee 2%, housewife 19%.

(d) Health

(d.1) Epidemiology — The results showed that there were 124 cases of malaria reported in the District of Salitral from January–June 1992 (MINSA, Sullana-Piura). In the treatment of the reported cases, the family intervened in almost half, providing support. Only three cases reported the intervention of traditional healers, while four cases reported relying on "prayers." In almost every case (31), trained malaria personnel were called upon, as follows: Village Collaborator (12), Health Outpost (11), Health Centre (6), Provincial Hospital (2). In the treatment category, 11 of the 32 cases reported using traditional herbs, mostly for relief of symptoms. The standard full treatment with chloroquine and primaquine was reported in 14 cases, while 16 reported having taken only chloroquine for 1–3 days.

(d.2) The Malaria Program — At this time, no formal educational program existed, and the transfer of knowledge concerning malaria took place in a very limited, incomplete manner during contact with patients receiving drug treatment.

(d.3) Community Attitudes and Beliefs about Malaria — This informal malaria program built up dependence and passivity in the community. Directly observed treatment was the rule. Survey respondents believed there was no mortality connected with malaria and commented that if malaria were life-threatening the community might be more responsive to the problem. During the family survey, a vast majority (28 of 36 families) stated that one could die from malaria, but only one respondent knew of a fatality connected with malaria. Twenty-one participants in the survey (58.3 per cent) stated that malaria was a common health illness, while only 10 (27.8 per cent) considered it to be a serious health problem. This contradiction needed to be further explored in the community.

(d.4) Community Knowledge of Malaria Transmission — Concerning the transmission of malaria, most people commented on the relationship between mosquitoes and water in the fields. They mentioned the need to protect oneself from being bitten, and not to spend too much time in water ("and becoming cold") during the wet, rainy months, especially in rice paddies. It was also commonly stated that one could get malaria in the fields, and also in the house during the evening or night hours. There seemed to be no apparent knowledge of the role that an infected person plays in the malaria transmission cycle, and the subsequent need to control and cure human carriers.

Through apparent empirical observation, people were aware that malaria attacks all age brackets, though less frequently small children, infants in particular. It was also remarked that more than one person could be affected at the same time in the same household. The isolated few who were more informed about malaria seemed to be so as a result of conversations with health workers during past treatment of the disease.

(e) Community Participation in Health — When discussing the possibility of the involvement of schools in health projects such as biological malaria control with directors and teaching staff of these schools, the response was highly positive. The school played an important role in a number of health activities.

Phase 2: Intervention in Schools (1994–95)

The researchers partnered with the ABIMSA youth group, which had been previously active in promoting health education, in this educational aspect of the project. After the intervention in 1995, we surveyed 50 of the students involved. Overall, accurate knowledge of malaria rose from 10 per cent to 32 per cent. Additionally, 25 per cent of brigade members were able to distinguish between *Anopheles* and *Culex* larvae, and 54 per cent correctly identified the transmission cycle. All of the students identified the effects of Bti, 60 per cent of the brigade members knew all stages of the Bti procedure, and 82 per cent conveyed their new knowledge to their families using direct observation techniques. This conveyance of knowledge is proof of the key role that schools play in making malaria control activities sustainable over time.

Prior to the production and application of Bti by the students, the test ponds contained no bacillus that were toxic to larvae. The Bti-coconut produced by the students contained about 2.2×10^5 spores/mL, and the average larvicidal effect was 100 per cent mortality of larvae at 6 and 12 hours with a concentration of 2.2×10^3 spores/mL. Four ponds (N°1) received 2 coconuts and four ponds (N°2) received 4 coconuts. After 96 hours, the *Anopheles albimanus* population decreased significantly. Mortality was 89.45 per cent and 80.71 per cent in experimental ponds N°1 and N°2, respectively. The anopheline larvae remained largely absent for 12 days.

Local personnel controlled the effect and persistence of Bti and larvae in each pond for 15 days. The concentration of Bti at 0 hours was 5×10^3 spores/mL in pond N°1 and 2×10^3 spores/mL in pond N°2. By the fifth day concentrations were 3.4×10^2 spores/mL and 2.2×10^2 spores/mL in ponds N°1 and N°2, respectively.

Phase 3: Intervention in the Community (July 1994–April 1996)

Following the intervention, we found that there was a positive correlation between accurate knowledge of malaria transmission and the presence of a participating student in the household. Almost 90 per cent were in favour of continuing the experience with the students, to "control the malaria problem better" and to "share knowledge about the problem with the rest of the community." When evaluating the production and application of Bti by the community, we found that 70 per cent of the Bti-coconuts were toxic, 25 per cent of the Bti-coconuts were contaminated by *Aspergillus niger* and gram negative *Bacillus*, and 5 per cent of the Bti-coconuts were broken open. We found that, as in the experiments done by the students, the *Anopheles albimanus* population decreased after 72–96 hours. The percentage of mortality was 60–80 per cent in 50 per cent of the treated ponds. The anopheline larvae remained largely absent for 12–14 days, but after this period, the larval population of the ponds recovered. As for the control ponds, 33 per cent of them were contaminated with Bti. In 33 per cent of the control ponds the *An. albimanus* population increased by 30 per cent; 34 per cent of the control ponds maintained the *An. albimanus* population as before the application.

Phase 4: Evaluation

1. Short-Term Evaluation (1993–95)

Evaluation one year after the educational intervention showed, as mentioned above, that 89 per cent of the participants were in favour of continuing the experience with the students in order to "control the malaria problem better" and to "share knowledge about the problem with the rest of the community." Meanwhile, 84 per cent knew the effects of Bti action, and 71 per cent knew all the stages of the Bti inoculation procedure and materials.

The evaluation also showed that students' knowledge about malaria and Bti improved post-intervention, when comparing the survey of 1992 to one done in 1994. When asked what happens to a larva when Bti is put into the pond, 83 per cent of students answered correctly in the 1994 survey, while in 1992, 0 per cent answered correctly. When asked to draw a sequence of how Bti is prepared in coconuts, 62 per cent of the students had some notion of the preparation process.

The community's knowledge also improved between 1992 and 1995. Their understanding of the malaria transmission cycle in 1992 was 13.9 per cent, and after the educational intervention it was 58.3 per cent. When asked whether mosquitoes transmit malaria, prior to the intervention, 91.7 per cent of answers were correct, and after the intervention this number increased to 93 per cent. To "What is Bti?" correct answers were 100 per cent.

2. Medium-Term Evaluation (1998–2003)

In 1998, three years after the last intervention, and without any research presence in the area, the communities were asked "What is Bti?", and we found that the number of correct answers had decreased to 59.57 per cent.

3. Long-Term Evaluation (2003–4)
We found that people from Salitral had more knowledge than the people from the control population of Querecotillo about larvicidal Bti and control methods (personal protection and environmental management). There are statistically significant differences between Salitral and Querecotillo.

Overall, our biological control of malaria project increased knowledge, improved attitudes, and transformed practices. These changes can be clearly seen in that the populations of Salitral now listens to the recommendations of the health minister, and this district has reported no cases of dengue since the intervention, while Querecotillo has every year (2001 = 153.68, 2002 = 2.28, 2003 = 4.11 API). Salitral has had less malaria in recent years (1990 = 61.58, 2000 = 20.04, 2002 = 52.72, 2003 = 6.08 API). There are two NGOs in the region which are oriented towards a healthy community, whose members are former school brigade (1993) members.

Conclusion
According to the social studies conducted in the community prior to the intervention there was very little knowledge of malaria transmission and control, and an absence of sustained community participation in activities directed at health problems, most of their efforts being directed at maintaining a functional school system. We found that local malaria volunteers had not been trained in how to conduct health education in the communities. The communities' ideas about the control of mosquitoes and treatment were constituted of a blend of the magic and naturalistic.

The existing formal health program did not emphasize education of the community on malaria; our study and previous ones[25] confirmed this. Education is vital where formal health services are scarce and there is little knowledge of causes of malaria, its prevention, and its treatment.

Educational techniques and tools used during the intervention with local reference groups (ABIMSA and Wedding at Cana) were useful in implementing adequate and interactive learning and teaching strategies. Our experience showed that it is possible to gain and maintain people's interest and participation in health issues over several years. The project also showed that it was possible to teach and learn with limited, inexpensive training materials. The knowledge people gained after the educational intervention was greatest with regard to the biological control using Bti. They also increased their knowledge about the malaria transmission cycle, vector life cycle, and adequate selection of treatment for the ponds. They learned to identify the species and larval stages of *Anopheles, Culex,* and *Aedes* mosquitoes, how to inoculate coconuts with Bti, how to apply the Bti-coconut preparation to the ponds, and how to evaluate the affects of the preparation on mosquito larval populations, as well as how to keep accurate records of their activities in their workbooks for reporting. They also learned how the researchers evaluated their results.

An interesting trend we noticed was the division of labour by gender that resulted from the project: more women than men participated in the biological control of malaria.

One key to successful dissemination of knowledge on biological control of malaria is to make appropriate use of indirect methods such as practical activities. In our case, this included following the mosquito cycle in safe plastic containers, motivational and informational videos, workshops, and fieldwork.

Our research shows that the contribution of local populations of endemic areas to controlling malaria through the production and application of Bti appears to be feasible. The results show that whole coconuts provide a suitable medium for the production of Bti by the community. Chillcot (1985) reported that the Bti production using coconut water was not inferior to production using standard media. Previously, a serious limitation of the usefulness of Bti was its cost, but here we have shown that the production and application of Bti at a low cost appears to be feasible.

In conclusion, the Bti-coconut system and community participation is an effective weapon against naturally occurring populations of *An. albimanus.* When compared with similar untreated areas, the Bti-coconut treatment provided significant control over the insect populations within 24 hours following the treatment and continued to provide control for at least 12 days after treatment. The results of this study indicate that the Bti-coconut system has the potential to be a rational alternative control strategy for malaria vectors in Peru.

Notes

1 WHO, "World Malaria Day: A Day to Act," http://www.rbm.who.int/world malariaday/.
2 Kakkilaya, "Malaria Risk in South America," http://www.malariasite.com/ malaria/samerica.htm (last updated April 14, 2006).
3 Oficina General de Epidemiología-MINSA, "Situación epidemiología de la malaria en el Perú hasta el año 2002."
4 Ventosilla, Huarcaya, et al., "A Statistical Model for Assessing the Relationship between Meteorological Variables and the Incidence of *Plasmodium falciparum* and *Plasmodium vivax* in a Peruvian Endemic Area."

5 Dirección General de Epidemiología-MINSA, "Indicadores de vigilancia epidemiológica, Perú SE. 53 – 2008."

6 Ibid.

7 Wilkerson, "*Anopheles* (Anopheles) *calderoni* N. SP: A Malaria Vector of the Arribalzagia Series from Peru (Diptera: Culicidae)."

8 Calderon-Falero and Valle, "Especies de la fauna anofelina, su distribución y algunas consideraciones sobre su abundancia e infectividad en el Perú."

9 Ministerio De Salud (Minsa), "Doctrina, Normas y Procedimientos para el Control de la Malaria en el Perú."

10 OMS, "Resistencia de los vectores de enfermedades a los plaguicidas."

11 Balta et al., "Evaluación de la susceptibilidad y resistencia a los insecticidas en mosquitos adultos del género *Anopheles* de las regiones maláricas del Perú," 42. See also, Dirección General de Epidemiología-MINSA, "Malaria por *P. vivax* y *P. falciparum:* Sala Situacional 2009"; and Herrera et al., "Estudio de susceptibilidad en Piretroides usados en control vectorial período 1998–2000," 37.

12 Wirth, "Tenephos Resistance in Mosquito Larvae: History & Consequences," 39.

13 Kroeger et al., "Operational Aspects of Bednet Impregnation for Community-Based Malaria Control in Nicaragua, Ecuador, Peru and Colombia." See also Ventosilla and Guerra, "Producción piloto usando cocos enteros y su aplicación en el campo de *Bacillus thuringiensis* var. *israelensis* para el control biológico de *Anopheles* spp. e zonas endémicas de Malaria en Perú," 61.

14 Chilcott and Pillai, "The Use of Coconut Waste for the Production of *Bacillus thuringiensis var israelensis*," and Ventosilla, Marin, and Guerra, "Mecanismo de acción de bacilos esporulados entomopatógenos."

15 Orduz et al., "A New Serotype of *Bacillus thuringiensis* from Colombia Toxic to Mosquito Larvae."

16 Rabinovitch, "Breves aspectos da malaria no Brasil e posibilidades do control biológico de Anophelinos."

17 Kroeger et al., "Operational Aspects of Bednet Impregnation for Community-Based Malaria Control in Nicaragua, Ecuador, Peru, and Colombia."

18 Ventosilla, Torres, et al., "Conocimientos, actitudes y practicas en el control de malaria y dengue en las comunidades de Salitral (después de seis años de educación: 1992–1998) y Querecotillo en el Departamento de Piura."

19 Lee et al., "Distribution of *Bacillus thuringiensis* in Korea."

20 Ibid.; see also Ventosilla, Torres, et al., "Conocimientos, actitudes y practicas."

21 Ventosilla and Guerra, "Producción Piloto"; see also Ventosilla, Torres, et al., "Conocimientos, actitudes y practicas."

22 Ventosilla, Marin, and Guerra, "Mecanismo de acción; see also Ventosilla, Torres, et al., "Conocimientos, actitudes y practicas."

23 Rubio-Palis and Zimerman, "Ecoregional Classification of Malaria Vectors in the Neotropics."

24 Ventosilla and Guerra, "Producción piloto."

25 Kakkilaya, "Malaria Risk in South America," http://www.malariasite.com/malaria/samerica.htm (last updated April 14, 2006).

CHAPTER NINE

Participatory Research on Information and Communication Technologies for Development and the Logic of the Network Approach

Heloise Emdon

Introduction

The International Development Research Centre's Acacia program is a program which provides grants and capacity-building support to Africans conducting research relating to the Information Society in Africa. The research undertaken with the financial and capacity-building support of the Acacia program is starting to demonstrate that, in Africa, the use of information and communication technologies (ICTs) is transformative. As Program Manager of this organization, I see ICTs as resources to which public access is both desirable and necessary; my main concern as an advocate and funder of research for development is the elimination of social, economic, and policy-related barriers to the participation of Africans in the use of ICTs.

The values espoused by the International Development Research Centre (IDRC) through the Acacia program are consistent with the spirit of participatory research, which is concerned with the engagement and meaningful involvement of the individuals and organizations that make up the community or nation in which the study or intervention is being carried out. This commitment to a participatory approach to research is perhaps most clearly manifested in the collaborative manner in which most Acacia-supported research projects are implemented. Networks are the keystone of Acacia's efforts to build a field of knowledge around ICTs for development because they facilitate capacity-building by offering opportunities for the mentoring of less experienced researchers by seasoned researchers. Multinational networks also allow researchers to learn from their counterparts facing similar challenges in other countries.

Members of Acacia-supported networks represent a range of stakeholder groups committed to researching the impact of ICTs on the advancement of the economic, social, and legal interests of their local communities, nations, and regions. Most are Africans living in Africa, and they include, primarily, academics and researchers from various disciplines, representing universities across the continent, but also practitioners and civil society activists.

Acacia-supported research networks set their own research agenda and determine their own research approach. Collectively, they treat a wide spectrum of issues concerning the Information Society in Africa, as demonstrated in the following list of Acacia networks:

- *Research ICT Africa*, whose overall goal is to provide ICT policymakers in Africa with evidence-based information, so that they can establish an environment that enables the wider participation of Africans in the information society. It started in seven countries, and now includes research teams from 20 African countries.
- *African Virtual Open Initiative Resources*: Their aim was to develop research and research capacity on free and open source software (FOSS) and FOSS processes in Africa. It started in eight countries, and grew to include several more.
- *Wireless Africa*, which endeavours to develop and test a business model for community-owned networks in 10 countries through the examination of the policy environment and needs and priorities of the communities involved, among other activities.

- *Gender Research in Africa into ICTs for Empowerment,* which is building the capacity of the network to investigate the relationship between men, women, ICTs, and empowerment. It also aims to enrich the research methodology with additional action-directed, participatory, and qualitative methods, and to expand the reach of the network to include researchers in the Middle East and North Africa. Those from the Middle East have rallied to participate in the network, swelling the number of researchers to 28.
- *Pan-African Research Agenda on the Pedagogical Integration of ICTs,* which aims to better understand how ICTs can improve the quality of African education from the primary to the tertiary level in 10 African countries.
- *Consolidating Research and Education Networking in Africa,* whose goal is to enable the UbuntuNet Alliance (a consortium of national research and education networks founded by National Research and Education Network leaders from Kenya, Malawi, Mozambique, Rwanda, and South Africa) to help integrate African universities and research institutions into the global research and education community by providing them with intra-African connectivity, and sufficient and affordable international bandwidth. The program is now active in 22 countries.
- *Local Governance and ICTs,* which endeavours to assess the current state and outcome of electronic local governance initiatives in Africa. It focuses on how ICTs are being used to improve internal organization processes, provide better information and service delivery, promote principles of good governance, and encourage public participation and consultation.
- *Open Architecture Standards and Information Systems,* which helps African countries develop and maintain low-cost sustainable health information systems and use these information systems to address health issues at both the facility and the public health level by reinforcing the existing implementation of an open-source medical record system (OpenMRS). The program is operational in Mozambique, South Africa, Zimbabwe, and Rwanda, as well as some Millennium Development Villages in Kenya, Uganda, Tanzania, and Rwanda. This work includes supporting open standards and expanding the OpenMRS developers' network.
- *Poverty and ICTs in Urban and Rural East Africa,* which aims to provide new empirical evidence on the effects of ICT usage on household poverty in Kenya, Rwanda, Tanzania, and Uganda.

- *African Copyright and Access to Knowledge Project,* whose aim is to build capacity in Africa to research and better understand the copyright environment that would facilitate citizens' access to digital and hard copy learning materials. It brings together a research team from Egypt, Ghana, Senegal, South Africa, and Uganda to analyse whether national copyright legislations are taking advantage of the exceptions and limitations allowed by international copyright treaties.
- *Pan-African Localization Network,* which addresses the issue of localization and local languages in ICT.
- *Uganda Health Information Network and Mozambique Health Information Network,* whose projects involve the use of low-cost handheld computers and employ the existing cellular telephone system for the collection of data and the transmission of medical information relevant to frontline health workers.
- *Publishing and Alternative Licensing Model of Africa,* which seeks to explore the application and outcomes of flexible licensing regimes in the publishing industry in Africa, and to better understand how they can facilitate citizens' access to knowledge in the digital environment and how the adoption of new and innovative business models of publishing can help African countries improve the publishing of learning materials.
- *Knowledge Access for Rural Interconnected Areas Network,* which seeks to improve the operation and outcome of International Fund for Agricultural Development (IFAD) projects aimed at fighting rural poverty in the Middle East and North Africa (MENA).
- *eAgriculture Network for Africa (eARN Africa),* which aims to fill gaps in the literature and supporting policy on the application of ICTs by increasing smallholders' access to agricultural information.

The breadth of these research areas demonstrates that the means through which Africans are broadening their participation in the information society for the betterment of their lives are diverse. The remainder of this chapter includes an overview of my personal path towards international development and a discussion of two of these research areas which are key to African participation in the information society: ICT policy and regulation, and women and ICTs.

My Early Path: Exploring the Relationship between ICTs and Women's Development

My career in the field of development began with the Development Bank of Southern Africa (DBSA), a development finance institution that provides loans for telecommunications infrastructure, among other social and economic infrastructure initiatives. Of the public infrastructure funded by the DBSA in the early 1990s, it financed public sector telecommunications companies ("public sector telcos"), as well as the entry of many private and public–private mobile operators into Southern Africa. It also helped build the capacity of the newly formed regulators in Southern Africa.

One of the challenges during the struggle for democracy in post-Apartheid South Africa was to ensure that the disenfranchised populations of the country had access to existing telephone and broadcast infrastructure. Having previously worked as an economics and public sector journalist, I found the injustice of the situation particularly compelling, given that access to the communications infrastructure was largely divided along racial lines. I carved out a niche for myself as an analyst of the telecommunications sector in order to help redress these inequalities.

In support of the DBSA's guiding principle of focusing on the development impact of its investments, I began researching the social benefits derived by communities as a result of better communications infrastructure. It was through this work that I became interested in understanding how the mostly women-run phone shop entrepreneurs, who were becoming increasingly numerous and visible, were benefiting from these new livelihood opportunities.

Vodacom, South Africa's largest cellular phone company, implemented the Community Services Program following a 1994 government mandate and license obligation to provide telecommunications services in underserviced, disadvantaged communities.[1] The program, which saw that the establishment of phone shops—many of them being operated out of converted shipping containers—in rural and poor communities, offered a ready-made business opportunity for entrepreneurs to offer cellular service locally as phone shop owners and operators. Many of those who were seizing these entrepreneurial opportunities were women, and I started collecting their stories from the field and relaying them to the DBSA Board Chairman.

Jay Naidoo, then chairman of the Development Bank of Southern Africa, had been called on as an advisor to the United Nations Economic and Social Council (ECOSOC), and had been invited by then-Secretary General of the United Nations, Kofi Annan, to be part of a group of advisors examining the nexus between the information society in Africa, including the digital divide, and the Millennium Development Goals. While documenting the findings of a consultation conducted by Ecosoc in South Africa, based on the value of ICTs in Africa which would inform an ICT-focused Human Development Report I interviewed women who had become phone shop entrepreneurs thanks to the cellular phone companies creating business opportunities for new entrepreneurs. Their stories suggested that income from these businesses had transformed their livelihoods; there were clearly new economic possibilities in these economically disadvantaged communities. These stories seemed to augment what we had learned from the Bangladesh "Village Phone ladies," who were benefiting from the Grameen Foundation's Village Phone Programme. Established in 1997 with the objective of expanding mobile phone service in rural communities, this program provided microfinance clients with loans on the order of $350 so that they could sell phone services to fellow villagers.[2] In the light of the publicity surrounding this program and my own related research in Southern Africa, it was in the back of my mind that African women's ICT stories, which could not be found in the formal literature, needed to be further explored and shared with a wider audience.

New Opportunities for Enabling International Development Research on Policy and ICT Access and Use in Africa

IDRC decided to close its Regional Office for Southern Africa (ROSA) in Johannesburg, South Africa, in 2001. Richard Fuchs, then-director of the Information and Communication Technologies for Development (ICT4D) program area, recognized that South Africa played an important role in the innovation that was occurring in ICTs in Africa, and he lobbied for the continuation of the ICT4D program in Southern Africa. IDRC started negotiating with the DBSA to house the program there. Around the same time, the IDRC program officer who had been working in ICT4D at ROSA decided to form an NGO to promote school networking in Africa. This turn of events presented me with a new career opportunity which would allow me to apply the skills and regional knowledge I had developed while working at the DBSA to other parts of Africa as well. I successfully applied for the position of program officer, and thus began the next phase of my career, working from South Africa for a Canadian Crown corporation to provide grants and capacity support to African researchers focussed on ICT4D.

From Local to Global

I was based in Johannesburg, South Africa, which was relatively better off in terms of institutions that could manage large grant funds, academics, and practitioners who saw the benefits of collaborating with other researchers in Africa—a diverse continent because of its 54 different countries. Seriously hampered by fragmented policy approaches that made cross-border interconnectivity expensive and that did not facilitate regional integration, which was the goal of the political leadership, and especially the vision adopted by the New Economic Partnership for African Development (NEPAD), the telecommunications regimes of Africa's 54 countries acted with sovereignty and independently from one another. This independence resulted in excessively high costs related to inefficient rent-seeking state-owned monopolies, and dependency on excessively high international bandwidth. South Africa was among the leaders in liberalization, which resulted in rapid increase in the use of mobile phones, which quickly expanded beyond the wealthy to the less prosperous small entrepreneurs and micro-businesses, and to communities picking up network signals in villages that had not been previously served. The availability of mobile telephone service, and a well-regulated market which would ensure interconnection between new operators, meant that people who had never owned a phone before were joining the ever-expanding network of mobile phone users. Other African countries would emulate South Africa as it followed a cautious route of "managed liberalization," trying to balance ideological concerns against market forces.

All the countries along the Indian Ocean and their hinterland neighbours that had no cross-border networks were dependent on satellite connectivity. Acacia developed a map for IDRC to table at the G8 Digital Opportunities Force (Dot.Force). It was a picture worth a thousand words, called "The Internet: Out of Africa," illustrating that countries were dependent on the high cost of satellite, and, using a kilobits-per-capita index, demonstrating just how deep the digital divide was, and how great the lack of economies of scale was for African countries dependent on satellite connectivity. We started to realize how excessively expensive our research partners' university bandwidth was—in some cases they paid up to one thousand times more for one one-hundredth of the bandwidth than Northern universities would pay for connecting, communicating, learning, and innovating. The countries in question had a pent-up demand for new and affordable services, for infrastructure that would reach beyond the country's capitals, for services that were independent of unreliable energy networks and that would enable affordable connectivity to the Internet.

By facilitating and networking potential researchers with each other, individuals and organizations that were paying these high prices for universities to function soon found themselves united by a common cause and joined forces to start unpacking the policy antecedents, in order to understand why these deficits were so persistent. The ICT4D approach was new, introduced during the 1997 meeting in Midrand, South Africa, where the G7 agreed to support Africa's entry into the information society for Africa's development. The IDRC created the Acacia program with a very ambitious budget forecast to implement pilot projects. Universal service funds stocked with a revenue stream from the newly licensed mobile operators, or telcos, were also just getting started in Africa, thanks to some earlier IDRC-supported policy work towards promoting the achievement of "universal access" in telecommunications. This notion was being debated in some countries to define policy goals for socially and economically marginalized populations and how to achieve these goals. The development challenges were reflected nationally, and, at most, subregionally. The IDRC's earlier pilot projects to test various approaches to universal service had been tackled locally in four countries — Uganda, Mozambique, South Africa, and Senegal. In the second phase of Acacia, when I joined, a decision had been made to develop more regional projects. Telecommunications and the infrastructure that connected countries and people for the exchange of information in a rapidly globalizing world was on a regional and global scale, and we needed to develop an understanding of this scale by connecting our research partners, and facilitating larger research visions and goals. The opportunity which allowed us to build bigger projects had the effect of creating networks that were able to observe national development challenges in the context of comparative and collaborative work. It created overlaps of knowledge about how to introduce new technologies into rigid and fairly unprepared countries. The researchers had two mandates: to investigate their national sector's performance against policy objectives and the outcomes among consumers, and to feed this back to the national policymakers. The Research

ICT Africa (RIA) network was able to collect the data and start the country comparisons. They started working towards building ICT indicators for Africa. All of this work was happening against the backdrop of the two rounds of the World Summit on the Information Society (WSIS), which took place in 2003 and 2005 and during which governments were convened around action lines in order to overcome the digital divide. Many of the network leaders we have worked with have become internationally acclaimed and in some cases nationally respected.

ICTs for Development in Context

My interest in the benefits of ICT4D stemmed from the fact that there was so much expectation and hype around the introduction of ICTs in developing countries, but very little understanding of why the progress was so slow. There was a high demand for access and local content, but little understanding that these all depended on policies that encouraged or discouraged private or public investment into new infrastructure. Technical innovations were bringing down the average cost of providing average and even remote services. It was necessary to restructure policy in order to create such an environment of accessibility. Many African countries envisioned following a separation-of-powers model wherein the policy, regulation, and operations of telecommunications structures were separated out from the old state-owned monopoly structure in order to make room for new participants, including mobile phone companies. Even among those who believed in the developmental potential vested in ICTs, few understood the market structure issues, and very little was known or understood about the investment constraints in this sector in Africa.

During my time at the DBSA, I had been working with the LINK Centre, an independently funded institute housed at the University of Witwatersrand, South Africa. The LINK Centre provided training in policy and regulatory matters to Southern African regulators, policymakers, and companies in an environment in which telcos were being privatized and becoming more aggressively monopolistic, and in which liberalization was occurring to accommodate the new cellular telephone entrants. Policymakers and regulators were playing key roles in reshaping Africa's economies, but little was known about the effects of certain policy commissions and omissions.

The LINK Centre's interest was in building the capacity of the newly formed regulators to enable them to become good "referees," capable of implementing government policy and ensuring fair competition among new market players. Alison Gillwald, the Centre's director, was concerned about the trend of adopting policy and regulatory guidelines wholesale from developed countries. She also recognized the need for research on the rapidly privatizing telco market, which was far from beneficial. If anything, South Africa's experience with partial privatization of the fixed-line operator suggested that even an inefficient state-owned telco was marginally better than a privately controlled monopoly. This revelation came during a time of rapid diffusion of mobile phone usage, thanks to another innovation coming from South Africa: prepaid mobile accounts.

Against this telecommunications backdrop in Africa, my position with IDRC gave me the opportunity to provide resources to organizations such as the LINK Centre which were training regulators and operators in this shifting market structure. The Acacia program wanted to increase participation in the use of ICTs by encouraging policy changes that would increase access to, and the provision of, ICTs. Furthermore, IDRC program officers were being challenged to create regional projects, and, in light of IDRC's mandate to support the development of researchers' capacity, the LINK Centre was a natural choice for an institutional partner.

We recognized the potential for facilitating the exchange of ideas between the LINK Centre and other African research organizations. Gillwald was keen to do the research, and also to collaborate with other researchers in the countries where regulators were being trained. Through her networks, soon after the first network proposal was submitted to the IDRC in 2003, seven country partners presented themselves as interested in collaborating on the research. The acceptance of this proposal marked the formation of the Research ICT Africa (RIA) network, and by 2004, twelve researchers from African universities had come forward to join the network based on the strength of the sector performance policy reviews and household studies that RIA was doing to try to establish an index of ICT access and usage in Africa.

RIA brings together scholars and practitioners from Africa with the aim of conducting research in order to develop the information and analysis necessary for evidence-based ICT policy and regulation. In coming together in the pursuit of knowledge, RIA researchers, many of whom were previously strangers, found common research threads to develop. Today, the network has global status, and the researchers themselves have benefited from the synergy created by the group, as well as its reputation as an authority on ICT policy and regulation. The network was part of the global LIRNE.net (Learning Initiatives on Reforms for Network Economies) and participated in global task forces and international events such as the World Dialogue on Regulation Africa Expert Forum, which was financially supported by IDRC through the Acacia Program. Furthermore, through the leadership of the LINK Centre, members have learned new methodologies and have created a common language and forums in which to express themselves and communicate their findings to those in a position to improve the ICT policy environment.

RIA's research outputs have provided African researchers, governments, regulators, operators, multilateral institutions, community organizations, and trade unions with the knowledge they need to develop appropriate policies to use ICTs effectively to support sustainable development in the areas of health, education, and livelihoods. Equally important to the way in which its research findings have been used is the fact that RIA generated this knowledge through the participation of African scholars across the continent, whose research and communication skills were fostered through the network's activities. Network members have produced independent primary research which has informed ICT policy and regulatory processes. Through regular interaction with policymakers, and thanks to its solid research outputs and publicly accessible data, RIA is posing challenging questions to politicians, regulators, and the private sector alike.

Prior to the formation of the RIA network, the limited research in the area of ICT policy and regulation in Africa was fragmented and typically undertaken through isolated and disconnected projects. RIA has changed this by establishing a research program and agenda that has continuously built on previous achievements to monitor policy and regulatory outcomes. The severe lack of telecommunications infrastructure, a condition from which most African countries suffered, has changed dramatically. This is thanks to changes in policy, the benefits of prepaid mobile service, and, most importantly, the transformation of the telecommunications market structure from enforcing state monopolies to enabling the entrance of mobile competitors, and eventually competition for the delivery of facilities and services. Today, the convergence of technologies in some countries is resulting in new licensing regimes. In less than a decade since 1996, more than 30 per cent of Africans have access to mobile communications, but only 1 per cent enjoy Internet connectivity.

In South Africa, the highly skewed racial distribution of communica-tion infrastructure presented a policy challenge for a newly democratic government. At the time, the globally accepted approach to achieving uni-versal access was to pilot telecentres, which would provide voice, Internet, and training services. The Internet was becoming a public resource, and the Acacia program had already started piloting telecentre projects aimed at providing Internet infrastructure in communities in low teledensity areas. These projects were challenged by a lack of legislation which would allow these models of public access to thrive. Therefore, one of my first undertakings with IDRC was to help foster research in the policy and reg-ulatory domain in Africa. I also wanted to understand not only the social context but also the benefits that communities could derive from this infrastructure based on the anecdotal evidence discussed above.

The RIA researchers have developed innovative methodologies to understand national policy effects and have applied innovative ways of collecting nationally representative household data. This work has resulted in the production of two seminal publications outlining baseline studies demonstrating the realities of ICTs users and policies. The publications are a collection of sector performance reviews and *Towards an African e-Index*, edited by Alison Gillwald,[3] which is a demand-side analysis of ICT use in Africa. The latter publication gives an overall perspective of how poor communities innovatively use high-cost telecommunications, espe-cially mobile phones, to make the service pay for itself. It also gives nation-ally stratified samples of statistics from 10 countries, a feat which has never before been achieved. The sector performance reviews have also been very important for the evolution of ICT programs. It was the research per-formed for these reviews that helped the researchers appraise the perform-ance of ICT policies. These reviews have been used widely as models by many other African countries. For example, Uganda now sponsors this same research annually so it can ascertain the performance of its policies.

RIA researchers have also experienced professional advancement inside their own universities. Some of the network members were professors, while others headed the IT services and satellite procurement for univer-sity bandwidth. One of the professors told me that he had been working for years without a salary from his university. The small stipend and opportunity to work with postgraduate students as field researchers renewed his commitment to his career. When the network grew even larger with interest from French-speaking countries, as several economists joined the network. The research they were doing enabled many members to publish, and soon several researchers were able to apply for promotions after years of no research income and few, if any, opportunities to publish.

The research approach was initially a mentorship and supervisory role undertaken by Gillwald, who later extended the project staff to include researcher coordinators who have assisted in the large nationally representative household studies undertaken with graduate students. Each country team also sought to engage with its country's statistical office, some of which even accompanied the research teams into the field or provided analytical support.

The network funding was calculated according to the scale of the household studies but was achieved at a fraction of the cost of large statistical studies. According to Gillwald, "The upside of the resource constraint is that the need to do the kind of quantitative research usually undertaken by national statistical offices in other parts of the world prompted the development of innovative, cost-effective research methodologies that made possible the gathering of information simply not available before. Even where, for example, accurate mobile subscriber numbers existed, an actual figure for the levels of concentration in metropolitan, urban, and rural areas; a breakdown of expenditure on fixed and mobile and Internet; and multiple means of communication used by consumers to remain affordably in contact is available in the public domain for the first time."

In addition to wanting its funding to build research capacity in applied development problem-solving, IDRC expected its research partners to influence policy. However, the findings of researchers examining the public domain does not always entail good news for governments wishing to build partnerships with regulators, national departments, and statistic offices, who attempt to take over the resource-intensive data collection and inputting, with the hope of retaining access to the data for analysis.

The RIA project initially started off very ambitiously on the assumption that most of the collaboration among its members could be done online, especially given the researchers' focus on ICTs. It became apparent very early on that the unreliable access, lack of bandwidth, and unevenness of the skill-base of the network made face-to-face collaboration necessary in order to reconcile expectations, to transfer skills, and to simply engage with one another. Gillwald explains this requirement in this way: "The rigor required, especially in the national household survey and focus groups, would not have been possible without the in-depth training done in each country through the selection of the sample from the nation census and the piloting of the questionnaire. IDRC's willingness to invest vast sums of money in this means that we have a continental resource that has subsequently built on the national household surveys, surveys among SME (small and medium enterprises) in each of the research countries to ascertain their reliance and use of mobiles, the Internet and fixed lines. The learning curve for all of us on the quantitative work of this scale has been steep and much has been learnt and fed into the research design of the cycles of surveys in successive phases of the research networks funding."

The value of the RIA experience was worthy of sharing with other developing countries. To this end, RIA started collaborating with LIRNEasia (Learning Initiatives on Reforms for Network Economies), a sister network of telecommunications policy researchers that also started under the auspices of the global LIRNE program which spawned RIA. LIRNEasia has been funded by the Pan-Asia Networking program, a sister program in IDRC's ICT4D Program Area. The household surveys have enabled the RIA network to research the percentage of households' expenditure on cell phone bills, to examine how they are using mobiles for banking or money and funds transfers, and to test the price flexibility of consumers, as well as the potential demand for more calls if their cost decreased. The RIA have aimed to develop skills in leading focus-group discussions, so as to gain more qualitative data from targeted groups, such as women users, SIM card swappers, bleepers, and many more.

RIA's Sector Performance Review represents another template of policy research which has been shared across the network as a framework for conducting research, including methodologies, to build a body of work by building research capacity. RIA have researched the cost of interconnection rates, compared the cost of mobile phone accounts, provided evidence of why the cost of telecommunications in Africa remains inordinately high, and described examples of progress, such as the East African roaming charges being dropped, or the fact that Mauritius Telecom challenged the dominant monopoly pricing on the submarine international cable linking Africa with Europe and Asia.

RIA's research is often very different from donor-led studies that seek to find solutions for the donors. Such studies are often more appealing for potential funding bodies because the outcomes are more tangible, such as the policy and regulatory work funded in Africa which focuses on economic models and solutions, rather than confronting the less measurable or more controversial political challenges that often are the real source of problems within the relevant sectors.

RIA collaborated on a number of indicator and impact analysis projects through cross-continental comparative analysis that provided evidence to African countries with similar challenges. IDRC and LIRNE.net put RIA in touch with DISRI, a Latin American research network. These collaborations have enabled the networks to share a number of innovative methodologies with one another, such as a digital poverty index, which has had significant global impact, and LIRNEasia's Telecommunications Regulatory Environment, which is regularly used in Asia and Africa to canvass the opinions of telecommunications operators and experts. This set of indicators has provided graphic input needed to demonstrate the perceived weakness and ineffectiveness of regulators that implement and regulate ICT laws to diversify participation in delivering services. The TRE scores in Africa are consistently low and negative, indicating a core challenge to Africa's slow rollout of infrastructure, compared with other developing regions.

Gillwald points out that South Africa, in some ways, has more in common with Latin American countries, such as Argentina, than it does with other African countries. As such, a comparative analysis of South Africa and Latin American countries would be more meaningful. However, coordinating the work of a network whose members reside in two continents with different resources demands input and feedback, upkeep of websites, and online discussions, all of which are challenges that can seriously deplete the resources of the network.

Indeed, the challenge of mobilizing research capacity has even been experienced during RIA's efforts to collaborate between African countries. However, this collaboration among RIA researchers in different African countries sharply contrasts with projects wherein multilateral or donor agencies commission research using expatriate consultants who often do desk research from Europe or the United States.

RIA was responsible for the African contribution to the International Telecommunications Union and Orbicom report *From the Digital Divide to Digital Opportunities: Measuring Infostate for Development*.[4] Its research has also been used in the OECD-African Development Bank's 2009 *African Economic Outlook*, which was presented at the 44th African Development Bank Annual Meeting.

At the time of writing in 2009, the RIA network boasted membership in 20 countries, spanning sub-Saharan Africa, as well as North Africa. As demonstrated in the discussion above, RIA's influential research outputs have allowed the network to leverage its collective skills in order to better understand the policy and regulatory constraints on ICT access and usage in Africa and influence policy for change through the communication of that knowledge.

Women's Stories

While the RIA research network was doing primarily quantitative analysis of the supply and demand for services in Africa, including quantifying the usage of ICTs and assessing the gaps in policy and regulatory capacities, there remained a need to understand the contextualized stories of ICT use. It was evident to me that this required supporting strong qualitative research that would examine societal change. Around 2004, IDRC began discussing with the Association for Progressive Communications (APC), which has a program in women's usage of ICTs, the possibility of jointly convening a workshop for established and budding researchers in order to examine the possibility of researching and documenting Africa's participation in this changing environment, with a particular focus on women. The workshop marked the birth of the Gender Research in Africa into ICTs for Empowerment (GRACE) network.

Workshop participants agreed that such research was indeed important, and they concluded that they wanted to investigate whether women's experience with ICTs had been empowering, an idea that was really at the heart of the inquiry's theory of change. This theory of change stemmed from anecdotal evidence suggesting that new economic development options resulted from women's increased access to ICTs. One of the key questions to be answered was, "Were women taking opportunities to use ICTs, and if so, how, and with what benefits and challenges?"

The focus on *women's* usage of ICTs was inspired in part when IDRC's Richard Fuchs mentioned that he was interested in how the role of women in the North American workplace (and society at large) had changed as a result of the introduction of computers, and asked me what changes I had observed in Africa. I wanted to know why a preponderance of the people investing in mobile phone shops in South Africa were women. I also wanted to unearth the voices of women that had been omitted from the big-pictures household data being collected by RIA. Furthermore, I was interested in the fact that the Grameen Foundation's "Village Phone Ladies" embodied the global paradigm at that time. I felt compelled to facilitate the telling of women in Africa's ICT stories. I believed that if we could tell the contextually rich stories of women, the theories would emerge. At that stage, we didn't fully understand that technology is not gender-neutral; this understanding only emerged as GRACE researchers and global experts like Nancy Hafkin began examining the ways in which women used ICTs. However, the Acacia program always perceived a need to incorporate a gender analysis in our ICT-based interventions. We felt a need to look at women as a subset of the population in hopes of determining whether they were being disadvantaged by the technological focus of the revolution in communication.

The GRACE network's approach to research can be contrasted with the empirical-analytical approach of the more quantitative approaches in research projects which test and measure against a fixed hypothesis. Many Acacia-supported projects involve a group of researchers, typically under the direction of an academic, using a common template of questions or areas of inquiry in order to build a shared research approach for capacity-building. The GRACE network's approach, on the other hand, is more akin to the contemporary interpretative-hermeneutical style of analysis, which recognizes that meaning is constructed by working with an open-ended hypothesis set by the researchers.

The objective of the GRACE network's work has been to listen to the voices of women respondents, which are often previously unheard, and to draw out their deep stories through participatory research. This kind of research moves beyond numeric data which revolve around questions of "Whether?" or "How many?", and incorporates the "What" questions calling for substantial description, as well as moving beyond this to the "Why?" questions, to discover respondents' perspectives, and create the opportunity for more inductive theory development at the analytical stage.

The other key facet which distinguishes the GRACE network's activities from those of other research inquiries is that the GRACE researchers were trained in methods that would allow them to uncover the respondents' ideas for solving problems, or for creating a "transformed reality" rather than focusing primarily on her current reality. Essentially, the researchers asked respondents to dream of a future where the problems they experience in their present reality are no longer relevant, and then asked what role (if any) would be played by ICTs in that future vision. The future-oriented approach taken by the GRACE network was very innovative and allowed respondents to reflect on their present situation, while helping them define more clearly the social, cultural, and economic constraints in their present lives. In this regard, the work of the GRACE researchers contributed to theory development.

Several years of this kind of work culminated in the publication in 2009 of a book entitled *African Women and ICTs: Investigating Technology, Gender and Empowerment.*[5] Written by GRACE researchers from across Africa and edited by the network's leaders, Ineke Buskens and Anne Webb, the stories told in the book confirm the theory that certain thresholds of development must be achieved before ICTs become useful. They also demonstrate the value of Amartya Sen's theory of capabilities and women's agency, in that access to physical resources such as ICTs does not constitute empowerment. Even women in relatively resource-poor situations can become agents of change with the help of ICTs. Arguably, the book's most important contribution is the understanding that our gendered world is reflected in the way ICTs are used. It also shows us that ICTs do not transform patriarchy; on the contrary, the patriarchal underpins the way in which ICTs are used.

Conclusion: Next Steps

As described in the previous sections, Acacia-supported networks such as RIA and GRACE have made significant contributions to the understanding of the access and usage of ICTs by Africans. In addition to promoting the participation of Africans in the information society through the generation and dissemination of knowledge, these and other Acacia networks have increased and enhanced the participation of African researchers in the creation of a field of knowledge around the current reality and the potential for ICT development and usage in Africa.

Building on the strength of their accomplishments, RIA and GRACE are pressing on with their respective research missions. A third phase of the RIA network project began in late 2008, and its goals relating to the network itself include establishing a network structure suitable for growth and the integration of country teams from North Africa. RIA will also continue to help its members build their capacity through a PhD scholarship program, and support for peer-reviewed publishing, international conference participation, and training. The overall goal of the Phase III project is to provide ICT policymakers in Africa with evidence-based information so that they can provide an enabling environment for wider participation of Africans in the information society.

The Acacia program is also exploring other options for supporting participatory research in other domains in which ICTs hold great promise, such as using participatory forms of mapping natural resources using geographical information systems; improving health outcomes with improved patient and health facility data; improved interaction between citizens and governments through improved information systems for government. Though researched from the perspective of improvements, the social contexts are of utmost importance in order to measure the impacts of these technologies on society. In summary, the participatory approach to building the capacity of African researchers to investigate ICT4D issues, and to propose and promote solutions, has resulted in positive change in the communities in which Acacia-funded networks work.

Notes

1. Reck and Wood, "Vodacom's Community Services Phone Shops."
2. D'Ansembourg and Tambo, "GrameenPhone Revisited."
3. Gillwald, ed., *Towards an African e-Index,* http://www.idrc.ca/uploads/userS/ 11339841321Toward2.pdf. Other RIA research publications can be found on the Acacia website at http://www.idrc.ca/en/ev-116784-201-1-DO_TOPIC .html or at www.researchictafrica.net/.
4. Sciadas, ed., *From the Digital Divide to Digital Opportunities.*
5. Buskens and Webb, *African Women and ICTs.*

CHAPTER TEN

The Role of Private Academic Centres and Foreign Aid in Developing Social Sciences during Military Dictatorship

Diego E. Piñeiro

Until 1973 Uruguay had one of the best records of democracy in Latin America. Then, in February that year, after years of mounting conflict, the Uruguayan military staged a quasi-coup, backing the president, Juan María Bordaberry, and rapidly taking control of the various branches of government. In June, the General Assembly was replaced with a Council of State, and the president empowered the military to take whatever measures they deemed necessary to ensure public services were maintained. The backlash from various sectors of Uruguayan society caused the civilian-military dictatorship to launch attacks on trade unions, political organizations, and all those considered to be dissidents. Supported by the U.S. government, a twelve-year reign of terror ensued. People were assassinated, disappeared, indiscriminately arrested, and tortured, and the country set a record for having the highest per capita number of political prisoners in the world. Also during that time, academics at the Universidad de la República, an autonomous institution, were force either to sign a declaration that they were not a communist, or they were fired from their jobs. By the end of the dictatorship in 1985, hundreds of people had been murdered or disappeared by the Uruguayan armed forces and police, and approximately 15,000 people were imprisoned for political crimes. This chapter deals with my personal experience working in rural development and also examines the role of private academic centres and foreign aid during Uruguay's difficult years of military dictatorship (1973–85).

Let me begin with some brief biographical information to provide context. Born and raised in Argentina, I could not be unaffected by the social and political conditions in which I grew up. I graduated as an agricultural engineer in 1969 from the University of Buenos Aires, and the university during those years was in a state of permanent upheaval, battling for its autonomy against the continuous military coups that considered university students to be at the heart of political unrest. When the military invaded and intervened at the University of Buenos Aires in 1966, I was one of the student leaders who opposed this extreme measure.

Upon finishing my studies I became involved in a Catholic movement working with peasants in the northern provinces of Argentina. When a group of peasants invited me to help them organize a peasant farmers union in a remote northern province, I did not hesitate to accept. I moved north with my family and I lived there for five years working as a counsellor for the Formosa Peasant Leagues Union. In Formosa I helped very poor farmers with two of their major concerns, namely, resisting the encroachment of ranchers on peasant land, and seeking better prices for their main crop, cotton.

In 1976, for safety reasons, my family was forced to leave Argentina because of a new military coup and the cruellest dictatorship that the country has suffered. We crossed the border to Uruguay to stay with relatives despite the fact that Uruguay was also under a military regime. I began a new chapter in my life, fleeing one dictatorship only to find myself under the dark shadow of another.

Upon arrival in Uruguay, I was unemployed for several months until I was finally offered an opportunity to work in a private academic centre called the Uruguayan Information and Studies Centre or CIESU (*Centro de Informaciones y Estudios del Uruguay*). In order to work with the centre, I was required to prepare a project and compete for funding. Based on my past experience, I turned to small farmer's organizations in Uruguay and worked on a project which was ultimately funded by an international funding agency. In this way I managed to stay on at CIESU and in Uruguay, which leads me to the discussion of Uruguay and academic life in the private research centres during its military dictatorship.

Uruguay's longstanding democratic tradition was shattered by the military coup of 1973. Up until that time, Uruguay had very strong political parties, a century of uninterrupted democratic government with power rotating between the two traditional parties, an extended welfare state, and a relatively high standard of living. However, political struggle, a fading economy, a strong union movement that opposed strict economic "adjustment" measures, and the appearance of an urban guerrilla (the "Tupamaros") finally led to a right-wing civilian–military coup.

Uruguay had (and still has) only one public university, the University of the Republic, which is governed by students, professors, and alumni who are democratically elected by faculty, students, and alumni for four-year terms. At the time of the military coup, private universities were prohibited, and even now 80 per cent of all university students attend the University of the Republic. Since the public university was one of the centres of civilian opposition to the right-wing government, soon after the military coup in June 1973, the university was taken over. In October 1973, the democratically elected rector and the deans were displaced; many were jailed, and others managed to leave the country. During the following months, political persecution, tight controls on teaching, budget constraints, and the closure of two departments—Sociology and Psychology—convinced many professors that it was time to leave the university.

The Faculty of Social Sciences in general, and the Department of Sociology in particular, developed relatively late in Uruguay. Sociology as a university specialization was only formally recognized in 1971 within the Faculty of Law, and very few professors were sociologists themselves.[1] At that time, the country had only 11 academics with a background in sociology, and at the time of the military coup in 1973, only 12 sociology students had graduated from the program. Clearly, sociology was in jeopardy as an academic field when the military took control of the university, dismissed dozens of faculty members, forcing many into exile and replacing them with individuals who were friendly to the new regime.

In 1975, CIESU was founded by a group of these sociologists who did not want to leave the country (and could stay), some of the new sociologists, and a group of final-year sociology students who had been expelled from the university. As is the case in many of these endeavours, a leading figure emerged who became an essential reference point for the entire group. In this case it was Carlos Filgueira, former director of the then closed Social Sciences Institute (*Instituto de Ciencias Sociales*), aided by his wife, Suzana Prates, a well-known gender studies sociologist.

I should also point out that something very similar happened with academics who worked at the Economics Institute in the Faculty of Economic Sciences. Even though this faculty was not closed, many of its professors left the country, while others founded the Centre for Economic Research or CINVE (*Centro de Investigaciones Económicas*). Two years later, in 1977, another academic centre, the Interdisciplinary Centre for Development Studies or CIEDUR (*Centro Interdisciplinario de Estudios para el Desarrollo*) brought together economists, agronomists, and sociologists. These three centres, together with the Latin American Centre for Human Economics or CLAEH (*Centro Latinoamericano de Economía Humana*) and the Pedagogical Experimentation and Research Centre or CIEP (Centro de Investigación y Experimentacion Pedagogica) from the Catholic sector, formed a community of academic centres that were affiliated with the Latin American Social Science Council or CLACSO (*Consejo Latinoamericano de Ciencias Sociales*), which played a very important role in obtaining funding for its members during these years.

In 1976, CIESU could finally stand on its own, thanks to an institutional grant from the Ford Foundation. External funding became the norm for social science research funding in the following years and during the military dictatorship, since it was completely impossible to obtain either private or public funds nationally.

These institutions offered the only alternative to academic research, since the University of the Republic was controlled by the dictatorship. They organized critical thought and systematic research, and also became a shelter and a formative environment for both new and older generations of social scientists.

However, undertaking this kind of research was extremely difficult and required much ingenuity on the part of researchers. Surveys, interviews, and opinion polls had to be submitted to the police for authorization or were directly banned. Access to statistical information produced by official institutions was only available from published sources, and special permission was required to carry out recalculations or comparison of any statistical information. In these cases, researchers were required to explain for what purpose they would use these new calculations and comparisons, and very rarely were these types of analysis allowed. These limitations, combined with the scarcity of published statistical and methodological evidence-based information, oriented research towards theoretical analysis and case studies, which were easier to perform.

Dissemination of the results of social research and its products was also difficult. For the most part, it was done through self-edited working papers, since no publisher wanted (or dared) to publish books of that kind. Public seminars or workshops were seldom allowed. Often, however, researchers were invited to meetings in other countries where their research was published. So paradoxically, social research from private Uruguayan centres was better known outside the country than in it.

The productivity of these five academic centres was impressive. During the first years of the dictatorship many subjects of inquiry had to be avoided for security reasons. However, after the 1980 plebiscite, which rejected the military dictatorship's proposed modifications to the Uruguayan constitution, research restrictions gradually decreased and researchers could diversify their range of subjects. In this way, private academic centres were gradually able to build a network of social sciences researchers inside the country. This, in turn, contributed decisively to ending the personal and institutional isolation characteristic of social environments dominated by fear. With the collaboration of foreign funding agencies, this network established very strong connections and benefited from its participation in several international academic networks.

I would also like to comment on a frequent subject of discussion that arose privately among members of the social research academic centres during this period. The discussion centred on the reasons why both private and public international agencies were funding our centres. Some social scientists rejected this type of funding and directly refused to join the private academic centres. Others felt that it was probably not the ideal source of funding for the centres but realized it was the only means which would allow them to continue their work. They also thought that it was important to maintain a window open to social inquiry during Uruguay's years of darkness. Others had their own particular scale of values and accepted financing from some donors and not from others. To some researchers, funding agencies represented the democratic forces within developed countries, while, to others, this type of financial support was simply the mild face of imperialism. After all, the involvement of the U.S. government in aiding military dictatorships through its agencies had been amply proven and publicized by that time.

Canadian funding, and especially funding from IDRC, was welcomed because of Canada's longstanding commitment to democracy. During the dictatorship, IDRC assisted academic social science research in several ways, namely, by funding research projects, by inviting scholars to seminars and meetings in other countries, by organizing public seminars in Uruguay with the presence of foreign scholars and officials from IDRC, and by aiding in the dissemination of research findings through the publication of working papers and books. The regular visits that IDRC officials made to Uruguay were always welcomed as an opportunity to discuss what we were doing, and to receive information on what was going on in other academic centres. The visit that the former president of IDRC, Dr. Ivan Head, paid to Uruguayan academic centres (circa 1981) was extremely helpful in legitimizing our existence.

In 1980, the military dictatorship committed a gross error. It called a plebiscite to modify the Constitution in order to allow them to stay on in power. The population rejected the modification, which began a slow erosion of the military's political power. Gradually, political restraints began to weaken. At CIESU, this meant that we dared to start a social sciences teaching program. At the University of the Republic, this type of instruction continued to be banned; therefore we requested and obtained external funding to begin a very modest teaching program. We accepted approximately 10 to 12 students into a two-year program, and we managed to teach two groups of this size before the dictatorship ended. As civilian support for the military dictatorship gradually disappeared, elections were finally held in 1985. That same year, the public university was returned to its legal authorities, and social sciences teaching resumed.

In 1980, IDRC funded a project that I proposed through CIESU to study the different ways in which family farmers were resisting the adverse conditions brought about by a neo-liberal economic program designed by the military government. It was through this research that I was ultimately able to obtain a masters degree at the University of Wisconsin in 1984. Upon my return to Uruguay, I continued my research in rural sociology in very close connection with family farming organizations. In 1987, I began teaching in the Faculty of Agronomy, and in 1990, in the Faculty of Social Sciences. Since then, my work has been related to research and teaching in rural development, concentrating on subjects such as family farming, rural organizations, rural workers, and more recently, the environment and sustainable development.

In 1990, the University of the Republic founded the Faculty of Social Sciences of which I have recently been elected dean for a four-year term. With five departments, we teach the specializations of Sociology, Social Work and Political Sciences. Additionally, we have academic groups working in Economics, Demography, Economic History, and International Relations, while other social sciences are taught in the Faculty of Humanities. We also teach 15 programs at the postgraduate level, offering both masters and doctoral degrees. In 2010, we began a totally new specialization in Development that is an interdisciplinary endeavour between several established departments of the faculty. At this time the faculty has 3000 students and 300 professors, approximately 100 of whom are full-time. Each year, we receive approximately 800 new students.

Most of the scholars who found shelter in the private academic centres during dictatorship returned to the university and were the central figures who helped create the Faculty of Social Sciences in 1990. The composition of the Sociology Department in the Faculty of Social Sciences provides an example of how these returning scholars had been spread across the globe. At the university, professors are ranked in five categories from Grade 1 to 5, 5 representing the highest level achievable in one's academic career. At this time, the Sociology Department has seven Grade 5 professors, five of them coming from the private academic centres — three from CIESU and two from CIEDUR. The remaining two returned from exile in 1985. Among the Grade 4 professors, three of the five professors are young academics who were our students in the Social Sciences courses that we held in CIESU during 1984–85, who then went on to do their PhDs in Brazil and France, and then returned to the university. In the Political Science department, of the five Grade 5 professors, three come from the private academic centres. I believe it is safe to say that if it were not for the private academic centres and their contribution to the development of serious academic research even during a harsh military dictatorship, and their modest but crucial role in training new academics, the history of social sciences in Uruguay would be quite different at this moment. Partnership funding from private and public agencies such as IDRC played an important role in recovering social sciences in my country, and we are grateful for this contribution.

In conclusion, I would like to point out that by supporting private academic centres during the Uruguayan dictatorship, IDRC also contributed to the return of political democracy. Some of the academics who stayed in

Uruguay were sheltered in these centres, and later went on to develop high profile academic, business, or political careers. I am one example of an academic who took refuge in an IDRC-supported research centre, and I have achieved significant success at the Universidad de la República once it was restored to its former status. Similarly, I have many colleagues who have also found their way home and into positions of authority. The best example of this development is our former minister of Economics and Finance, Danilo Astori, who, before the coup, was the dean of the Faculty of Economics at the Universidad de la República, and who became the vice-president of Uruguay in 2009. Like I did, Danilo Astori took refuge in a foreign-funded research centre. There are many other academics in Uruguay and throughout the Southern Cone region whose work was disrupted by political events but saved by the farsighted approach taken by IDRC and other funding agencies that sought to maintain research capacity in fields such as sociology and economics.

Notes

1 This information, along with the following examples related to the private academic centres, is taken from Suzana Prates, *Los Centros Autónomos en Ciencias Sociales en el Uruguay: Trayectoria y perspectivas* (Montevideo: CIESU/EBO, 1987).

Long-Term Solutions

The complexity of the challenges of poverty in our rapidly changing world are daunting because solutions to everyday problems often seem to be just beyond the grasp of countries with so many needs and so few resources. Without the dedication of individuals like the researchers in this book, innovation and research into problems of poverty would be the preserve of scientists from industrialized countries of the world. The contributors to this book are people who in most cases have studied abroad but have chosen to return to their home countries where they live and work. In so doing, they have sacrificed the benefits of working with big budgets in state-of-the-art facilities. As researchers who have a profound understanding of the social, political, and cultural backdrop to the problems that are the focus of their attention, they are essential to finding lasting solutions. This is why their work is so significant.

The authors invited to tell their stories in *Long-Term Solutions in a Short-Term World* are activist researchers who have made significant contributions in their fields of study. Through their stories readers are introduced to the kinds of problems researchers from the developing world regularly confront in advancing science and effecting change in societies where resources are scarce. In each case, the contributors have been obliged to adapt their research to local conditions and developed methodologies to help them avoid obstacles particular to a society or place. Global challenges combine with local conditions to make the research discussed in the preceding chapters both timely and significant. The solutions to problems in one country cannot always be implemented in exactly the same way in other contexts, but the knowledge gained through research for development can be adapted to solving similar problems elsewhere.

Although they work in different countries and in different fields of science, their focus is on solutions that are long-term and transferable to other parts of the world. Some solutions are more direct in their application to the alleviation of poverty, but each of the projects described in this volume has contributed to a better understanding of the problems at hand. These stories of dedication and innovation serve as an introduction to the concept and impact of participatory research for development. Participatory research is a means of intervention to foster development and change within communities. This type of research requires researchers to engage with communities, governments, and other relevant actors so that they may come together to find solutions to common problems. To do this, participants must reflect critically on the cultural, economic, historical, political, and social contexts within the topic under investigation.

Education and commitment are the main threads that run through *Long-Term Solutions in a Short-Term World*, and the authors are people who make sacrifices that inspire those around them to try harder, to reach further in the quest to provide a better future for the inhabitants of our planet. These researchers share a worldview that is evident in the way each of them approaches the problems of development on which they focus. Their involvement with communities and commitment to helping the poor demonstrate their commitment to change and improvements to the living standards of the people with whom they work. As a group, all are conscious that they are in a position to make a lasting contribution. Their knowledge, combined with their commitment to making a difference, is the foundation to building capacity in poor countries in order to effect meaningful change.

A good example of impact that is not easily quantified is the story of Indirha Zapata Atoche, who was only nine years old when a team of researchers arrived in her hometown of Salitral, a remote community on Peru's semi-tropical north coast where malaria rates were extreme. At such a young age, Indirha was not clear about the purpose of the visit by this group of foreigners, but she knew that it had something to do with the study of a common sickness, and she remembers being struck by how exotic the visitors seemed. When the group left after a few days of work in Salitral, one researcher, Dr. Ventosilla, continued to return to the village, and Indirha had an opportunity to get to know more about her and her work. This is because, as part of her research, Dr. Ventosilla developed a community-based program that helped to educate the population about malaria. A key component of the community program was the education of young people like Indirha as part of a long-term strategy to increase the general understanding of malaria and the ways to prevent it. A youth group was formed with the objective of involving the next generation in the fight against malaria, and Salitral evolved into a leading example of how community-based research can provide long-term solutions to the most vexing of problems.

Indirha Zapata was too young to be a part of the youth group when it was first formed, but after a few years she joined and soon became one of its most active members. Indirha learned to identify larvae, use the bacterium Bti with coconuts to create a natural pesticide, and participate in the eradication of malaria in her community. She became an active part of Dr. Ventosilla's project and, for a girl who was living in a very poor community where opportunities for advancement were few and far between, the chance to participate in research on the prevention of malaria was something almost inconceivable. As a result, Indirha developed a strong interest in science and upon finishing high school, an accomplishment in itself, she went on to take a technology course in biology and health. She is among the first young women of her generation in Salitral to advance beyond high school, and her future is shaped by the experience of working with, not for, Dr. Ventosilla and her team.

Indirha was in Salitral on the day we visited the town to see for ourselves the legacy of the research conducted by Dr. Ventosilla on malaria prevention. It was a rainy Saturday morning, but Indirha was out with the youth group conducting an education campaign in the community to remind people not to leave containers out where they could collect water because they then become perfect incubators for the mosquito larvae that will eventually spread disease. As a leader of the youth group, Indirha taught other young people by example, knocking on doors, speaking to residents, and getting her hands dirty by hauling old containers out to be recycled. During a break in the action, she told of her experience of developing an interest in science and of her desire to use her knowledge to help others in her community and elsewhere in Peru. The passion she had for doing what she could to help her community was evident, and it was clear that Indirha understood that she had succeeded in overcoming some of the obstacles to a better future for herself. This is why Indirha was out in the streets that Saturday morning, serving as a role model and leading teens through the educational process she herself had followed on her way to a higher education.

Indirha's story, and that of her community, offers an example of how research for development can have multiple outcomes that are not easily quantified as part of the original study. Salitral's focus on a natural method of eradicating malaria has led to a better understanding of the dangers posed by pesticides and herbicides, and it is no wonder that the community became the first in Peru to begin producing organic bananas for export. It is also not surprising that a visit to the local health centre revealed that rates of malaria and dengue fever, a more recent scourge affecting Peru, are far below the regional average. Make no mistake that the problems faced by the residents of Salitral in their daily struggle against poverty are still as great as those of any of the neighbouring communities. Except that in this one town, fewer pesticides are used and the rates of diseases caused by mosquito bites are low. Along with other efforts by community members to raise levels of awareness about environmental issues and provide opportunities for their children, the youth group's activities set Salitral apart from neighbouring towns. While this may be only a small step forward, it is an important step because on the day we visited there were many future Indirhas among the youth who went door to door in Salitral.

The example of this one small community in northern Peru is indicative of many of the results of the research contained in this volume. Each story has shed light on outcomes from research that are both surprising and rewarding. The growth of co-operatives among Berber women in Morocco, the spread of e-learning in Central America, studies on the impact of trauma on Palestinian youth, and the knowledge gained from developing a detailed understanding of the social economy of a garbage dump in Dakar are examples of how research supported by funding from a Canadian institution is creating new knowledge for the benefit of the poor. The International Development Research Centre is a unique institution that has created opportunities by supporting researchers for the past forty years, proving that international development through research can have a positive impact on the lives of those who are most in need.

However, as with all scientific research, results are not always evident, and progress is made over time using many different building blocks. The results of research designed to address a problem of development are often the platform for further research. For this reason, none of the authors would claim to have solved a given problem because they know that development is an extremely complex process and that there is no magic bullet. Stable funding and the participation of the people for whom the research is being conducted are the keys to sustainable development. IDRC's role is to build research capacity in the developing world. IDRC assists researchers with short-term financing in order to position them to take advantage of opportunities offered by larger institutions. For this reason, the authors of several of the chapters in this book have already moved away from IDRC support, and by doing so have created opportunities for other scientists in need of research funding.

Forty years after the Trudeau government made Maurice Strong the first president of IDRC and Lester Pearson's dream came true, IDRC continues to play a unique and important role in supporting research for development. Building on decades of success, taking advantage of its arm's-length relationship with government, and always searching for innovative research to support, IDRC continues to play an important role in demonstrating Canada's commitment to development. No other governmental organization has the same mandate or impact as IDRC in the field of international development. As an organization it remains true to Maurice Strong's dictum that narrowing the knowledge gap is the key to narrowing the development gap. To accomplish this IDRC continues its support for research on long-term solutions.

Given the times we live in, with the major shifts in the world economy, seemingly endless conflict in several parts of the world, and a population that continues to grow at a rapid rate, our short-term world needs more long-term solutions that are the result of research that seeks to address the concerns of community stakeholders. More than ever before, the future of humanity depends on people working together to find solutions to the problems that affect us most. *Long-Term Solutions in a Short-Term World* provides concrete examples of both the challenges and the benefits of research for international development. As a companion to the existing literature on international development or as an entry point for understanding some of the obstacles inherent in efforts to confront the problem of poverty in the modern world, the articles in this book provide readers with examples of how building research capacity in the developing world can make a difference. Research for development is a means of providing the tools needed to allow people to help themselves. The stories told in this book are most important for the current generation: for young people like Indirha Zapata who are looking for inspiration so that they, too, can take their place in the ongoing struggle to make the world a better place.

General Bibliography

Acemoglu, D., S. Johnson, and J. Robinson. "Institutions as the Fundamental Cause of Long-Run Growth." In *Handbook of Economic Growth*, edited by Phillipe Aghion and Steven M. Durlauf. Elsevier, 2005.

Aghion, Philippe, and Peter Howitt. "A Model of Growth through Creative Destruction." *Econometrica: Journal of the Econometric Society* 60, no. 2 (1992): 323–51.

D'Ansembourg, Benoit, and Ichiro Tambo. "Grameen Phone Revisited: Investors Reach Out to the Poor." *The DAC Journal* 5, no. 3 (2004): 15–56.

Aruri, Naseer H. "Dialectics of Dispossession." In *Occupation: Israel over Palestine*, edited by Naseer H. Aruri. London: Zed Books, 1984.

Austin, Alvyn J., and James S. Scott, eds. *Canadian Missionaries, Indigenous Peoples: Representing Religion at Home and Abroad*. Toronto: University of Toronto Press, 1986.

Baker, Ahmad, and Nadera Shalhoub-Kevorkian. "Effects of Political and Military Trauma on Children: The Palestinian Case." *Clinical Psychology Review* 19, no. 8 (1999): 935–50.

Balta, R., L. Gonzáles, J. Lucer, J. Pinto, L. Troyes, S. Moreno, A. Vicente, G. Diaz, E. Chalco, C. Del Águila, M. Santa Cruz, L. Boyer, S. Villegas, L. Sánchez, and V. Herrera. "Evaluación de la susceptibilidad y resistencia a los insecticidas en mosquitos adultos del género *Anopheles* de las regiones maláricas del Perú. 64° aniversario del Instituto Nacional de Salud." Paper presented at II Congreso de la Red Nacional de Laboratorios en Salud Pública, Lima, Perú, September 28–29, 2000.

Barro, R. J. "Economic Growth in a Cross-Section of Countries." *Quarterly Journal of Economics* 106, no. 2 (1991): 407–43.

Barro, R. J., and X. Sala-i-Martin. "Convergence." *Journal of Political Economy* 100, no. 2 (1992): 223–51.

Baumol, W. J. "Productivity Growth, Convergence and Welfare: What the Long-Run Data Show." *American Economic Review* 76, no. 5 (1986): 1073–85.

Behrman, Jere R., Nancy Birdsall, and Miguel Székely. "Pobreza, desigualdad y liberalización comercial y financiera en América Latina." University of Pennsylvania, Carnegie Endowment for International Peace, Inter-American Development Bank, May 2001. Available online at http://www.iadb.org/res/publications/pubfiles/pubWP-449.pdf.

Berthélémy, J. C. "Clubs de convergence et équilibres multiples." Paper presented at Conférence ABCDE de la Banque Mondiale, Dakar, 2005.

Birdsall, Nancy. "Education: People's Asset." CSED Working Paper no. 5, September 1999.

Birdsall, Nancy, Carol Graham, and R. H. Sabot. *Beyond Tradeoffs: Market Reforms and Equitable Growth in Latin America.* Washington, DC: Published for Inter-American Development Bank by Brookings Institution Press, 1998.

Birdsall, Nancy, and Juan Luis Londoño. "Asset Inequality Does Matter: Lessons from Latin America." OCE Working Paper. Washington, DC: Inter-American Development Bank, Office of the Chief Economist. March 1997. Available online at http://www.iadb.org/res/publications/pubfiles/pubWP-344.pdf.

Black, C. E. *The Dynamics of Modernization.* New York: Harper and Row, 1966.

Bothwell, Robert. *The Penguin History of Canada.* Toronto: Penguin Canada, 2006.

Brass, Paul. "The Political Uses of Crisis: The Bihar Famine of 1966–67." *The Journal of Asian Studies* 45, no. 2 (1986): 245–67.

B'Tselem. "Beating and Abuse of Palestinians by the Israeli Security Forces." http://www.btselem.org/english/beating_and_abuse (accessed February 14, 2009)

B'Tselem. "Restrictions on Movement." http://www.btselem.org/English/Freedom_of_Movement (accessed February 14, 2009).

Buskens, Ineke, and Anne Webb. *African Women and ICTs: Investigating Technology, Gender and Empowerment.* London: Zed Books, 2009. Also available online at http://www.idrc.ca/en/ev-135944-201-1-DO_TOPIC.html.

Calderon-Falero, G., and J. Valle. "Especies de la fauna anofelina, su distribución y algunas consideraciones sobre su abundancia e infectividad en el Perú." *Revista Peruana de Epidemiología* 8 (1995): 5–23.

Carr, Nicholas. "IT Doesn't Matter." *Harvard Business Review* 81, no. 5 (May 2003): 41–49.

Castells, Manuel. *La sociedad de la Red.* Vol. 1 of *La era de la información, sociedad y cultura.* México: Editorial Siglo XXI, 2002.

Cavell, Nik. "Canada and the Colombo Plan." *The Empire Club of Canada Addresses,* 112–28. Toronto: Empire Club Foundation, 1953.

Chilcott, C. N., and J. S. Pillai. "The Use of Coconut Waste for the Production of *Bacillus thuringiensis* var *israelensis.*" *MIRCEN JOURNAL* 1 (1985): 327–32.

Chisholm, Brock. "World Health." *The Empire Club of Canada Addresses,* 334–45. Toronto: Empire Club Foundation, 1951.

Cissé, Oumar. *L'argent des déchets: L'économie informelle à Dakar.* Paris: Karthala, 2007.

Cohen, D., and M. Soto. "Why Are Some Countries So Poor? Another Look at the Evidence and a Message of Hope." OECD Development Centre Working Papers, no. 197, October 2002.

Coleridge, Peter. "Palestinian Adolescents Coping with Trauma, Phase II: A Formative Assessment." CBR report, November 2007. http://idl-bnc.idrc.ca/dspace/handle/123456789/37570 (accessed May 10, 2009).

Comisión Económica para América Latina y el Caribe. *Transformación productiva con equidad: La tarea prioritaria del desarrollo en América Latina y el Caribe e los años noventa.* Santiago, Chile, 1990.

Community-Campus Partnerships for Health. http://www.ccph.info/ (accessed February 14, 2009).

Desakota Study Team. *Re-imagining the Rural–Urban Continuum: Understanding the role ecosystem services play in the livelihoods of the poor in Desakota regions undergoing rapid change.* Research Gap Analysis prepared by the Desakota Study Team (DST) for the Ecosystem Services for Poverty Alleviation (ESPA) Program of Natural Environment Research Council (NERC), Department for International Development (DfID) and Economic and Social Research Council (ESRC) of the United Kingdom. Kathmandu, Nepal: Institute for Social and Environmental Transition-Nepal (ISET-N), 2008.

Dirección General de Epidemiología-MINSA. "Indicadores de vigilancia epidemiológica, Perú SE. 53 – 2008." *Bol. Epidemiol.* (Lima) 17, no. 53 (2008): 971. Also available online: http://www.dge.gob.pe/Boletin_sem/2008/SE53/se53-06.pdf.

Dirección General de Epidemiología-MINSA. "Malaria por *P. vivax* y *P. falciparum:* Sala Situacional 2009." (SE) Nro, 2008. Also available online: http://www.dge.gob.pe/vigilancia/sala/2008/SE53/malaria.pdf.

Editors. "Cast Lead in the Foundry." *Middle East Report,* December 31, 2008. http://www.merip.org/mero/mero123108b.html (accessed December 31, 2008).

Emmerij, Louis, Richard Jolly, and Thomas G. Weiss. *Ahead of the Curve? UN Ideas and Global Challenges.* Indianapolis: Indiana University Press, 2001.

Falk, Richard. "Israel's War Crimes." *The Nation,* December 29, 2008. http://www.thenation.com/doc/20090112/falk?rel=hp_currently (accessed January 2, 2009).

Fonseca, Clotilde. "From ICT to Digital Creation and Productivity: Releasing the Potential of Technology for Education and Capacity Building." In *Access, Empowerment & Governance: Creating a World of Equal Opportunities with ICT,* edited by Rinalia Abdul Rahim, Daniele Waldburger, and Gabriele Siegenthaler Muinde, 121–43. Kuala Lumpur: Global Knowledge Partnership, 2005.

———. "Moving beyond the Digital Gap: Investing in the Young to Create New Learning and Socio-Economic Opportunities." In *Harnessing the Potential of ICT for Education: A Multistakeholder Approach (Proceedings from the Dublin Global Forum of the United Nations ICT Task Force),* edited by Bonnie Bracey and Terry Culver, 46–62. New York: United Nations Publications, 2005.

―――. "Informática educativa en Costa Rica: Hacia un uso innovador de la computadora en la escuela." In *Política social y educación en Costa Rica*. Serie de Políticas Sociales no. 4, edited by Alicia Gurdián Fernández, 457–94. San José, Costa Rica: UNICEF, 1999.

Fonseca, C., and R. Murillo. "Summary of Principal's Response: A Perspective from Costa Rica." In *The ITEC Project: Information Technology in Education of Children; Final Report of Phase 1*, edited by Betty Collins, 163–70. Paris: UNESCO, 1993.

Franks, Isaiah. "Isaiah Franks to Secretary." 26 June 1961. JFK Library, Papers as President, National Security Files, Carl Kaysen, Box 372, File: Economic Policy – Subjects – OECD Development Center, 3/61–6/61.

Fundación Omar Dengo. *Educación y tecnologías digitales: Cómo valorar su impacto social y sus contribuciones a la equidad*. San José, Costa Rica, 2006.

―――. "Construir el futuro." San José, Costa Rica: RV Producciones, 2004.

―――. *Testimonies: Impact of the National Educational Informatics Program from the Point of View of Its Beneficiaries*. 2004.

Fundación Omar Dengo, ed. *Multi-Stakeholder Partnerships and Digital Technologies for Development in Latin America and the Caribbean: Three Case Studies, Fundación Omar Dengo, Acceso Foundation, and ChasquiNet Foundation*. San José, Costa Rica: Ediciones Innov@, 2007.

Giacaman, George, and Dag Jørund Lønning, eds. *After Oslo: New Realities, Old Problems*. London: Pluto Press, 1998.

Giacaman, Rita. "Editorial: Coping with Conflict." *Education for Health* 18, no. 1 (2005): 2–4.

Giacaman, Rita, H. F. Abdul-Rahim, and L. Wick. "Health Sector Reform in the Occupied Palestinian Territory (OPT): Targeting the Forest or the Tree?" *Health Policy and Planning* 18, no. 1 (2003): 59–67.

Giacaman, Rita, H. Saab, Viet Nguyen-Gillham, A. Abdullah, and G. Naser, "Palestinian Adolescents Coping with Trauma." Birzeit University, November 2004.

Giacaman, Rita, H. S. Shannon, H. Saab, N. Arya, and W. Boyce. "Individual and Collective Exposure to Political Violence: Palestinian Adolescents Coping with Conflict." *European Journal of Public Health* 17, no. 4 (2007): 361–68.

Gillwald, Alison, ed., *Towards an African e-Index*, Research report for the RIA, 2005, http://www.idrc.ca/uploads/user-S/11339841321Toward2.pdf.

Goldman Sachs Group. "BRICs." http://www2.goldmansachs.com/ideas/brics/index.html.

Gonsalves, Tahira, and Stephen Baranyi. "Research for Policy Influence: A History of IDRC Intent." Report for the Evaluation Unit. Ottawa: International Development Research Centre, January 2003.

Gutiérrez Saxe, E., coord. *Estado de la región en desarrollo humano sostenible, Informe 1*. San José, Costa Rica: PNUD, Unión Europea, 1999.

Gyawali, D. *Rivers, Technology and Society: Learning the Lessons from Water Management in Nepal*. London and Kathmandu: Zed Books with Himal Books, 2003.

Gyawali, D. *Water and Conflict: Whose Ethics Is to Prevail?* In *Water Ethics, Marcelino Botin Water Forum 2007*, edited by M. R. Llamas, L. Martinez-Cortina, and A. Mukherji. London: CRC Press Taylor & Francis Group, 2009.

Gyawali, D., J. A. Allan, et al. *EU-INCO Water Research from FP4 to FP6 (1994–2006): A Critical Review.* Luxembourg: Office for Official Publications of the European Communities, 2006.

Gyawali D., A. Dixit, and M. Upadhya. *Ropeways in Nepal: Context, Constraints and Co-Evolution.* Kathmandu: Nepal Water Conservation Foundation and Kathmandu Electric Vehicle Alliance, 2004.

Gyawali, D. "Economic Security in a Predominantly Informal World: South Asian Realities and Global Elation with Liberalisation." In *Regional Economic Trends and South Asian Security,* edited by Iftekharuzzman. Colombo: Regional Centre for Strategic Studies/New Delhi: Manohar Publishers, 1996.

Gyawali, D., Othmar Schwank, Indra Thapa, and Dieter Zürcher (eds.), *Rural–Urban Interlinkages: A Challenge for Swiss Development Cooperation.* Zürich: INFRAS/ IDA, 1993.

Haaretz. "Humiliation at the Checkpoints." August 8, 2008. http://www.haaretz .com/hasen/pages/ShArt.jhtml?itemNo=315603&contrassID=2&subContrass ID=3 &sbSubContrassID=0&listSrc=Y (accessed August 8, 2008).

Halloran, Mary, John Hilliker, and Greg Donaghy. "The White Paper Impulse: Reviewing Foreign Policy under Trudeau and Clark." Paper presented at the 77th annual conference of the Canadian Political Science Association, June 2–4, 2005. Also available online: http://www.cpsa-acsp.ca/papers-2005/Halloran.pdf.

Hammami, R., and J. Hilal. "An Uprising at the Crossroads." *Middle East Report* no. 219 (2001): 2–7 and 41.

Haussmann, R., L. Pritchett, and D. Rodrik. "Growth Accelerations." Harvard University, August 2005.

Herrera, V., R. Balta, C. Rivas, P. Purizaga, W. Sandoval, and G. Villanueva. "Estudio de susceptibilidad en Piretroides usados en control vectorial período 1998–2000." Paper presented at II congreso de la red Nacional de Laboratorios en Salud Pública, the 64th anniversary of the Instituto Nacional de Salud, Lima, Perú, September 28–29, 2000.

Hillmer, Norman, and J. L. Granatstein. *Empire to Umpire: Canada and the World in the Twenty-First Century.* Toronto: Thomson Nelson, 2007.

Hurley, James Joseph. "Ceylon and the Colombo Plan." *The Empire Club of Canada Addresses,* 58–70. Toronto: Empire Club Foundation, 1956.

IMF. "Building Institutions." *World Economic Outlook,* September 2005.

Instituto Nacional de Salud and Ministerio De Salud (MINSA). "Susceptibilidad de los vectores de malaria a los insecticidas en el Perú. Informe técnico de la evaluación de la susceptibilidad a los insecticidas en mosquitos adultos del género Anopheles de las regiones maláricas del Perú." Documento Técnicos N° 5, Enfermedades emergentes y Reemergentes, 2002: 9–46. Also available online: http://www.bvcooperacion.pe:8080/biblioteca/bitstream/123456789/707/1/BVCI0000720.pdf.

International Development Research Centre. Archives. International Development Research Centre, Ottawa.

Jolly, Richard, Louis Emmerji, Dharam Ghai, and Frédéric Lapeyre. *UN Contributions to Development Thinking and Practice.* Indianapolis: Indiana University Press, 2004.

Kakkilaya, B. S. "Malaria Risk in South America." http://www.malariasite.com/malaria/samerica.htm (last updated April 14, 2006).

Kaufmann et al. "Governance Matters, Governance Indicators for 1996–2004." World Bank Policy Research Working Paper 3630, June 2005.

Khalidi, Rashid. *Palestinian Identity: The Construction of Modern National Consciousness.* New York: Columbia University Press, 1997.

Khalidi, Walid, ed., *From Haven to Conquest: Readings in Zionism and the Palestine Problem until 1948.* Washington: Institute for Palestine Studies, 1971.

Kimmerling, Baruch. "Sociology, Ideology, and Nation-Building: The Palestinians and Their Meaning in Israeli Sociology." *American Sociological Review* 57, no. 4 (1992): 446–60.

Kroeger, A., R. Meyer, M. Mancheno, M. Gonzalez and K. Pesse. "Operational Aspects of Bednet Impregnation for Community-Based Malaria Control in Nicaragua, Ecuador, Peru and Colombia." *Tropical Medicine and International Health* 1.2, no. 6 (June 1997): 589–602.

Kurlantzick, Joshua. "Planners & Seekers." Review of *The White Man's Burden: Why the West's Efforts to Aid the Rest Have Done So Much Ill and So Little Good*, by William Easterly. *Commentary Magazine,* June 2006. Also available online: www.nyu.edu/fas/institute/dri/Easterly/File/commentary_plannersandseekers.pdf.

"Leapfrogging in Costa Rica." International Labour Organization, November 12, 2001. http://www.ilo.org/global/About_the_ILO/Media_and_public_information/Broadcast_materials/Video_News_Release/lang — en/WCMS_ 074403/index.htm.

Lee, H.-H., J. D. Jung, M. S. Yoon, K. K. Lee, M. M. Lecadet, J. F. Charles, V. Cosmao Dumanoir, E. Franchon, and J. C. Shim. "Distribution of Bacillus thuringiensis in Korea." In *Bacillus thuringiensis*, Vol. I, edited by T.-Y. Feng et al., 201–15. Taipei, Taiwan: Biotechnology and environmental Benefits Hua Shiang Yuan Publishing, 1995.

LeGrand, Catherine. "L'axe missionnaire catholique entre le Québec et l'Amérique latine: Une exploration préliminaire." *Globe: Revue Internationale d'Etudes Québécoises* 12, no. 1 (2009): 43–66.

Levinson, Paul. *Digital McLuhan: A Guide to the Information Millennium.* London: Routledge, 2001.

Levy, Gideon. "The Neighborhood Bully Strikes Again." *Haaretz,* December 29, 2008. http://www.haaretz.com/hasen/spages/1050459.html (accessed December 29, 2008).

Lucas, R. "On the Mechanics of Economic Development." *Journal of Monetary Economics* 22 (1988): 3–42.

de Macedo, Jorge Braga, Colm Foy, and Charles P. Oman. *Development Is Back.* OECD Publishing, 2002.

de Macedo, Jorge Braga, and J. O. Martins. "Growth, Reform Indicators and Policy Complementarities." NBER Working Paper, no. 12544, September 2006.

Maddison, Angus. *The World Economy: Historical statistics.* OECD Publishing, 2003.

Meier, Gérald M. *Leading Issues in Economic Development,* 6th ed. New York: Oxford University Press, 1995.

Merello, J., P. Ventosilla, J. Chauca, H. Guerra, B. Infante, and E. Peréz. "Coconut and Yucca Agars to Produce *Bacillus thuringiensis var israelensis*." Paper presented at the 65th Annual Meeting of the AMCA and the 87th Annual Meeting of the New Jersey Mosquito Control Association, Inc., Atlantic City, NJ, March 12–16, 2000.

Milne, Seumas. "Israel's Onslaught on Gaza Is a Crime That Cannot Succeed." *The Guardian*, December 30, 2008. http://www.guardian.co.uk/commentisfree/2008/dec/30/israel-and-the-palestinians-middle-east (accessed January 1, 2009).

Ministerio De Salud (MINSA). "Doctrina, normas y procedimientos para el control de la malaria en el Perú." Dirección General de Salud de las Personas, Dirección del Programa de Control de Enfermedades Transmisibles, Control de la Malaria y Otras Enfermedades Metaxénicas, Lima, Perú, 1996.

Moench, M., E. Caspari. and A. Dixit (eds.) *Rethinking the Mosaic – Investigations into Local Water Management*. Kathmandu: Nepal Water Conservation Foundation and Boulder, CO: Institute for Social and Environmental Transition, 1999.

Morrison, David R. *Aid and Ebb Tide: A History of CIDA and Canadian Development Assistance*. Waterloo: Wilfrid Laurier University Press, 1998.

———. "The Choice of Bilateral Aid Recipients." In *Canadian International Development Assistance Policies: An Appraisal*, 2nd ed., edited by Cranford Pratt. Kingston: McGill-Queen's University Press, 1996.

Muirhead, Bruce. "Differing Perspectives: India, the World Bank and the 1963 Aid-India Negotiations." *India Review* 4, no. 1 (2005): 1–22.

Muirhead, Bruce, and Ronald Harpelle. *IDRC: 40 years of Ideas, Innovation and Impact*. Waterloo: Wilfrid Laurier University Press, 2010.

Muirhead, Bruce, et Ronald Harpelle, *CRDI: 40 ans d'idées, d'innovations et d'impacts*. Québec: Les Presses de l'Université Laval, 2011.

Muirhead, Bruce, and Ronald Harpelle. "The IDRC and Middle East: An Innovative Development Model." In *Canada and the Middle East*, edited by Bessma Momani and Paul Heinbecker, 145–60. Wilfrid Laurier University Press, 2007.

Myrdal, Gunnar. *Asian Drama: An Inquiry into the Poverty of Nations*. New York: Twentieth Century Fund, 1968.

Nguyen-Gillham, Viet, Rita Giacaman, Ghada Naser, and Will Boyce. "Normalizing the Abnormal: Palestinian Youth and the Contradictions of Resilience in Protracted Conflict." *Health and Social Care in the Community* 16, no. 3 (2008): 291–98.

North, D. *Institutions, Institutional Change and Economic Performance*. Cambridge: Cambridge University Press, 1990.

Oficina General de Epidemiología-MINSA. "Situación Epidemiología de la Malaria en el Perú hasta el año 2002." Vol. 12, no. 8 (February 16–22, 2003): 1.

Olivier de Sardan, J. P. *Anthropology and Development: Understanding Contemporary Social Change*. London: Zed Books, 2005.

OMS. "Resistencia de los vectores de enfermedades a los plaguicidas. 15° informe del Comité de Expertos de OMS en Biología de los Vectores y lucha antivectorial." *Serie de Informes técnicos* 818 (1992): 2–20.

Orduz, S., W. Rojas, M. M. Correa, A. E. Montoya, and H. De Barjac. "A New Serotype of *Bacillus thuringiensis* from Colombia Toxic to Mosquito Larvae." *Journal Invertebrate Pathology* 59 (1992): 99–103.

Overdijk, Maarten, and Wouter van Diggelen. "Technology Appropriation in Face to Face Collaborative Learning." University of Utrecht, Learning in Interaction Research Center. Available online at http://igitur-archive.library.uu.nl/fss/2007-1213200540/OverdijkVanDiggelen%20ECTEL%202006.pdf.

Pappé, Ilan. *The Ethnic Cleansing of Palestine.* Oxford: Oneworld Publications, 2006.

Peyton Lyon, V., and Tarequ Y Ismael, eds. *Canada and the Third World.* Toronto: Macmillan, 1976.

Prensky, Marc. "Digital Natives, Digital Immigrants." *On the Horizon* 9, no. 4, MCB University Press (October 2001): 1–2.

Programa de las Naciones Unidas para el Desarrollo. *Informe sobre desarrollo humano: El adelanto tecnológico al servicio del desarrollo humano.* PNUD, 2001.

Punamaki, R. L. "Relationships between Political Violence and Psychological Responses among Palestinian Women." *Journal of Peace Research* 27, no. 1 (1990): 75–85.

Rabinovitch, L. "Breves aspectos da malaria no Brasil e posibilidades do control biológico de Anophelinos." *Biotecnología* 4 (1989): 1–4.

Reck, Jennifer, and Brad Wood. "Vodacom's Community Services Phone Shops: Providing Telecommunications to Poor Communities in South Africa." Case study for the World Resources Institute, August 2003. http://www.digitaldividend.org/pdf/vodacom.pdf.

Rodrick, Dani. "Rethinking Growth Policies in the Developing World." Lucas d'Agliano Lecture in Development Economics, Torino, October 2004.

———. "Growth strategies." Working Paper, Harvard University, August 2004. Available online at http://ksghome.harvard.edu/~drodrik/growthstrat 10.pdf.

Rodrick, Dani, Arvind Subramanian, and Francesco Trebbi. "Institutions Rule: The Primacy of Institutions over Geography and Economic Integration." NBER Working Paper no. 9305. Boston: Harvard University, 2002. Mimeographed.

Romer, Paul M. "Increasing Returns and Long-Run growth." *Journal of Political Economy* 94, no. 5 (1986): 1002–37.

———. "Endogenous Technological change." *Journal of Political Economy* 98, no. 5 (1990): S71-102.

Rubio-Palis, Y., and R. H. Zimerman. "Ecoregional Classification of Malaria Vectors in the Neotropics." *J. Med Entomol* 34 (1997): 499–510.

Sachs, J., and A. Warner. "Economic Convergence and Economic Policies." NBER Working Papers Series, Working Paper no. 5039, February 1995.

Salomon, Jean-Jacques. "The Uncertain Quest: Mobilising Science and Technology for Development." *Science and Public Policy* 22 (February 1995): 9–18.

Sciadas, George, ed. *From the Digital Divide to Digital Opportunities: Measuring Infostate for Development.* Orbicom, 2005, published in association with NRC Press, Canadian Institute for Scientific and Technical Information, http://www.itu.int/ITU- D/ict/publications/dd/material/index_ict_opp.pdf.

Sen, Amartya. *Development as Freedom*. New York: Knopf, 1999.

―――. *Teorías del desarrollo a principios del siglo XXI*. Lecture at the University of Seville, Seville, Spain, 1997. Available online at http://personal.us.es/ezamora/ Docencia_archivos/Teorias%20del%20dessarrollo%20siglo%20XXI-amartya% 20sen.pdf.

Sharma, S., J. Koponen, D. G Gyawali, and A. Dixit. *Aid under Stress: Water, Forests and Finnish Aid in Nepal*. Helsinki and Kathmandu: Himal Books for Interdisciplinary Analysts and Kathmandu: Institute for Development Studies, 2004.

Shu'aybi, A., and K. Shikaki. "A Window on the Workings of the PA: An Inside View." *Journal of Palestine Studies* 30, no. 1 (2000): 88–97.

Smillie, Ian, and Henny Helmich. *Non-Governmental Organizations and Governments: Stakeholders for Development*. Paris: Development Centre of the Organisation for Economic Cooperation and Development, 1993.

Solow, R. M. "A Contribution to the Theory of Economic Growth." *Quarterly Journal of Economics* 70, no. 1 (1956): 65–94.

Summerfield, Derek. "Effects of war: moral knowledge, revenge, reconciliation, and medicalised concepts of 'recovery.'" *British Medical Journal* 325 (November 9, 2002): 1105–7.

―――. "A Critique of Seven Assumptions behind Psychological Trauma Programmes in War-Affected Areas." *Social Science & Medicine* 48 (1999): 1449–62.

Tamari, Salim. "What the Uprising Means." *Middle East Report* 152 (1988): 24–30.

Thompson, M. *Organising and Disorganising: A Dynamic and Non-linear Theory of Institutional Emergence and Its Implications*. Devon, UK: Triarchy Press, 2008.

Thompson, M., and D. Gyawali. "Uncertainty Revisited or the Triumph of Hype over Experience." New introduction to *Uncertainty: On a Himalayan Scale*, by M. Thompson, M. Warburton, and T. Hatley. London: Ethnographica, 1989. Republished, Kathmandu: Himal Books and Laxenburg, Austria: Oxford University's James Martin Institute for Science and Civilization and the International Institute for Applied Systems Analysis, 2007.

Thompson, M., R. Ellis, A. Wildavasky, and M. Wildavsky. Cultural Theory. Boulder, CO: Westview Press, 1990.

Tomlin, Brian W., Norman Hillmer, and Fen Osler Hampson. *Canada's International Policies: Agendas, Alternatives, and Politics*. Toronto: Oxford University Press, 2008.

United Nations. "Question of Palestine: History." http://www.un.org/Depts/dpa/ ngo/history.html (accessed March 20, 2008).

United Nations Department of Public Information. "Socio-economic achievements of the Palestinian People, 1993–Present: Building a Public Administration under the Palestinian Authority." In *The Question of Palestine and the United Nations*. http://www.un.org/Depts/dpi/palestine/ch9.pdf (accessed December 29, 2007).

Uzawa, H. "Optimal Technical Change in an Aggregative Model of Economic Growth." *International Economic Review* 6 (1965): 18–61.

Vaillancourt, Jean-Guy. "Les groupes socio-politiques progressistes dans le Catholicisme québécois contemporain." In *Les mouvements religieux aujourd'hui*.

Theories et pratiques, edited by Jean-Paul Rouleau and Jacques Zylberberg, 261–82. Québec: Presses de l'Université Laval, 1984.

Valcárcel, Marcel. "Génesis y Evolución del Concepto y Enfoques sobre el Desarrollo." Research Report. Lima, Peru: Pontificia Universidad Católica del Perú, Department of Social Sciences, 2006.

Ventosilla, P., and H. Guerra. "Producción Piloto usando cocos enteros y su aplicación en el campo de *Bacillus thuringiensis* var. *israelensis* para el control biológico de *Anopheles* spp. e zonas endémicas de Malaria en Perú." *Revista de Medicina Experimental del Instituto Nacional de Salud* (Segunda Epoca, Lima, Perú) 14, no. 2 (1997): 61.

Ventosilla, P., E. Huarcaya, P. Gutierrez, and J. Chauca. "A Statistical Model for Assessing the Relationship between Meteorological Variables and the Incidence of *Plasmodium falciparum* and *Plasmodium vivax* in a Peruvian Endemic Area." *International Journal of Environmental Health* 2, no. 1 (2008): 37–44.

Ventosilla, P., D. Marin, and H. Guerra. "Mecanismo de acción de bacilos esporulados entomopatógenos." In Talleres No 3. *Taller Latin-Americano: Control de vectores,* 131–33. Trujillo, Venezuela: Centro de Investigaciones José Witremundo, 1994.

Ventosilla, P., and M. Snyder, "Guía Metodológica: Controlando el paludismo." Report for International Development Research Centre (IDRC)/ Instituto de Medicina Tropical Alexander von Humboldt-UPCH, Lima, Perú: Ed. SAYWA s.r.l., 1992.

Ventosilla, P., E. Torres, L. Harman, K. Saavedra, W. Mormontoy, J. Merello, B. Infante, and J. Chauca. "Conocimientos, actitudes y practicas en el control de malaria y dengue en las comunidades de Salitral (después de seis años de educación: 1992–1998) y Querecotillo en el Departamento de Piura." *Mosaico Cient* 2, no. 2 (2006): 65–69.

Walt, W. Rostow. *Les étapes du développement économique.* Paris: Seul, 1960.

Water Nepal 4, no. 1 (September 1994).

Wilkerson, R. C. "*Anopheles* (Anopheles) *calderoni* N. SP. a Malaria Vector of the Arribalzagia Series from Peru (Diptera: Culicidae)." *Mosquito Systematics* 23, no. 1 (1991): 25–38.

Williamson, O. "The New Institutional Economics: Taking Stock, Looking Ahead." *Journal of Economic Literature* 38 (September 2000): 595–613.

Wirth, M. C. "Tenephos Resistance in Mosquito Larvae: History & Consequences." Paper presented at the 65th Annual Meeting of AMCA and 87th Annual Meeting of the New Jersey Mosquito Association, Inc., Atlantic City, NJ, March 12–16, 2000.

World Bank. "Doing Business 2007: How to Reform." Washington, DC: World Bank and International Finance Corporation, 2007.

World Health Organization (WHO). "World Malaria Day: A Day to Act." http://www.rbm.who.int/worldmalariaday/.

Contributors

Zoubida Charouff is a professor at the Mohammed V University in Rabat, Morocco. Her interest lies in the phytochemistry of Moroccan medicinal plants and the evaluation of their chemical components in nutrition and cosmetics. A woman of action and conviction, she has contributed to the betterment of rural women's lives through money-making schemes using medicinal plants, through literacy, training (in management, marketing, and communication) and through the protection of the environment. Zoubida Charrouf was behind the first argan oil co-operatives in Morocco, which now employ more than 2500 women who form task groups to collect and begin the process of argan oil production, followed by extraction of the oil, and an economic interest group (GIE) Targanine that is concerned with the marketing of the products. She has been active in obtaining geographical guidelines for argan oil as there are many false claims both inside and outside Morocco. She is the author of over a hundred publications and articles on argan oil.

Oumar Cissé is a civil engineer who holds a master's degree in environmental studies and a PhD in urban planning and environment from the University of Montreal. Since 1997 he has served as Executive Secretary of the African Institute for Urban Management (IAGU). His previous positions include a stint as municipal engineer and environmentalist at the

Urban Community of Dakar, where he founded the subdirectorate of the environment in 1992. He is a researcher in urban environments, specializing on issues of urban waste, and has trained African professionals in urban areas as a lecturer at the Institute of Urban Planning at the University of Montreal since 2000 and associate professor at the international French-language Senghor University in Alexandria, Egypt, since April 2007. Dr. Cissé has acted as an international consultant (UNDP, CIDA, UN HABITAT) and authored several articles and international communications in urban environment. He has also served as president of the Network of African Institutions Urban Management (ANUMI) since 2003 and was coordinator of the Regional Centre of the Basel Convention on hazardous waste in French-speaking Africa from 2004 to 2006. The main areas of intervention are municipal waste, environmental planning, public–private partnership in urban services, urban agriculture, and international co-operation in urban areas. Dr. Cissé is the main initiator and coordinator of the "Discharge Mbeubeuss: Analysis of Impact and Development of Channels of Waste and Urban Agriculture to Diamalaye (Malika)" project funded by IDRC under its Urban Poverty and Environment initiative (PURE).

Heloise Emdon leads Acacia, an International Development Research Centre program that works with African partners to apply information and communication technologies to Africa's social and economic development. Before joining IDRC, Ms. Emdon was a communications sector analyst for the Development Bank of Southern Africa (DBSA). At the bank, she worked on telecom and broadcast investment projects and operational policy as well as other ICT-related projects in Southern Africa. She also led, for the DBSA, a development-oriented community radio pilot project in a remote peri-urban and rural South African community. Ms. Emdon also has ten years of experience as a journalist for the print press, as well as experience with a news agency.

Clotilde Fonseca is the director and founder of the Programa de Informática Educativa de Costa Rica. The program was created in 1988 by the Fundación Omar Dengo and the Ministry of Public Education. She was also the executive director of the Fundación Omar Dengo from its founding in 1987 until 1994 and from 1996 to the present. She was also the president of Instituto de Asistencia Social de Costa Rica (1994–95). Clotilde

Fonseca is a member of the Consejo Consultivo del Ministro de Ciencia y Tecnología (2000–1) and the Proyecto del Estado de la Nación (2001). She has also served as a consultant to numerous international agencies and was a professor at the Universidad de Costa Rica. Clotilde Fonseca is the author of *Computadoras en las escuelas de Costa Rica* and the author of several articles.

Rita Giacaman is a professor of public health at the Institute of Community and Public Health, Birzeit University, occupied Palestinian territory. She is a founding member of the institute and has worked there for 31 years. During the 1980s, she participated as a researcher and practitioner in the Palestinian social action movement, which led to the development of the Palestinian primary health care model. During the 1990s, she participated in building the Palestinian community-based disability rehabilitation network. Since 2000, Rita has been focusing on understanding the impact of chronic warlike conditions and excessive exposure to violence on the health and well-being of Palestinians, with an emphasis on psychosocial health; and ways in which interventions could generate the needed active and positive resilience and resistance to ongoing warlike conditions, especially among youth. She has published extensively, including articles in scientific journals, chapters in books published internationally, as well as several volumes and reports published locally.

Dominique Guillaume is a professor of medicinal chemistry at the University of Reims Champagne-Ardenne (France). He is an expert in natural product chemistry and has been working with Professor Z. Charrouf (University Mohammed V-Agdal, Morocco) on the argan tree since 1995. Dominique Guillaume's initial work on argan tree secondary metabolites focused on the search for biologically active molecules, but he rapidly oriented his activity toward argan oil. His work has led to the design of analytical methods of ascertaining argan oil purity and quality. These methods have been implemented in the argan oil women's co-operatives and have undoubtedly permitted the commercial success of argan oil. Dominique Guillaume has authored or co-authored more than 100 scientific papers, is a regular reviewer for several scientific journals, and is consultant to two start-up companies working in the therapeutic and nutrition field.

Dipak Gyawali is a member of the Royal Nepal Academy of Science and Technology. By profession he is a hydroelectric power engineer (Kafedra Gidroenergetiki, Moskovski Energeticheski Institut, USSR,1979) as well as a resource economist (Energy and Resources Group, University of California, Berkeley, 1986) specializing in water and energy issues. For the past two decades he has been an independent researcher and consultant on development issues and has been pursuing his own interdisciplinary research agenda on society–technology–resource-base interface. After the democratic changes in Nepal in 1990, he was called by the new government to help define a new energy development policy in the changed context in Nepal. He is currently a director of Nepal Water Conservation Foundation and the editor of its journal *Water Nepal,* as well as a member of the Oxford Commission on Sustainable Consumption.

Ronald Harpelle is a professor of history at Lakehead University, where he is also the co-director of the Advanced Institute for Globalization and Culture. His association with IDRC dates from 1998, when he was awarded a Canada and the World grant to undertake a study of the West Indian community of Central America. With Bruce Muirhead, he authored a commissioned history of IDRC.

Bruce Muirhead is a professor of history and the associate dean of graduate studies and research in the Faculty of Arts at the University of Waterloo and senior fellow at CIGI. He is the co-author of a history of the International Development Research Centre and has undertaken the writing of a history of Canadian official development assistance policy from 1945 to 1984 with a grant from the Social Sciences and Humanities Research Council. He continues to work on the topic of the development of Canadian foreign economic policy in the 1960s and 1970s.

Viet Nguyen-Gillham has a background in social work and psychotherapy. She has a PhD from Boston University in sociology and social work and has worked internationally in conflict areas (Thailand, Bosnia, Guinea/ Sierra Leone, East Timor, Palestine) in programs related to refugees, torture victims, and social development. She is currently working as an independent consultant and researcher in mental health and community development at the Institute of Community and Public Health, Birzeit University.

Diego Piñeiro is dean of the Faculty of Social Sciences, Universidad de la República, in Uruguay. He has worked and published extensively in the area of rural sociology. With a PhD in sociology, Piñeiro has received research grants from several organizations, including CLACSO and the Ford Foundation. Because he was a researcher in Uruguay during the military dictatorship, Piñeiro's later work reflects the importance of supporting research during times of repression.

Yoke Rabaia conducts research with the mental health unit of the Institute of Community and Public Health, Birzeit University, in the occupied Palestinian territory. She is also working on her PhD dissertation with the VU University Medical Centre, Amsterdam, the Netherlands.

Palmira Ventosilla is an expert on tropical disease vectors and for years has toiled to control malaria by targeting the spread of the Anopheles mosquito. With funding from IDRC, Ventosilla and her colleagues at the Alexander von Humboldt Institute of Tropical Medicine in Lima have developed a low-cost, environmentally friendly alternative to pesticides through biological control of mosquito larvae. Through an educational program using posters, comics, and games, the three major schools of Salitral, the town where the program is based, are involved, and the whole community has been reached; future plans include expansion to more towns, schools, and ponds. Palmira Ventosilla also volunteers with the American Society for Microbiology (ASM) project in Mozambique to evaluate the range of microbiology capacity within Mozambique.

Index